UTOPIA IN THE AGE OF SURVIVAL

Utopia in the Age of Survival

Between Myth and Politics

S. D. CHROSTOWSKA

STANFORD UNIVERSITY PRESS
Stanford, California

STANFORD UNIVERSITY PRESS
Stanford, California

© 2021 S. D. Chrostowska. All rights reserved.

No part of this book may be reproduced or transmitted in any form or by any means, electronic or mechanical, including photocopying and recording, or in any information storage or retrieval system without the prior written permission of Stanford University Press.

Library of Congress Cataloging-in-Publication Data
Names: Chrostowska, S. D. (Sylwia Dominika), 1975- author.
Title: Utopia in the age of survival : between myth and politics / S.D. Chrostowska.
Description: Stanford, California : Stanford University Press, 2021. | Includes bibliographical references and index.
Identifiers: LCCN 2021018478 (print) | LCCN 2021018479 (ebook) | ISBN 9781503629981 (cloth) | ISBN 9781503629998 (paperback) | ISBN 9781503630000 (epub)
Subjects: LCSH: Utopias. | Critical theory. | Political science—Philosophy.
Classification: LCC HX806 .C47 2021 (print) | LCC HX806 (ebook) | DDC 335/.02—dc23
LC record available at https://lccn.loc.gov/2021018478
LC ebook record available at https://lccn.loc.gov/2021018479

Cover design: Rob Ehle

Cover painting: *The Raft of the Medusa*, Théodore Géricault, 1818–19. 490 cm × 716 cm (16 ft 1 in × 23 ft 6 in). Via Wikimedia Commons.

Text design: Kevin Barrett Kane

Typeset at Stanford University Press in 10/14 ITC Galliard Pro *for* BRIAN STOCK

CONTENTS

PROLOGUE
1

CHAPTER 1 The Utopian Hypothesis
From Radical Politics to Speculative Myth
24

CHAPTER 2 The Emancipation of Desire
Preludes and Postludes of May '68
55

CHAPTER 3 The Utopia of Survival
Critical Theory against the State
83

EPILOGUE
The Displaced Imagination
100

POSTSCRIPT
113

Acknowledgments 123
Notes 125
Bibliography 175
Index 195

UTOPIA IN THE AGE OF SURVIVAL

PROLOGUE

"IS THIS DYSTOPIA?" Sometimes a simple stencil of bold red letters sprayed across a lamppost in a shabby part of town under lockdown stops us in our tracks. As though its message were addressed exclusively to us.

It might be some part of the phrasing that for a moment holds all our attention. For me, it was the word *this*. Was the dystopia our society, now and here? Or was "this" the contemporary world as a whole? And did it matter which? Is there a real difference between these alternatives?

The question on the streetlight was patently rhetorical. It acted as a dramatic provocation by implying an answer so evident it hardly needs stating and is not expected. Yet at least one passerby whom it similarly arrested was compelled to respond. What the querying hand had left tacit another felt bound to spell out, making definitive what had merely been intimated. As if to suggest that the answer, undesirable though it might be, was unavoidable, and that not supplying it clearly, passing the question over in silence, was irresponsible, smacking of indifference at a time when, things falling apart as they were, the exact opposite attitude was called for. And so, for their own sake or ours, somebody affixed below, scribbled in black marker, a resounding—an unequivocal—"Yes!"

But let us return to the reflection that "IS THIS DYSTOPIA?" seemed designed to provoke. It was, of course, a simple yes-or-no question. Under the new dispensation and prevailing social conditions, the presence of that critical word *dystopia* all but presupposed an affirmative reply. Publicly asserting, making the implicit explicit, at once proved the query's dialogic efficacy and spurred others to answer it for themselves, blocking neither repetition nor continuation of dialogue. That, by withholding the obvious, the questioner had meant to spare us from what we might not wish to hear is just as unlikely as that the answer was given to rub our faces in an inconvenient truth.

And once we accept the truth, what next? To this the question had even less to say. The realization, however, that our world and dystopia are the same sets our mind in motion. Its likeliest effect is a negative reaction, a resistance. A mental step in the right direction is already progress. Simple questions are easy to dismiss and underestimate. If this one gave me pause, it is because confronting the actual state of the world, here or everywhere, evokes (betrayed) utopian aspirations, highlighting our epic lack of success.

If this is dystopia, which way to utopia?[1] The question central to this book is equally straightforward. There can be no doubt that utopian thinking persists. Its energies have not been extinguished. But how is such thought possible in our dystopian world (or worlds)? Is it reasonable to hope for utopia, to continue and renew our hopes for its realization, in a place where more and more of us each day struggle to survive, let alone to pursue happiness? Is there an appropriate, reality-congruent, pragmatic utopian thinking we should adopt that might get us out of this mess? Under the circumstances, when the best we can realistically hope for is slowing down irreversible and often unintended widespread damage, does it still make sense to think utopian thoughts?

Throughout modernity, *utopia* has been a handy term of criticism among educated elites. Early modern and Enlightenment political philosophers, theorists of the social contract, were wary of being taken for writers of utopias.[2] In polemics and politics, *utopia* branded the adversaries of those who thought themselves realists for desiring and fighting for the possible, only to be stigmatized as utopian in their turn. In 1849, within a year of the French Revolution of 1848 and the bloody June Days Uprising, the socialist revolutionary Auguste Blanqui, accused of inciting popular violence, defended himself thus against the charge of utopianism:[3]

> Utopia! impossibility! devastating word nailed to our foreheads by our enemies that means "murderer"! homicidal appeal to the egoism of the living generation, which does not accept being cut down in bloom and buried in order to fatten future generations . . . ! This weapon is terrible, we know a thing or two about it; but it is disloyal. There are no utopians, in the overdrawn acceptation of the word. There are thinkers who dream of a more fraternal society and seek to discover their promised land in the shifting mists of the horizon.[4]

Two decades later, in prison, and haunted by the brutal suppression of the Paris Commune as by its promise of a more fraternal society, Blanqui would pen his "astronomic hypothesis," *Eternity by the Stars*, finding a desperately utopian vision in the shifting mists of the heavens.

A similar enthusiasm for the Commune sustained two German thinkers who, in 1848, had met the "nursery tale of the spectre of communism" then haunting Europe with a jointly authored manifesto of the Communist Party. In it, they had distanced themselves from visionaries too busy dreaming to act historically and wanting initiative when it came to agitating for change.[5] "Since Marx," twentieth-century philosopher of utopia Ernst Bloch observed in his magnum opus, *The Principle of Hope*, "mere utopianizing, apart from still having a partial active role in a few struggles for emancipation, has turned into reactionary or superfluous playful forms. These do not lack a seductive quality of course, and are at least useful for diversion, but this is precisely why they have become mere ideologies of the existent, beneath a critical-utopian mask."[6] Such historical glimpses go to show that utopian thought had its peaks and valleys even—especially—for its exponents.

A century after the revolutionary wave of the Spring of Nations had swept across an "Old Europe" of principalities, kingdoms, and empires, the liberal philosopher Isaiah Berlin, posing as a man of sense in the postwar years, merely stated a commonplace when he equated utopianism with escapism, anachronism, and impracticality. He laid out the reasons for his dislike of the *homo utopiens*, the generic utopian thinker, as follows:

> What is it that we mean when we call a thinker Utopian, or when we accuse a historian of giving an unrealistic, over-doctrinaire account of events? After all, no modern Utopian can be accused of wishing to defy the laws of physics. It is not laws like gravitation or electromagnetism that modern Utopians have ignored. What then have addicts to such systems sinned against? Not certainly the laws of sociology, for very few such have as yet been established, even by the least rigorous, most impressionistic of "scientific" procedures. Indeed, the excessive belief in their existence is often one of the marks of lack of realism—as is shown on every occasion when men of action successfully defy them and knock over yet another false sociological model. It seems truer to say that to be Utopian is to suggest that courses can be followed which, in fact, cannot, and to argue this from theoretical premises and in the face of the "concrete" evidence of the "facts." That is certainly what Napoleon or Bismarck meant when they railed against speculative theorists.[7]

For Berlin, acting on utopian ideals was, if not an outright demerit, at any rate a potential liability. Yet he could not deny its power to effectuate a radical break, letting in new and practical ideas for the betterment of society. "The passionate advocacy of unattainable ideals may, even if it is Utopian,"—or, more accurately, because it is utopian—"break open the barriers of blind tradition and transform the values of human beings."[8]

Utopia has not gone away as a term of abuse. In its old haunts, its notoriety seems secure. It has, however, become something of a buzzword. That its positive invocations have, in our age, filtered into mass and commercial culture testifies to the idea's growing social relevance. To say that they are, most of them, skin-deep and gratuitous is not to dismiss all such uses out of hand. *Utopia* on a can of organic tomatoes or a bag of California-grown artisanal cannabis might mean its producer truly believes their product contributes to improving society, for buyers of their brand anyway. Björk's 2017 album, *Utopia*, is a surreal treatment of bona fide utopian images. As Pierre Boulez once remarked of liberal society, "The economy is there to remind us, in case we get lost in this bland utopia: there are musics which bring in money and exist for commercial profit; there are musics that cost something, whose very concept has nothing to do with profit. No liberalism will erase this distinction."[9] He might have added: in the bland "utopia" of value pluralism, where one thing is as good as the next, there are musics that hunt for an exit.

Each place *utopia* makes an appearance is different. Despite the word's entry into market vernacular, its positive connotation—as the opposite of *dystopia*—is still not generally a given. Yet there is plenty to suggest that something of what it stands for has acquired, if not cachet, then at least greater visibility and sex appeal it did not previously have. In view of these developments, it is no longer credible to associate the idea of utopia with intellectual elitism. Judging by its popularity as a transcultural signifier of a positive, forward-looking attitude or of well-being, the meaning of the term has lost much of its former focus. It is diluted, diffuse, nebulous, floating above ideal political systems and programs of social engineering, to which it once exclusively referred. Yet for that very reason, *utopia* today has occasion to awaken the social imagination in contexts where it would otherwise remain unknown.

How has the trace of something that previously, in the Cold War era, set off alarm bells and called up images of failed totalitarian experiments, come to pervade everyday life without raising an eyebrow? Utopia's wider acceptance has as much to do with neutralizing or rendering innocuous its incitement to transformation as with its evocativeness. We have the *Weltgeist* to thank for it. For the world spirit so arranged things that the "utopia" of the free market could colonize whole areas of life, from entertainment to fitness to sex. Utopia has lent its name to everything from 1980s video games and yoga studios to the latest multispeed vibrators. Looking around us, capitalism more than deserves the title of "cauldron of utopias," its concoction a witches' brew of satisfaction guaranteed. Utopian semiosis mostly without commitment to alternative holistic social visions thrives on the value pluralism of globalized societies. Because it operates through commodity fetishism, its utopias do not pose a threat to the established economic order, being themselves perfectly fungible and reconcilable. Once they are attached to commodities, radical utopian ideas and values, such as social harmony, health and well-being, joy and pleasure, lose their link to the will actually to remake social bonds. The play of utopian gestures, no matter their political complexion, is easily assimilable to uncontroversial standards of pleonectic social happiness built around limitless and predatory economic growth, underwritten these days by a green or techno-capitalist agenda. More-of-the-same automatically gets utopian credit for a smart aesthetic (e.g., packaging makeovers for beauty products) and clever marketing (calling a new mega-mall American Dream, or selling biomass, destructive for the environment, as a "renewable").

A hard look at the situation is enough to turn believers into cynics. To those who oppose it, the diversion of socialist utopias to capitalist ends or the appropriation of utopian elements for financial gain does not justify abandoning all utopian thinking. And even if we feel utopianism as a conscious striving for social perfection to be unsalvageable, and we must indeed let it go, we may be simultaneously setting the bar for ourselves higher, not lower. For it is now clear that, to get out of the present dystopia, humans must be prepared for almost superhuman sacrifice and effort. We must be ready, in other words, to do the impossible, synonym for utopian. The ambition puts us back, willy-nilly, on the track of utopian thinking. Only the particulars of the destination have changed, been obsolesced—some would say *regressed*, adding that there is little that is recognizably utopian about the new end. It does not much resemble the utopias of old and might seem more moderate by comparison, but the impossible task to be accomplished is, all the same, the embryo of a just and harmonious society. The project's unwitting, higher level utopianism demonstrates an important truth about utopia, namely, that it is never really about devising a precise social blueprint to satisfy all. Today, the only feasible blueprint is a "blueprint for survival," as *The Ecologist* called it fifty years ago.[10] Forestalling social breakdown and catching up to the harm already inflicted on the environment is as ambitious a plan as we can hope to carry out. However otherwise emancipatory or utopian such a precise and modest-sounding goal may be, it is, by its very nature, limited. But so are all particular utopias.

One of the most stubborn misconceptions about the utopian genre of thinking, of which Bloch left us such a breathtaking inventory—from the freedom of the Cynics to the sensual hedonism of the Cyrenaics, from athletics to alchemy, from Zionism to ordinary daydreams—is that utopia consists in an imaginary place depicted in greater or lesser detail. This is the legacy of Thomas More's *Utopia*, which gave the Platonic *ideal state* a new twist.

The twentieth century's retooling of utopia has done a lot to complicate this picture. More may have presented his island of Utopia as actually existing but inaccessible to most—attainable in principle, hence doubly attractive. Yet, contrary to received wisdom,

Utopia itself was a jocoserious creation, rather than an earnest proposal for a model society, much less a guideline for development. Emphasis on the dialectical character of More's invention, then, fought against its vulgarization, on display in utopia's heyday in the nineteenth century. Especially following the miscarried utopian experiments in society-building that were Soviet Russia, Nazi Germany, and Maoist China, historians and theorists on the left, such as Bloch and Miguel Abensour, called into question the narrow conception, held by its twentieth-century critics, of utopia as an abstract rational model imposable on material social realities, be it at the price of mass suffering. Moving away from the totalizing visions that defined it in past centuries, utopian world-making thus became a heuristic device, an organon, critical and self-reflexive, provisional and open-ended.

Building on these novel conceptions, utopia came into its own as a sociological method. In Ruth Levitas's holistic analytic, rather than descriptive, approach—the "imaginary reconstitution of society"—utopia was to be understood in terms of *desire*, instead of the narrower *hope*. It generated "a method which is primarily hermeneutic but which repeatedly returns us from existential and aesthetic concerns to the social and structural domain."[11] In its *critical-creative* (as opposed to compensatory) role, utopianism still yielded "explicit alternative scenarios for the future," whose "explicitly hypothetical character," however, allowed for "provisionality, reflexivity and dialogic mode."[12] Conceptualizing utopia as method—in contrast to goal, concrete destination or telos, precise plan for empirical execution, or, at the other extreme, ideal for contemplation, regulative idea—presupposes looking at human society as a problem in need of a solution, a perspective that best responds to current realities.

Attempts to bring some order to the profusion of utopian scenarios, modalities, and their combinations have continued alongside theoretical updates like Levitas's. Darko Suvin, for one, proposed a trio of spatial categories, *locus, horizon,* and *orientation,* where *locus* designates the defined place (chronotope) of an agent in motion at any given point; *horizon*, the "furthest imaginatively visible goal," such as abstract, nonlocalized utopian programs and blueprints, toward which the agent is moving; and *orientation*, the direction of projection or movement that acts as a vector conjoining locus and horizon. The ideal is a dynamic utopia, in which the oriented locus never fuses with the horizon.[13] Indeed, the scholarly field of utopian studies, already vast and well plowed by the late twentieth century, shows no signs of enclosure. Thanks to efforts at definition, classification, and systematization, at redefinition and retheorization, *utopia* now names a great and growing family of phenomena. It is known not only as hope or desire, but also as impulse, propensity, spirit, mindset or mentality, mode, image, dream, vision, projection, project, method, process, and practice. Besides assuming myriad forms with a wide variety of ideational contents, utopia performs a number of functions: consolatory, educative, hermeneutic, critical, problem-solving, experimental, anticipatory, socially transformative, and so on.

Asking about the fate of utopia in dystopian times cuts a path through this wild conceptual garden and its intricate history. It is not obvious what utopia is anymore, or what it means for us. Answering the question obliges one to be unabashedly selective. Those looking to find their interest in or take on utopianism represented in these pages are bound to come away disappointed. Those who leave their prejudices at the door may later find them changed. Far from dashing or encouraging hopes, I propose different grounds and structures for them. Whether these prove useful in our current predicament, in all its economic, political, and cultural ramifications, is another matter, and material for another book—to be written post history. I say this with a tinge of sarcasm out of a distinct if common sense that things are coming to a head. Either way, human history—the history of human making—could end, if otherwise than hitherto prognosticated. What comes afterward is anyone's guess.

Despair, it seems, is hope's deepest well. As an underground resource, the images it produces of hoped-for relief or redemption are normally not the castles in the air fancied over the rainbow by starry-eyed philosophers and social planners. The question about the fate of utopia today is not so much whether there is enough hope as what are the ends to which hope is directed. Suffice it to say that not every socially inspired hope or action is utopian. The dichotomy between hope as reasonable expectation and utopia as wishful thinking or fantasy was recognized by the godfather of utopia himself.[14] The denigration of hope for its passivity, rooted in monotheistic theology, is all too familiar. The pantheist philosopher Baruch Spinoza conceived of this affective-cognitive state as mingled indissolubly with fear, hence pain, as lined with sadness, and as contrary to reason and virtue—not only not good, but sinful. As such, hope interfered with what he called striving (*conatus*) for self-preservation, with the augmentation of the human mind's power to think/imagine and the human body's power to act virtuously (perseverance being the principle or essence of all things, not just humans). Spinozan hope is a sign of "a defect of knowledge and a lack of power in the mind."[15]

Just when one thought that nothing could further ruin its chances as a psychic resource for action, the atheist thinker Raoul Vaneigem, whose lifelong utopianism is nourished by his interest in heretical and millenarian movements, scorned hope once and for all as "the leash of submission," for maintaining the hopeful in inaction. In this strongly negative light, hope is vain, inefficient, fixating on an object and fantasizing about it while leaving its attainment to others or to God, rather than taking steps to put it within reach.[16] Nonetheless and more fundamentally, without hope, the lived, mediate future would not exist at all. As Eugène Minkowski argued, aspiration (hope along with desire) constructs an "ample" future before us, irrespective of our reasoned attitude—pessimism or optimism—toward it. Permitting us to look far into the future, hope frees us from "the embrace of expectation" (whose *linear* prolongation it is not). It ought not, therefore, be spurned as vain, naïve, instinctive, or a proof of inexperience.[17]

Hope keeps company with anxiety: as an escape from anxious expectations.[18] During the crises of capitalism and climate, despite the "vast bureaucratic apparatus for the creation and maintenance of hopelessness" to which we are captive, there has been no shortage of alternative futures, not all of them alarmist or postapocalyptic.[19] In the aftermath of the 2008 financial crisis, interest at the White House in Thomas Piketty's best-selling history of growing wealth and income inequality (his recommendations to save capitalism from capitalists being limited to the "useful utopia" of a global progressive and redistributive taxation of capital) gave the left reason to hope that change was coming.[20] Marxists proposed a high-stakes, provisional, "minimum utopian program," and public left-leaning libertarians put on the table "realistic" ideas for social reconstruction in a "return of utopia."[21] For "party communists" and "disaster communists," international revolution as nonnegotiable is back on the table.[22] Visions of a new social order after capitalism abound.[23] If these are not signs of hope, what is?

We have seen time and again how the public emanation of hope can activate desire for a better world. In North America, from the civil rights movement to Black Lives Matter, from Martin Luther King Jr.'s "I Have a Dream" speech to Barack Obama's 2004 address at the Democratic National Convention, hope has been a potent stimulant. In Obama's discourse, hope became "audacious" to demarcate it from "blind optimism," that "almost willful ignorance."[24] It was no longer just ordinary, quotidian hope. It was manifest, providential hope, spiritually and practically potent. "Hope in the face of difficulty. Hope in the face of uncertainty. The audacity of hope! In the end, that is God's greatest gift to us, the bedrock of this nation. A belief in things not seen. A belief that there are better days ahead."[25] That 2004 speech, which brought hope home, greasing the wheels of Obama's race for the presidency, struck frankly utopian notes—utopian not only with hindsight, relative to the presidencies that preceded and, especially, that followed his, but utopian in the sense of expecting radical measures to improve life for a majority of the American people. The message put out by Obama in books, posters, and paraphernalia for the general election season of 2008 wedded hope to a presidential hopeful and thus to a tangible political opportunity, which lasted eight years, until 2016. Despite or because of the train wreck of Donald Trump's single term in office, it was reasonable to suppose that peak hope would be reached in the run-up to the 2020 election. The projected Democratic victory would rescue the country—and world—from utter chaos. And then the pandemic hit.

An unfit Republican in the White House proved that hope is not enough to save us. The election of his challenger, Joe Biden, proves the impotence of utopian slogans, be it MAGA, Make America Great Again, or (more to the progressive Democrats' taste) MEGA, Make Earth Great Again. What, then, we might ask, is the relationship of utopian hope to desire for *real* change, and, even more important, their relationship to will, to agency? Since imagination does prosper in hopeful idleness, some amount of some kind of hope—though on its own an insufficient motor—seems to be an indispensable ingredient of utopia-oriented transformative action. To the motivating spirit of negation within despair we can add the stimulating energy of angst and anxiety as generative of hope;[26] these passions can be said to set the agenda of our age and its structure of feeling. "If utopia arises from desire" for a better way of life, writes Levitas in *The Concept of Utopia*, "the transformation of reality and the realization of utopia depend on hope, upon not only wishful thinking but will-full action. The presence of hope affects the nature of utopian expression," yet does not entail realization. The utopian dream, desire for utopia, "becomes vision only when hope is invested in an agency capable of transformation" or seeing transformation as its task.[27] Levitas's account here simplifies what is actually a reciprocal relationship between hope and desire: hope being activated by utopia-spinning desire, and vice versa. But she is right to insist that, to be invested in transformative agency, to have a shot at socially transformative effects, utopian hope and utopian desire, dream, or wish must work in tandem. No matter which of these two affective entries it uses, utopia can supply an impetus to action as its wish-turned-hopeful-vision incites the will.

Writing these reflections about utopia exercised my hope for humanity. If they encourage the reader to exercise theirs to be in ever so slightly better shape for the future, they will have served their purpose. The workout begins with a fresh look at the problematic of utopia and its relevance to our time. Understood as a *myth*, utopia presupposes the existence, in fact the proliferation, of different versions of the good society, modified with each telling. Such an understanding is threatened from two sides. On the one hand, there is the abovementioned stereotype that utopia contains a more or less detailed plan for an imaginary society presented by its creator as more or less perfect. On the other hand, utopia is dogged by the belief that, as an image of a just and happy society, it should be practicable and submit to attempts to realize it. If the image, as a particular ideal, does not necessarily demand realization, the experiment, a real social possibility, does not necessarily require perfection, accepting compromise with ideals as the cost of realization. Plato can be said to have bequeathed us both alternatives: while Kallipolis in *Republic* and the "first-best" state in the later *Laws* (the more democratic of the two, with common property across the board) stand as ideals, the "second-best" regime of Magnesia represents a major compromise with the flawed reality of human nature. Reconciling the ideal and the real seems impossible, and utopia—Plato's as much as anyone else's—appears forever caught in an endless oscillation between them, however useful this may be for critical reflection on the existing social order.

Has the time finally come to release the concept, especially in common parlance, from swinging between idealization and realization, which has for so long plagued it? I invite the reader to consider embracing utopia—worn out though it may be—at once as indeterminate speculation about a qualitatively better future for human society and as a hypothesis, by assuming it to be possible. With this assumption, we hold on to a holistic expression of the highest earthly aspirations of humankind, aspirations we have no good reason to abandon when their realization seems further off than ever. These two facets of utopianism as advanced in the present book—that is, the speculative and the hypothetical, or utopia as conjecture about, and utopia as possibility in, the future—amount, in fact, to the shift, discussed earlier, from identifying utopia with concrete visions and practices aimed at their materialization, and toward understanding utopia as provisional conjecture about a future that would be qualitatively better, as different from anticipation of what lies ahead. Utopia in this second sense is the imaginative genesis of surmise about how the world might be substantially improved (not what it would be at its best), rather than just what might become of it. The change in conception is not as drastic as it may seem at first blush. Utopia retains its narrative roots (even its artistic blossoms, if "hopepunk" and the more straightforwardly utopian "solarpunk," new turns in speculative fiction, are any indication).[28] It also remains, as ever, critical of the status quo. What it gains, however, is social-theoretical grounding.[29]

Social speculation about a possible, radically other and better future (without committing to any determinate version of it) cannot be equated with reformism or with fiction disconnected from reality. It consists in dialectical play with what social analysis turns up as trends and forces, desires and concepts (conflicting or contradictory), affinities and tensions at any given moment at work in society. It starts from the present by asking: to what better futures can existing tendencies lead us? This is starkly different from the question: toward what super-dystopia is the world likely headed? Its point of departure is thus not an imaginary, wish-list future to be reverse-engineered, only to reveal that the present lacks the resources to build it. This means that utopia-as-speculation describes not a real, practical possibility (let alone expectation), but a hypothetical one. In this mythic guise, it is neither abstract nor concrete; neither fantastic nor experimental; an extrapolation neither from normative principles nor directly from history. The utopist assumes nothing about utopia except its future possibility. A more metaphoric way of putting it would be that, instead of flexing our hope by trying to seize this or that elaborate utopian project, we extend hope by letting go of such projects for good.

Hope draws strength from desire, as vice versa, and it is to training desire that I turn next. This is the desire for the good society that subtends and impels utopia as speculative storytelling and as something whose possibility—that it can be actualized, if in a form that will continue to elude us—we assume. Desire for utopia arises from the experiences and interests of an individual or members of a group and is, therefore, conditioned by particular felt wants and physical capabilities. To the extent that the state of the natural world today provides a shared premonition of doom, the historical moment affords a collective horizon of experience on an unprecedented scale. Never has there been greater consensus about what is wrong with the world, what is rotten and missing in it. Never, then, have there existed more fertile conditions for a universal desire for utopia. Yet the place of desire per se on the path to a better future, as the majority tend to envision it, has shrunk on the basis of the premise that present desires need to be radically constrained if humanity is to survive, still less to attain lasting happiness. Unless we want utopia to mirror economic austerity, such a plan is misguided and unsatisfactory as a way of modeling this radiant future. And that is simply because the transformation of our desires does not hinge on their repression or reduction, or, to put it differently, on having the same desires, only less pronounced or fewer.

The experience of survival, of our existence coming under acute or chronic threat, is instructive and valuable in this respect. Between the calculation of remaining resources and the adrenaline-fueled tunnel vision from which pain has receded, survival leads us to realign our priorities. We become aware of desires entirely dependent on objects unavailable to us or beyond our control, of whims and velleities that do little for us, of desires whose maintenance and fulfillment is secondary or detrimental to our welfare, and of those which are for us unnecessary, compared to others that are indispensable, essential. Instead of being deliberately reined in, retracted, reduced in amount and intensity, desires become spontaneously focused and rerouted toward the primary, the vital. Thus, in the most difficult and creaturely of conditions—which, throughout recorded human history, has been the breeding ground for heroes—we discover a potential source of utopian desire unchained (if incompletely) from desire's habitual deformation by the capitalist economy. Anything that jeopardizes survival temporarily loses its value; any relative excess we had grown accustomed to, or perhaps never had to do without, is the first to be forfeited. Its retention as a wish, in fantastic form, involves its abstraction and sublimation. Such desires as survive this sorting process, adapted to the exigencies of self-preservation, undergo alteration by amplification and even refinement. The objective limits placed on their indulgence render them more valuable. At the same time, the new perspective can serve to mount a critique of praxis aspiring to plenitude yet at best assuring organic self-preservation, as well as to call for solidarity and cooperation.[30]

Of course, even if survival might suddenly seem like a shortcut to utopia, survival alone will not take us all the way. Yet the modification and appreciation just outlined will do as a pattern for desire in that looked-for place, where the condition of the struggle for survival no longer obtains (the menace to existence being absent). Desire, overgrown in the wilderness of capitalism, needs no cutting back or stunting as such for the purposes of utopia. We can think of learning to live within our means in the interest of the general good as the training of desire on the espalier of our resources. Desire and its gratification have two sides: that structured by lack (compensatory, reserved, regressive), and that founded on expenditure and abundance (extravagant, expansive, progressive). The first side gives direction, the second force. Desire's training, or "education"—such as happens in survival—requires reorienting it away from its alienated form, as desire for commodities, and toward its nonalienated form, as desire for sensual and intellectual enhancement through social and creative activity. For all these reasons, utopia's aesthetic and political connections to survival are worthy of attention.

The materials and artifacts assembled in this book are by and large social-theoretical. They fall into the general category of critical-utopian thought, in which the critical social analysis *a pessimo* is characteristically complemented by a desire *ad optimum*. What follows is a look at select moments and currents in utopian thinking in a variety of spheres and registers. Political and critical social theory intersect in them with anthropology, literature, and practical action motivated by desires and hopes for radical social transformation. The common denominator is their relationship to survival, and since the latter is a deeply embodied experience, the book's through line is embodiment.

For some years now, I have been preoccupied with the historical divergence of politics and utopia.[31] I attribute their divorce not to the well-known critique of utopian socialism by Marx and Engels, but to the progressive theoretical *disembodiment* or *spiritualization* of the utopian project in the twentieth century. As the historical evidence against utopianism accumulated, positive sociopolitical visions and experiments of community building on broadly communist principles increasingly aroused justified suspicion. In effect, utopian thinking came to function defensively as a nonpolitical alibi, all but precluding active political engagement, in a range of heterodox Marxist and post-Marxist political theory (notably, in the work of left-libertarian Abensour, its considerable hermeneutic value notwithstanding). More recently, however, the rising rhetoric of hope, the embrace of prefigurative praxis in radical democratic social movements[32] like the movement to take back the commons, and other communal, physical elements of such action began to point to a possible reinvigoration of both utopianism and radical politics taking place on the theoretical and historical planes. Historicizing the long-standing discursive disconnect between utopian and radical democratic energies seemed to me necessary for bringing them together and thus preempting the bankruptcy of their respective visions. This rapprochement is also what drives the present book.

The range of periods and social contexts in which utopian values take root demonstrates the utopian tradition's plurality of signification and valence. But the tradition itself warrants remapping. In an earlier work, I looked back through the history of utopian literature to trouble the beginnings of modern European utopian thought and imagination. I found these beginnings not, as is customary, in *Utopia*, More's canonical Renaissance text, but in the popular late-medieval topos of Cockaigne: the profane corporal imaginary of a land of shared plenty, pleasure, and leisure, for the most part omitted from the major and wide-ranging studies of utopia.[33]

Cockaigne's importance as a myth, meanwhile, is paramount. The depiction, in one of the Kildare Poems (mid-fourteenth century), of society turned upside down, linking social justice with abundance, has been recognized in Marxist historiography as complementing the revolutionary thought behind the English Peasants' Revolt, which put equality first.[34] Cockaigne was "the Utopia of the hard driven serf, the man for whom things are too difficult, for whom the getting of a bare living is a constant struggle."[35] The satisfaction of bodily appetites, including erotic desire, that defines the plebeian *pays de Cocagne*—the most synthetic literary example of which is an anonymous, mid-thirteenth-century French poem—resurfaced powerfully in the somatic-utopian visions of the Marquis de Sade and, especially, of Charles Fourier. These authors projected (differently, to be sure) a dream society rooted in the lived body and its passions by availing themselves of Cockaigne's logic of the subversion of hierarchies, laws, and *moeurs*. My panorama aimed to correct the bias that the modern utopian tradition sprang from More and to draw attention to the intermittent resurgence, amid and in tension with city utopias, of *utopias of the body*.[36]

The present book expands this picture of a minor, mostly latent and neglected strand of utopianism as a resource for utopian thinking across the humanities and social sciences. As science works wonders and technological advances make some people dream of immortality, as nature refuses to be mastered and the environment to cooperate, the human body remains the real frontier of utopian dreaming against what Bloch called our "hardest nonutopia," namely, death. All pleasure wants to last forever, *alle Lust will Ewigkeit*, says Nietzsche. If there is an ultimate utopian telos, it is surviving the body as perishable, as *pourriture*—a survival that does not pass through suffering and resurrection. Mortals long elevated spiritual immortality to perfection because the body was experienced primarily as displeasure and pain. From a reduction in bodily suffering comes the appeal of a fleshlier immortality. Vampires, potentially immortal, are intermediate to the new conception, insofar as their dependence on mortal death for sustenance and everlasting life is for them a continual source of anxiety and fear of dying. The vampire survives mortality, rather than dwelling in immortality. During capitalism's crises, the figure of the zombie comes to life as dystopian critique: rather than surviving mortality, the living dead define the nadir of survival. The body reaches utopia as a wreck and is reconstituted there. Biological bodily survival in a social world harmonious with its environment is the minimalist utopia to true immortality's maximalist one, *ceteris paribus*. As the horizon of possibility, the utopian spirit adapts and even changes its mind.

The second chapter of this book looks at the role played by corporal desire in twentieth-century utopian conceptions of emancipation, focusing on the French context. The exposition commences with three "scenes." The first, the post-Marxist phase of Surrealism, is Fourierist in inspiration. The second zooms in on the Situationist International, deepening the Surrealist critique of repression and alienation while offering a theory of society as *spectacle* and, as a remedy, the passional revolution of everyday life. The third scene opens in May '68, with another wave of critique, this time going after the spurious utopia of sexual liberation. At stake here is desire's recuperation by (rather than knowing complicity with) capital, which peddles as freedom what has become an obligation, a new circle of the market hell, further alienating us from ourselves. The revolutionary energy of the "sixty-eighters," particularly as relates to sexual mores, put the body front and center, building on preexisting critiques of desire and lack.

The critical currents discussed, tendering utopian visions of sovereign passion, all represent resistance to the spiritualization of utopianism then under way, as well as to its melancholization owing to the disappointment with the Soviet experiment, from which the left has yet to fully recover. Registering the rampant economic growth and wealth of postwar French society, they adopted the notion of survival to theorize, first, the inferior form of life conforming to society's "programmed lack," and, subsequently, the lived experience providing a utopian springboard. The advent of environmentalism further underscored the importance of dialectically articulating survival with desire, tying radical ecological sense to antistate somatic utopia. These debates and struggles, in which ecological met critical-utopian consciousness, merit replaying on account of their remarkable relevance and sophistication.

The third chapter then extends this critique of survival in seeking to overturn the presupposition that "bare life" is incompatible with radical utopian politics. The project of moving beyond the state form, there to protect life from brutish existence yet incapable of honoring the social contract, continues to animate critical social theory *sensu lato*. Theorists of this tendency, I argue, ought to take a more dialectical view of survival: as a source of utopia, rather than simply as anathema to their down-to-earth political vision.

In some recent, broadly neo-, post-Marxist, radical democratic, and anarchist incarnations, critical theory has been guided by the recognition that human biological and cultural survival depends on our dual, critical *and* utopian, capacity to desire against and beyond the biopolitical state. Yet the converse—that the critical-utopian impulse springs also from the individual and collective experience of the struggle to survive—has yet to be widely acknowledged. The twenty-first-century utopian *politics of survival*, describing radical struggle with diverse modalities of bodily mobilization that responds to the biopoliticization of sovereignty, embodies both the promise and the risk of politics.

Finally, the epilogue is dedicated to bodies for and in utopia: the corporal constitution of community approximating the utopia to be universalized. What interests me is, on the one hand, the relationship of desires in the present to their idealized, utopian form; and, on the other, the configuration of the utopian imagination by bodily whereabouts, structured by *displacement* physical or imaginary. I move on to say that utopianism's strength as a myth continues to lie in its simultaneous "iconoclasm," its resistance to determinate content, rather than in its hell-bent pursuit, as in times past, of positive recipes, blueprints, or programs for the future. Utopia's normative "deficit," for which first-generation Critical Theorists Theodor W. Adorno and Max Horkheimer have been criticized, is also the dialectical guarantee of its truth. I briefly take up the body in Adorno's thought to highlight its importance as an ethical index. The historical problematics presented in the book and the corresponding modalities of utopian desire are those of utopias of the body, which liberate bodily passions instead of rationally mastering them. The final accent falls on the living conditions sufficient for utopia-inspired or utopianizing action and on what utopia might look like in our survival-centered age.

The ensuing pages tease out a set of utopian criticisms, sentiments, projects, and expectations, to suggest how these might inform, caution, and illuminate contemporary left politics. The utopian current, coded "warm" by Bloch on account of its link to imagination, passion, and will, has not always run alongside the "cold stream of analysis,"[37] which can strengthen utopianism's language and clarify its aims, but also chill its energies. If utopian thinking is once again "hot," it is because analysis has shown that the political stakes in the global ecosocial crisis are clearly greater than those of the nuclear threat's "balance of terror." The imminence of a planetary apocalypse becomes the index of wishful, optative immanence, of an urgent desire to overcome the causes of our ruin. But the sense of crisis to which we are prone and that (bound up with it) of possibility, following the rhythms of capitalism, are not new. Utopia is not a totalitarian nightmare or a liberal façade for the global exploitation of labor. It is a unified response to both crisis and the possibility for dramatic improvement arising from it.

Indeed, utopia can be many things at once. My intention in arguing for a different composite version of it is punctual and undogmatic. If the constellation of utopia includes garden-variety social blueprints, the asterism within reach of our naked eye excludes them. The pattern coming into view, closer to our concerns and outlook, is twofold. On the one hand, utopia is any embodied desire, here and now, for a good society; a desire capable of giving form to individual and collective action and thus becoming prefigurative of such a society, which nonetheless remains latent and dynamic, rather than being elaborated as a social plan.[38] On the other hand, utopia is a futureward myth that activates hope and orients, without purporting to normatively determine, action. A can-do attitude depends on having a purpose. Utopias, even those cast centuries into the future, should furnish only revisable goals.

Historically speaking, utopia is a wheel that, if it is not to come off and put society as such in peril, requires reinventing every few generations. This is the tenor of Slavoj Žižek's break with its earlier, "false" conceptions, the unrealizable ideal and the realizable libidinal utopia of capitalism (satisfying ever new desires): "The true utopia is when the situation is so without issue, without a way to resolve it within the coordinates of the possible, that out of the pure urge of survival you have to invent a new space. Utopia is not kind of a free imagination. Utopia is a matter of innermost urgency. You are forced to imagine it as the only way out, and this is what we need today." "It's a matter for survival. The future will be utopian, or there will be none."[39]

Even reinvented, however, the utopian wheel needs to be realigned from time to time. I understand my principal role to be that of a wheelwright. Those interested in a systematic, comprehensive review of available conceptions of utopia and a thorough treatment of individual themes united in this book will be better served elsewhere. The pages that follow, the fruit of (so far) fifteen years spent working through the problems of the utopian tradition from an essentially Critical Theory perspective, pull out merely a few of its threads of greatest relevance to the present. *Parti pris* and polemics are a vital, not a regrettable, part of this process; rather than creeping into it, they move it along.[40] It is not a matter of trailblazing, but, taking Herbert Marcuse's advice, of *weitermachen*, of carrying on.

A book about utopia these days is also necessarily inconclusive. To conclude would go against the openness and mobility of immanent utopian horizons. The only way to end is by inviting the reader to attend to their longing for a qualitatively better world both despite and because of the doubtful survival of the one we currently inhabit.

CHAPTER 1

The Utopian Hypothesis
From Radical Politics to Speculative Myth

THE FUTURE MIGHT NOT BELONG to us after all. This we must grant. Given the distinct possibility that history is not on our side, why not give up? Why continue denouncing, the world over, the world's wrongs? Why insist—as in the old days, when the future was a promise to us—that real change for the better is possible? The world to come must still be worth fighting for. No matter the actual odds of victory by the right side of history, which are low indeed. As long as the future is for us a *prima facie* value, we will not give up the little claim we have to it. What is more, we will fight without fail to get it right.

So goes the refrain of the international left today. Chanting it now, with so much water under the bridge, betokens a historical obstinacy, a resilient hopefulness, or at least immunity to cynicism. That same old tune has now a deep patina. Whole movements died with it on their lips, and others were considerably weakened. If new ones have taken it up, it is by adapting the lyrics or the melody.

The once so musical tomorrows have fallen silent. The future is not our echo chamber; it was not built to resonate. Contrary to what was expected, it did not deliver on the promise of its improvement. If the left still has a future, it is because there seems hardly any future left. The coming climate catastrophe looms ever larger as the projective sense of human possibility diminishes. It is up to the left—carrying this sense in its DNA, in its structure—to rebuild it, even on quicksand. A compromised future, which few want, for which demand is dwindling, can be won by the left.

And so, deaf, invincible or incapable of accepting defeat, the left sings itself a solace. It can still afford it. And singing, even a song such as this—played out, nostalgic, consolatory—is already half the battle. It's the other half that remains to be won.

The other half of the battle over the future is actually fighting it. Our fight should not be confused with anticipating victory or defeat, or with envisioning what comes after. Whatever you do, stay calm and do not lose your dialectic—a survival skill, no matter on which side of the struggle you happen to be. Reasoning on the principle that there are two sides to every coin, that well-meaning actions can produce harmful effects, and that, like luck, history itself can turn on a dime, reverse direction, is a skill that cannot be overestimated. The objective is beating history at its own endgame, in a battle of wits, of cunning. On only one condition: that the means used are consistent with the ends to be attained.

Those means on the left have been two, principally: *critique* and *utopia*. They form a double helix. Coiled around each other, the critical and the utopian impulses directed against capitalism are without a doubt the greatest socialist legacies for our politically sclerotic age. The question was and is theoretical as much as practical: how to turn the one into the other, critique *into* utopia? Time and again, theory complicates practice. Time and again, practice challenges theory to prove its validity in efficacy. A theory that is its own practice is not practical enough for it. But does practice incontestably prove itself? Less by its consequences than deontologically. Its rectitude derives from following its own right principles.

The spectacle of mass mobilizations in social movements such as Extinction Rebellion or its offspring, Birthstrike, seems to show that social practice, if it possesses hope and strategic skills, can do without social theory. The momentum of activist practice is taken as a sign of theory's weakness, its lag. Following up on posttruth and postcritique, the allure of posttheory is getting things done. But the idea of putting doing above thinking, thereby dissociating them, is still theory, if at an impasse.

The promise of such mobilizing is undeniable. It has to do with the immensity of the stakes. We are invested in avoiding a probable catastrophe. The planetary ship is sinking, and if we must go down with it, we shall not be idle but fighting. The distant future matters little at this stage. Giving it thought seems more and more an unearned privilege, a luxury, a foolhardy pastime, to be indefinitely postponed. When the house is on fire all around us, and the alarm is sounding louder every day, utopian dreaming differs little from the ironic meme "this is fine": its sole message is its opposite. In a universal emergency, nuances are the first to go. The question of how to get from *here* to utopia is no longer asked—should not be asked—for utopia (*ou-topia*) is *nowhere*, and here, meanwhile, is *everywhere*.

When critique does not go far enough, the question becomes how to stay where we are, so as to not cede this place, as bad as it is (it will only get worse if we do). It is not at all a question of turning around or reversing direction; past the point of no return, by definition, there is no going back.

And critique today either does not go far enough or, when it does, its reach is mighty disappointing. It does not reach out to us, to rouse us from our apathy, confusion, cynicism, demoralization, depression, or inertia. To prove its credentials as praxis, critique must do more than reach inside; it must also reach out, and far. That is not its job, but its true vocation. Absent such far-reaching critique, whatever "utopias" still come into view are partial or infantile. The crusade of human rights, the dropout cultures from anarchoprimitivism to VR gaming, and the scientific fantasy of transhumanism all come to mind.

Social criticism today finds itself at a crossroads. Will it be—as R. Buckminster Fuller, sounding the alarm, put it some fifty years ago—utopia or oblivion? Until this fork in the road, until this compounded crisis, immanent critique, appealing to existing social values and abandoning the perspective of a revolutionary break with the existing order, has been hobbled by too deep a suspicion and disenchantment with progress, placing its hopes instead in redemption and a "weak" messianism. That realization and the imperative to avoid both human oblivion and dialectical indecision are the strongest they have ever been since the guideposts of Heaven and Hell faded and fell by the wayside. All the more so given that the two roads, having crossed, continue to run parallel; so close, in fact, that from utopia to oblivion it is but a small step or misstep. To go down the path to utopia is to think dialectically without going round in circles, which is to say—with Adorno at his most lucid—"to think at the same time dialectically and undialectically."[1] Otherwise, utopian impulses will always already be taken for dystopian.

Falling off this utopian path will put us by default on the one to oblivion, which passes through tribalism and social entropy, and, true to its name, leads to forgetting. No differently from a critique overly entangled in the struggles and values of the present and losing sight of a universal utopia, however, a critique distracted from contemporary social complexities by setting its sights on particular visions of utopia abandons the dialectic and forgets the mobile horizon in the name of which it was formulated. This, indeed, is the dual focus or obligation Fredric Jameson advised.[2] For action to take shape, for real change to happen, for history to be made rather than merely endured, every reality check requires a utopia check and vice versa.[3] The challenge continues to be to think society as a dynamic whole, its conflicts inextricable from its desires, its histories from its utopias. Utopia or oblivion: the future of society or its impossibility; the choice is not even, properly speaking, an alternative.

Two roads for social critique, then: one leading nowhere, the other to the cemetery. Only this road to nowhere can take us far enough. When it has, it becomes utopia.

The technique of social movements on the left is showing and sowing discontent and dissent physically, outside, in the field. The voluntary weaponization of bodies, such as gluing them to a protest site to prevent forcible removal, is taken for a new, performative model of critique. But such critique—vehement, ruthless, almost visceral—is not new. It had merely fallen out of practice.

No one these days really doubts the use of social criticism. Radicals, from the showboat to the knee-jerk, avail themselves of it all the time. But theory—who needs it? Is a crisis that every year grows more acute the time and place for systematic reflection about the society in which we live? Insofar as there are still spaces and a moment to lose for social critique, the answer is yes. To become again far-reaching, sidestepping the grave by taking the path toward utopia, critique must renew its vocation as a genuinely social practice. The social theory indispensable for this renewal will come up short if it is not, at the same time, a critical theory of utopia.

What Politics?

So posed, the question raises doubts about its own terms. "What kind of politics do we need?" simply takes politics for granted and presupposes a choice among its known modalities. But do we even need politics? And what do we mean by it? What limits do our working definitions of "politics" presuppose? Formulating questions that raise such far-reaching doubts betrays a degree of noncommitment to the status quo, an intimation of alternative arrangements. In them, both criticism and imagination are at work or at play. This work-play is one of reconceptualization and redefinition.

The path from critique to utopia—from reasoned and impassioned discontent to something like lasting happiness—must to some extent and in some sense become political, inasmuch as politics is the public exercise of freedom to bring about systemic sociopolitical change. How else, if not by some kind of politics, would the conversion of social critique into a significantly better social order be accomplished and secured? There are those who say that a revolution in social relations must eschew, not just existing forms of politics associated with the state form, but the political altogether; that the way to social utopia worthy of the name does not pass through political contestation; and that we will know that we've gotten there when, having climbed it, we can kick away the ladder of politics. We may, indeed, start by opposing politics as we know it: the monopoly of the state, in distinction to, for example, social movements, whose convergent character bypasses the fractured left of the party system. We might expend energy on transforming everyday life, social values, and social dynamics, and on prefiguring in this way the good society beyond politics, where, for Friedrich Engels, "the government of persons" would be replaced by "the administration of things."[4] But any expansive form of such a profound and wide-ranging transformation is almost certain to come up against state politics and into conflict with it, becoming caught in its wheels either by choosing from among existing avenues for political engagement or by inventing new, oppositional ones. Let us not fetishize the state as *the* historical form standing between us and utopia. A revolutionary politics motivated by the conviction that a far better world lies *just the other side of* the state's ruins is a dead end. With nothing constructive to offer, it lacks a utopian register.

To learn from the errors of twentieth-century left-wing leadership and assumptions of power is not to make of Lenin, Stalin, Mao, or Castro targets at a fun-fair shooting range or models for toilets and trashcans. Such creative contempt for history should be the privilege of utopia: ours only once we get there.[5] The catalog of horrors perpetrated in the name of left utopia circulates here below like that of Sears, Roebuck & Co. on the imperiled utopian island of Pala dreamed up by Aldous Huxley.[6] Any new leftist politics worth the trouble cannot be magically protected from the blunders of the old. A hubristic attitude toward past disasters (of which those born after 1970 legitimately feel innocent) in order to gain credibility signifies, more than anything else, that the left is too weak to bear the burden of its failure in living memory. Yet the converse, despondency, part of the same drama, is just as telling.

To think and do politics outside the box containing its state-sanctioned varieties, which mostly lack the hope needed to make a fresh go of radical emancipation, is a good start, as such politics have, by and large, kept utopia in quarantine. Writing in the *New Left Review* some years back, T. J. Clark struck the first clear notes of a new "left-wing melancholy," into which a part of the left has settled as into an armchair. When it comes to influence in the political domain, the most Clark grants left intellectuals is that their "groaning establishes the key of politics for a moment, and even points to a possible new [politics]"—adding that, occasionally (as in, for the nonce), the survival of the left depends on its ability to transpose politics to a new, *tragic* key.[7] In short, an "anti-utopian politics."[8] Clark's predilection is for tragedy without catharsis; for the inevitability, and thus certainty, of an inflexible natural, mythical law. As Walter Benjamin well saw, the "essence of mythic happenings is recurrence," an eternity of torment as punishment.[9] This is what a pessimism without solace looks like. A pessimism that will have none of Antonio Gramsci's or Negri's accommodations: an optimistic will or intellect, respectively.[10]

It is a pessimism as great as the disappointed hopes on which it is founded. For not long before his *profession de foi*, Clark (a onetime member of the Situationist International) looked forward to a future with utopian overtones, when once ineffective political ideas could be activated, restoring them to their proper use and aim. "Political writing is always instrumental as well as utopian. Guy Debord's is no exception. Only sometimes writing has to reconcile itself to the idea that its time of instrumentality—its time as a weapon—lies a little in the future."[11] By 2012, however, in the wake of Occupy and the Arab Spring, Clark had come to favor left-wing politics rebuilt around the refusal of utopian hope, seeing in utopianism *tout court*—which, as late as 1998, he had judged inextricable from radical political reflection—an encumbrance when it came to political strategy. If he had not altogether lost faith in the left intellect, he had appreciably scaled down his expectations for its reach and range.

To Clark circa 2012, the left has no future to speak of on which it can pin all its hopes. The very orientation toward a future infantilizes politics. Only by looking its own failure in the face, disdaining the grand promises of modernity, does the left have an actual future before it. There is a need for a new, disabused telos. Clark's prescription for left politics is here the struggle to assemble material for a society, rather than the former inexorable march toward a radiant millennium.[12]

"What would it be like," Clark muses, "for left politics not to look forward—to be truly present-centred, non-prophetic, disenchanted, continually 'mocking its own presage'?" To be willing "to dwell on the experience of defeat"? "A politics actually directed, step by step, failure by failure, to preventing the tiger from charging out" is his idea of "the most moderate and revolutionary [politics] there has ever been." He does not shrink from calling it "reformism."[13] It is Clark's version of "the year of dreaming dangerously," his dystopia to Žižek's utopia.[14]

"Utopianism . . . is what the landlords have time for." "Fantastical predictions" about the end of capitalism serve no purpose: "No doubt there is an alternative to the present order of things. Yet nothing follows from this—nothing deserving the name political. Left politics is immobilized, it seems to me, at the level of theory and therefore of practice, by the idea that it should spend its time turning over the entrails of the present for signs of catastrophe and salvation." The left's "root-and-branch opposition to capitalism" requires digging up the present. To the adolescent (unreconstructed) leftist, ridding the present of capitalism would be tantamount to the flourishing of utopia, as though nothing more needed to be done. The "Great Look Forward" of deluded anticipation.[15] But the way forward is buried, that much is certain.

Between 1998 and 2012 in Clark's intellectual trajectory, hopeful futurity has thus gone missing. Only the present matters: the spadework to uproot capitalism in the here and now. With a radically foreclosed horizon of expectation, there can be no more question of utopian futures, new or old. Tarrying with them or dwelling nostalgically on the sense of utopian possibility, which existed for earlier generations of thinkers but not for ours, is counterproductive. For the left to survive—by transposing politics to a tragic key—its "groaning" must be loud and clear. The left's future, in other words, needs to be staked firmly and sensibly on the first part of socialism's twofold legacy, that is, on *critique*: on a criticism of existing conditions and their tendencies that stops short of extrapolating a vision of the future from them. For as long as the paralysis of theory and practice that Clark diagnosed holds—and I do not think that it does—there can obviously be no critical theory of utopia. If his *Heaven on Earth* (2018), to which the 2012 piece became the coda, is any indication, even the possibility of such a theory of utopia is incorrigibly "utopian." But naïve affirmation is out of character for critical theory; its spirit is thoroughly *sentimental*, as it rests on a reconstruction of the Enlightenment project.

Even those on the left who agreed with Clark that a healthy dose of pessimism is just what the doctor ordered continue to nourish, however gingerly, a hope for the return of utopia, or something like it. Witness Enzo Traverso, in whose *Left-Wing Melancholia* (2016) utopia is both pronounced dead and resurrected. If, according to him, 1990 marked the year when "the historical dialectic between the experience of the past and the utopic projection toward the future was broken," when "the horizon was removed from sight[,] and the past became a saturated memory of wars, totalitarianism, and genocides," then the late 1990s retrieved that dialectic as a still image, in Benjamin's sense. By that time, as confirmed an anti-utopian as Daniel Bensaïd was coming around (almost *malgré lui*) to a late, melancholy utopia.[16]

There are, to be sure, different shades of melancholy and ways in which it combines, or not, with contemplation and action. The experience is fundamentally ambivalent. No one knew this better than Benjamin. In contrast to the empathic sadness of the historicist historian, the melancholy method of the materialist historian—as Benjamin self-identified—is cautiously detached contemplation.[17] Earlier on, in the 1931 review-essay "Left-Wing Melancholy" (from which Traverso borrowed his title), the concept of melancholy does critical work. It serves to caricature the politically bankrupt "political lyricism" of left-radical writers, whose heaviness of heart derives from routinely "forfeit[ing] the gift of being disgusted," whose "negativistic quiet" makes of "political struggle" an "article of consumption," and whose "tortured stupidity" is despair's latest metamorphosis.[18] This melancholy is, as Wendy Brown clarified in her own, 1999 critique of left-melancholy traditionalism, Benjamin's "term of opprobrium for those more beholden to certain long-held sentiments and objects than to the possibilities of political transformation in the present."[19] In the heart of a left-wing melancholic, the past is a string of more or less unconscious losses, the deepest one being that of utopian promise. Thinglike and frozen, it cannot inspire; the heart and the world become immobilized. For this reason, melancholy habits of thought must be thrown off if we are again to "draw creative sustenance from socialist ideals" and develop a deep, radical critique of, or a "compelling alternative" to, the status quo.[20]

Where are we, twenty years on from Brown's call for resisting left melancholy? According to Traverso, "new collective hopes have not yet risen above the horizon. Melancholy still floats in the air as the dominant feeling of a world burdened with its past, without a visible future."[21] In 2016, apparently, we were still stuck with a "paralyzed dialectic," in what registered like an eternal present unable to project itself into the future; a world without those seductive pictures of the good society in the abstract that made utopia's name.[22] Since then, the left has been in receipt of one wakeup call after another. And have we not dwelled on and even worked through the left past long enough to be revolted by it? One is tempted to grant Clark full license to experiment with his tragic "tonality" just to trigger the contrary, immune response he would certainly not approve of. For the spell of melancholy seems to be lifting.

Certainly, the tension between the demands of the past, of memory, and the pull of the future, of forgetting or redemption, is less intense than it once was. But the retrospective and the projective sallies of thought—critically inseparable—have not entirely lost touch with one another. Assessments of crisis, of direness, stand as proof that, at the very least, utopia is missed. The retrospective impulse rarely limits itself to dwelling on past defeats, as Clark would wish it; past utopias are there to greet it. There is, indeed, too much defeat to hold in one's memory; an active mind cannot take it, and shrinks from its sheer enormity, its cascading relentlessness. Brooding melancholy (still in its nonclinical sense) loses its hold, the mood swings to its other, manic pole, unable to hold the mind to the morose tasks in store for it.

It may be hard to see how the persistent passive remembrance of the past and commemoration of history's victims become the impetus for a new left politics, instead of deepening resignation or complacency. The note on which this book terminates is that the path out of the past and the present through which it runs is necessarily sentimental. The sentiment that can serve as a compass is, however, nostalgia, rather than melancholy. Nostalgia is a mood so often maligned that I imagine readers recoiling at the mere mention of it. But just as there are different melancholies, so there are different nostalgias. The nostalgia of sentimental illusions keeps memory hostage, demanding the restoration of that which is missed. The nostalgia inextricably tied to utopianism, meanwhile, liberates memory. Like all nostalgias, it is selective and implicitly critical of the present; but what it longs for are utopian hopes and their expression. It feels a double responsibility, to the past and to the future.

The past is for it an inheritance, not a refuge. If its sources are the Golden Age and Paradise myths, it seeks to make good on ancient social ideals. Sometimes it is barely even legible as nostalgia, having already invested itself in a prospective vision, as when the Golden Age is declared to be not in the past but in the future.[23]

From these myths, however, utopian nostalgia keeps a contemplative distance, as though looking too closely would disenchant and destroy them, but, in reality, as a matter of principle: by associating too closely with the process of transmission, not just of select cultural treasures but of the whole archival *dispositif*, we risk—as Benjamin understood—colluding with the triumphal procession of history's victors, who count these objects among their spoils.[24] And that same distance nostalgia shares with critique. It is a stubborn myth about nostalgia that it short-circuits social criticism; in fact, nostalgic attachments can provide criticism with material, values, and aspirations relativizing our own and idealized ones, in a protest against what is. Socialism's *"nostalgie du juste,"* glimpsed by Emmanuel Levinas behind the audacity of utopian hopes, conserves the norms necessary for critique and action.[25] Nostalgia can make us look wistfully, admiringly, imaginatively upon so much mute heroism of the oppressed and compare it with our own condition. The past comes alive and does not haunt nostalgic memory as it does conservative, left-melancholic remembrance. But neither is its mystery unmasked by imitation. Try as we might to copy it, our collective hope will never "equal" that of old, though it may surpass it. It is in nostalgic *emulation*, in a devoted recovery of that lost sense of possibility, that despair reveals its precious veins of hope, and where the metal of courage is cured.

Similarly to Clark's present-centered tragic key, a potent left nostalgia critical of the present and hopefully futureward is a matter of attuning affect and reflection. But, unlike his refined pessimism without solace, nostalgia's solace gives birth to hope: an uncomplicated, despondent *hope without optimism*, and no less radical for it. Optimistic hope, erected upon the left's accommodation- and consolation-inducing historical defeat,[26] would be a true tragedy, the *hamartia* of naïve trust in an accelerating, greening global economy in its *n*th cycle of promise and frustration, bringing society closer to that irreparable *metabolic rift* Marx warned about. Present hope, of Terry Eagleton's dewy-eyed moralists and spiritual cheerleaders,[27] is insufficient; we need to stimulate and build up our desire for utopia, reinforcing it with the dramas of survival and dashed hopes in the past's broken social promises. In his defense of hope, Eagleton allows that "the Left's suspicion of hope" is "not entirely groundless"; some hope is deluded or false, producing images of the future that are pejoratively "utopian," disconnected from its construction.[28] Good hope is not deluded, nor, obviously, is it reconciled to the present.

What left-wing politics follows from this attunement (which is not a resolution, but an evolution of sentiment)? We could answer by saying that the question of *utopian politics*, of its general shape, is best left unanswered if such politics is to evade capture by state machinery. Let us look more closely at the orientation of this politics.

Myth

The present book concerns the utopian share of socialism's legacy, of that double helix formed by utopia and critique. Socialism—and, with it, left utopia—has gone in and out of fashion, falling out of circulation during decades of ideological dissensus and trenchant division within the leftist milieu, and now once again *à la mode* as a party platform in liberal democracies. Yet the larger project to which this volume contributes is a history, not of socialism, but of criticism; a history in which reason is as vital to critique as affect and myth.

When we speak of utopia, we evoke a modern myth, with premodern origins. It is what Hans Blumenberg, following Hans Jonas, called a *fundamental myth* (*Grundmythos*), with heterogeneous versions (each meaning to improve, to some extent, on its antecedents) of the same basic story.[29] And it is also, according to Northrop Frye, a *speculative myth*, that is, a myth "designed to contain or provide a vision for one's social ideas, not to be a theory connecting social facts together,"[30] and in this respect unlike that other myth of human social organization—the social contract. The latter explains its contemporary society based on social analysis and available historical evidence by projecting into the past an account of the emergence of social order; whereas utopia, still attached to political and social theory, imagines not society's origin but its telos. Yet the two myths are mutually complementary. Any serious myth of telos assumes a myth of origin (the best-known modern mythologist who attempted to tell both stories is, of course, Jean-Jacques Rousseau). The utopian "vision of something better has to appeal to some contract behind the contract, something which existing society has lost, forfeited, rejected or violated, and which the utopia itself is to restore." It comprises a longing for what precedes social order, and is thus inherently nostalgic. As Frye astutely observes, the contract myth's "overtones" are tragic, incorporating an element of the myth of mankind's fall. The utopia myth, meanwhile, is oriented toward comedy, presenting an ideal state of social integration and reconciliation.[31]

To these two we might add a third secular myth, conjoining them. It may have had its day, but the myth of History, especially in its progressive variant, held in its thrall a large part of humanity, which saw itself somewhere along the dusty road that leads from civil society to utopia.

In "Myth Today," his "semioclastic" analysis at the end of *Mythologies* (1957), Roland Barthes describes myth's emptying of reality and naturalizing of history, transforming history into universal nature. He sees myth as colonizing "en bloc" or "worming" itself into meaning, distorting it. Myth "is a language which does not want to die: it wrests from the meanings which give it its sustenance an insidious, degraded survival, it provokes in them an artificial reprieve in which it settles comfortably, it turns them into speaking corpses." Instead of historicizing, myth lends contingency the appearance of eternity.[32]

As an area of study and a metalanguage, mythology is, for Barthes, part semiology, part ideology. As he sets out to prove, bourgeois society, whose "norm" he considered "the essential enemy," was also "the privileged field of mythical significations." Structurally mirroring Western capitalism, his semiotic theory of myth is permeated by the very ideology it seeks, self-sacrificially, to expose and demystify. Consciously politicized, it understands the phenomenon of myth in terms of this particular ideological structure, as if the latter were the very matrix of myth rather than its historical transformation. For reasons that could be strategic, Barthes thus speaks the language of alienation, dissimulation, reification, commoditization, appropriation, colonization, exploitation . . . His weapon is adapted from that of his enemy. His mythology is at once ideology critique and a counter-mythology (body of myths); it produces experimental second-order myths. "The best weapon against myth is perhaps to mythify it in its turn, and to produce an *artificial myth*: and this reconstituted myth will in fact be a mythology. Since myth robs language of something, why not rob myth?"[33]

Does Barthes's *ruse de guerre* of a counter-mythology undo the loss of memory around objects (things, people, actions) used by first-order myth and, in restoring their history, restore their human significance? Does it repoliticize speech, reinstate complexity and contradiction? Does it bring back dialectics?[34] *Bref*, is it *revolutionary*?

There is another way in which Barthes participates in the late capitalist culture he is denouncing. "Revolutionary language proper" is, for him, "spoken in order to transform reality" and "no longer," as in the case of mythical language, "to preserve it as an image." In claiming that revolution "abolishes" and "excludes" myth, that the first-order or object language of revolution is antithetical to the second-order or metalanguage of myth,[35] he denies political revolution its left arm, which—as Georges Sorel recognized—is none other than myth. (Its right arm, of course, is social truth: functionally absorbed in the making of the world; both motivating and produced by revolutionary action as altered reality. The distinction between truth and myth becomes fluid, as prospective utopias, action-guiding or incarnated in action, are "often only premature truths,"[36] and truths, conversely, often start out as utopias.)

"As long as there are no myths accepted by the masses," Sorel wrote, "one may go on talking of revolts indefinitely without ever provoking any revolutionary movement."[37] Revolutionary myths dynamize the process of change. They "allow us to understand the activity, the sentiments and the ideas of the masses as they prepare themselves to enter on a decisive struggle."[38] Contemporary critics of Sorel's own revolutionary social myth of the *grève générale* (general strike) dismissed it as a utopia. Sorel dismissed utopia in his turn, without recognizing its participation in the revolutionary myth.[39] "Myths must be judged as a means of acting on the present [and] all discussion of the manner of materially applying them to the course of history is devoid of sense," even if anticipation does benefit from definition: "we are unable to act without leaving the present, without considering the future, which seems condemned to forever escape our reason. Experience shows that the *framing of a future in some indeterminate time* may, when it is done in a certain way, be very effective and have few inconveniences; this happens when it is a question of myths in which are found all the strongest inclinations of a people; of a party or of a class." Sorel's rejection of utopia rests on his understanding of it as descriptive and theoretical, in contrast to the dramatic and apocalyptic essence of social myth.[40] A utopia taking the form of a story would turn it into myth, a narrative of transformation ending in an ideal or qualitatively better social order to come. And it was obvious for Sorel that utopia, while distinct, associates closely with myth during a revolution:

> The real developments of the Revolution did not in any way resemble the enchanting pictures which created the

enthusiasm of its first adherents; but without those pictures would the Revolution have been victorious? The myth was heavily mixed up with utopias, because it had been formed by a society passionately fond of imaginative literature, full of confidence in the *little science* and very little acquainted with the economic history of the past. These utopias came to nothing; but it may be asked if the Revolution was not a much more profound transformation than those dreamed of by the people who in the eighteenth century were inventing social utopias.[41]

In Barthes's estimation, however, the myth-prone language of the left, even when mixed up with utopias, remains unrevolutionary (the left is "not Revolution").[42] And it will stay that way, presumably, unless its own myths become subject to a second-order mythification. The *critical mythology* proposed by Barthes "is certain to participate in the making of the world" as it "harmonizes" with reality's dream of itself (*tel qu'il veut se faire*)[43]—including, dare we say it, with the subversive myths (numbered though these may be) born in the oppressed, myths that reject the unjust present and are retro- and projective (utopian). Barthes's counter-mythification thus is and is not "political." The resultant "unveiling" "liberate[s]" myth, postulating the freedom of language and repoliticizing myth's objects. Yet for all that, or because of it, the operation remains a metalanguage, "'acts' nothing," being "at a distance from" the "entire community," from "everyday life," and from the "political dimension," which justifies it.[44]

The left itself becomes, in Barthes's hands, quasi-mythical, as does revolution. Again, the possibility left open is that this may be tactical, if not strategic, on Barthes's part. As he continues his dismantling, left-wing myth is criticized for being "incidental," "inessential," "rare, threadbare," and "poverty-stricken"—nonproliferating and transient—because tactical; "produced on order and for a temporally limited prospect, it is invented with difficulty." It reveals the falsity of its own obviousness; its artificiality shows through, instead of being concealed (as it would be in bourgeois myth): "Left-wing myth is always . . . a reconstituted myth: hence its clumsiness." Resisting bourgeois mythology and siding with the oppressed, it is "imperfect." For Barthes, the oppressed do not have access to the luxury of a metalanguage, needed to produce myth. So the left fabricates myths on their behalf. The "wretched of the earth" appear to him immiserated beyond repair; they are defined essentially by destitution, by lack. "The oppressed is nothing, he has only one language, that of his emancipation," he writes. Though poor, this language is revolutionary if it forgoes myth. It is the language of truth, not of lies; a language of actions, aiming for social transformation. "The oppressed *makes* the world, he has only an active, transitive (political) language; the oppressor conserves it, his language is plenary, intransitive, gestural, theatrical: it is Myth."[45] Where does this political, and indeed utopian, supposedly nonmythic speech of the oppressed arise, if not in their oppressed condition? Though it may not resemble anything we are used to calling a luxury, the language of emancipation is not "nothing," and is to be treasured. Barthes seems not to see the luxury in apparently unproductive, inoperative, useless imagination—the secret that capitalism, recognizing wealth solely in the reified form of a commodity, wants to conceal from us.

Barthes's mythologist, viewing this history of linguistic struggle from the left, "can live revolutionary action only vicariously: hence the self-conscious character of his function, this something a little stiff and painstaking, muddled and excessively simplified which brands any intellectual behaviour with an openly political foundation ('uncommitted' types of literature are infinitely more 'elegant'; they are in their place in metalanguage)."[46] A new, unsung hero, the critical mythologist participates in history but

> it is forbidden for him to imagine what the world will concretely be like, when the immediate object of his criticism has disappeared. Utopia is an impossible luxury for him: he greatly doubts that tomorrow's truths will be the exact reverse

of today's lies. History never ensures the triumph pure and simple of something over its opposite: it unveils, while making itself, unimaginable solutions, unforeseeable syntheses . . . For him, tomorrow's positivity is entirely hidden by today's negativity.[47]

As a critic of bourgeois ideology, he destroys past and present and, in so doing, creates—in this apocalyptic fashion, reminiscent of Sorel—a utopian future without ever knowing its shape.[48]

Utopia, which we have classed as a myth, is not calculation. It is not a mere tactic. Neither is it strategic (unlike bourgeois myth). It is not per se part of any "revolutionary strategy"—an oxymoron if ever there was one. The energy of the Revolution in France no doubt owed much to a belief in a utopian outcome; in anticipation of it, revolutionaries projected themselves beyond politics as a separate sphere of human activity. The Revolution's utopian momentum shows in the audacity of the 1793 Republican Constitution relative to the 1789 Declaration of the Rights of Man and of the Citizen. In the context of such radical political change, for which it served as a guiding principle, utopia itself can appear "depoliticized." The creation, beside legitimating mythical pasts, of modern popular myths (e.g., the Nation, the People, the Law, Natural Rights to Liberty and Equality, Revolution as a radical break with the past, the foundation of a new, republican civilization enshrined in a new temporality, measures, fashions, and so on) nowise prevented the overthrow of the system. The new, revolutionary-era mythology was at least auxiliary, conducive—less than decisive, more than accessory—to the events. Bronislaw Baczko speaks of a "fusion" of utopian representations of the ideal city with symbols and political myths "in the crucible of Revolutionary ideas," and of the Revolution as generative of such hopes and myths, notwithstanding the reformist character of the utopias of the period.[49] Utopia became thus an "integral part" of the myth of revolution as new beginning, a myth reproduced in the nineteenth century in the narrative of the "*unfinished* Revolution."[50]

Barthes, however, would have only a myth-free vanguard doing the revolutionary work. History (it, too, become quasi-mythical) is here destroyed along with the vanguards that subscribed to present-transcending, dialectical myths about past and future, utopia chief among them. Yet we know that, to revolutionary actors, the course of revolution itself appeared mythical: a change so natural, inexorable, a violent necessity, *anankē*-like, as if traced by a superior force, rather than by historical determinants and actors, its workers. In the experience of Pierre-Joseph Proudhon, socialist philosopher, journalist, worker, professional revolutionary, and critical participant in the Revolution of 1848,

> a revolution is a force against which no other power, divine or human, can prevail: whose nature it is to be strengthened and to grow by the very resistance which it encounters. A revolution may be directed, moderated, slowed down . . . A revolution cannot be repressed, cannot be deceived, cannot be denatured, or, and even more so, cannot be vanquished. The more you constrict it, the more you increase its resilience, and render its action irresistible. So much so that it is precisely the same, for the triumph of an idea, whether it is persecuted, harassed, beaten down in its beginnings, or whether it develops and spreads unobstructed. Like the ancient Nemesis, whom neither prayers nor threats could move, the revolution advances, with fatal and somber step, over the flowers cast by its devotees, through the blood of its defenders, across the corpses of its enemies.[51]

This is the myth of revolution, its real mythical image in the dialectic of history. If the pattern of history is cyclical, as the historical application of complexity science suggests,[52] it may be that history is fundamentally a species of myth, that uniquely human form of meaning-making. As such, it is a defense of human agency against material and social contingency or Blumenberg's "absolutism of reality."[53]

Where the left once saw a horizon of actualizable human possibility, walls of reluctance, timidity, and wariness have gone up. To break down these enclosures, it may be necessary to reach for the time-honored repertoire of left political myths: for the accord of the "Good Old Cause" as for the "Great Night" (*le Grand Soir*) of anarchists and communists;[54] for Marx's "old mole" (a thoroughgoing revolution, future success through adversity) as well as Sorel's *general strike* (last enacted on a national scale in France in May–June 1968); for mythicized events like the Paris Commune and '68, to say nothing of the series of popular and revolutionary heroes (Saint-Just, Marx, Louise Michel, Jaurès, Luxembourg, Zapata, Durruti . . .).

But what of the myth of utopia in our century? How did the left lose sight of its horizon? The parables of the proletariat's redemptive suffering, Christian-millenarian in inspiration, are no longer dispensed by political theology like hosts from a paten.[55] Before the weakening of its proletarian base, the millennial promise was integrated into the utopian wish sclerosed as blind faith that is the bourgeois ideology of limitless economic progress.[56] Disenchantment with its own theoretical power to control and reorganize society left the working class with thirst for utopia but no matching means or strategy of slaking it. Belief in utopia had to be vested in utopia's enemy—capitalism. Utopian desire ended up being expertly channeled into mass consumerism. The meager political means at the disposal of institutionalized socialism were largely bereft of a radical (as opposed to liberal) utopian orientation. Add to this the postwar disillusionment with socialist utopia and the new Western economic policy, and the dissociation of utopia and politics was complete. The three decades following World War II were devoted to the winnowing of utopian ambitions that raised the question of politics, and to a compensatory *realpolitik*. In the 1960s and 1970s, the *renewal* of utopian energies happened on the social plane, bypassing the political. At the close of the last millennium, Russell Jacoby issued his grim report about the "end of utopia": given the bleak reality "stripped of anticipation" in an age of political apathy, radical or revolutionary politics was no more.[57] But Jacoby was not ready to give up utopia without a fight. Utopian thinking, at least in its "iconoclastic" mode, remained, for him, "the essential precondition for doing something."[58] In 2012, Oskar Negt said it loudest: "Utopias are the power sources of every emancipation movement."[59] Utopia is a luxury lavished upon the disenfranchised.

This, of course, is not a new belief. Marcuse, for his part, was adamant that "without some doses of Utopianism, no real changes in history have ever been accomplished."[60] He saw nothing wrong with reforms whose cynosure was rupture with the continuum of domination, pollution, and dehumanization, so long as one did not neglect the "radical transformation of values."[61] Everything must begin with a stance first articulated by Maurice Blanchot, namely, that of the *great* or *absolute refusal*:

> precisely because the so-called utopian possibilities are not at all utopian but rather the determinate socio-historical negation of what exists, a very real and very pragmatic opposition is required of us if we are to make ourselves and others conscious of these possibilities and the forces that hinder and deny them. An opposition . . . that is free of all illusion but also of all defeatism, for through its mere existence defeatism betrays the possibility of freedom to the status quo.[62]

By the late 1960s, anyhow, utopia—in its pejorative sense, critically labeling the real possibilities of a socialist transformation as *im*possibilities—could be said to have run its course. With humanity already in possession of the material keys to utopia, its criticism had proven shortsighted. Marcusean "end of utopia" could

> also be understood as the "end of history" in the very precise sense that the new possibilities for a human society and its environment can no longer be thought of as continuations of

the old, nor even as existing in the same historical continuum with them. Rather, they presuppose a break with the historical continuum; they presuppose the qualitative difference between a free society and societies that are still unfree, which, according to Marx, makes all previous history only the prehistory of mankind.[63]

The idea of qualitative difference, too, was not new. Its precursor in social philosophy had been utopist Fourier's method of *absolute deviation* from the present, *l'écart absolu*.[64]

Utopianism has long motivated, upgraded, and brought up to speed socialism's quest for emancipation. Socialist utopia, where the means of production are held in common, has been its essential myth, whose seniority is a sign of its adaptability and indeterminacy. It can be filled with hopes again and animated. Left-wing political myths can build up our desire for something better and greater for all of us. But not all popular myths converting despair into hope are equally serviceable to the left. Those that rapidly proliferate as a mainstream media spectacle should be approached with caution; they may be convenient enough to serve nothing but the status quo. Take the savior myth, exemplified by the climate campaigner Greta Thunberg. To produce change, the movement around her needs to catalyze or articulate, not just the scandal of its hypocrisy, but a thoroughgoing critique of the very system enabling the destruction of the planet. Today's front pages are, of course, no basis on which to judge the future course of consciousness. Besides, Barthes said it best: "It is never a good thing to speak *against* a little girl."[65]

Wager

A critical theory of utopia is indispensable to critique as renewed, utopia-oriented social practice because left utopia (nostalgic and negating) is not some magic formula to be embraced uncritically. It requires us to analyze such things as (1) the core values and ideals grouped under the umbrella of utopianism and the total social transformation for which it stands; (2) the appeals to and invocations of utopia, or the sources, circumstances, forms, and uses of utopian mythopoesis; (3) the social contradictions that contemporary utopian thought, be it fiction or social theory, reveals and masks; (4) particular sites where belief in the speculative myth of telos works to enslave rather than emancipate; and (5) movements and contained experimental communities claiming some part of the utopian legacy or ethos, their negotiations with and function within the established social order.

Never before in human history have there been so many unmet needs. Capitalism, in its revolutionary capacity, multiplies immanent desires by multiplying commodities and the quantity of their consumers. The transformation of those needs that oppress us and—only then—their full satisfaction is imperative. The time has come for critical theorists to embrace utopianism as value-disclosing and critical, without simply assimilating it to theory's normative dimension and politically construed task of human emancipation. Utopia must be embraced for the myth that it is, and as both an extension and orientation of social criticism (which, as Nick Kompridis reminds us, should be "possibility-disclosing").[66]

This can render it useful, operative for renewing left politics.[67] Utopia strikes a chord with "groaning," as hope does with despair. It also, in one of its strands, strikes a chord with revolution. For Gustav Landauer, utopia and revolution are more than bedfellows:

> Each utopia contains two elements: the reaction against the topia from which it arises, and the memory of all utopias that have previously existed.
>
> Utopia is the unity of aspirations distilled to purity that will never reach their goals, but always a new topia.
>
> Revolution is the time interval between the old topia that is no more and the new topia yet to be established.
>
> Revolution is hence the way from one topia to another, or from one state of relative stability to another relative stability, over chaos, rebellion, and individualism (heroism and

beastliness; the solitude of the great and the forlornness of the atom in the mass).[68]

Revolution has been theorized as involving utopia, both as a reaction to the status quo and as (utopian) memory—here I would specify *nostalgic* memory, weighing upon revolution's children as wings do upon birds. Their "realization" is asymptotic; both are processes, ways to happiness whose coordinates undergo revision in the course of their pursuit.

Landauer tells us that utopia "stays alive underground," where it then "creates a complex unity of memory, volition, and feeling." This complex often goes by the name of revolution.[69] The utopian tradition has long been an underground—not to say unconscious—one, participating in the modus operandi of the revolutionary tradition of thought. Uniting the two are ambition, excess, and conspiracy. In their excess, they have been homogeneous as means to ends—perhaps never more so than during the Paris Commune. As *élans*, they are making a desperate comeback after decades of restraint and hanging back. Unlike the back-row groanings (to return to Clark's "concert-hall analogy"), they have all along lived in the pit, out of sight of everyone but the musicians.

There is no choice to be made between the myth of utopia and that of revolution. Whether and how they manifest is purely a question of dialectical cycles and timing. Utopia's time has come again, though maybe not revolution's. Revolution has too often lent its face to virtual spectacle, costing it its aura, and more. Through televising, advertising, and recycling in the twentieth century, its gesture has become both imitable and overacted. Save for its brief reemergence among the Yellow Vests and, still more recently, in the early phase of the American multiracial rebellion triggered by the killing of George Floyd by police, the revolutionary spirit seems to have lost its power as a rallying point to bewitch spectators and physically mobilize the masses.[70]

The eclipse of the utopian imagination from the 1980s on mirrored the fate of revolution among Western political theorists, who gradually swapped its vocabulary for *insurrection* (as the more visceral), *the coming community, destituent power, the common,* and *public assembly*.[71] Like Clark, Michael Hardt and Antonio Negri now go in for a version of *revolutionary reformism*—a "subversive reformism" as "an instance of political realism." They see the future as the object, not of struggle, but of a Pascalian "wager" (*pari*) so as to avoid the charge of utopianism when projecting "a process of transformation." Their calculation of the odds is based on witnessing "the accumulation of resistances, struggles, and desires for liberation." (They also argue for a "strategy of exodus" inheriting those of utopian communities, and, to their credit, call for a general or social strike, demonstrating that political realism need not shy away from social myths.)[72] Similarly, for Bensaïd, "the transformation of the world" is subsumed under a melancholic, Pascalian "bet" (*pari*), or a "strategic hypothesis" combined with a "regulating horizon," with which Traverso concludes his historical panorama.[73] The ending of *Left-Wing Melancholia* thus gestures toward utopia (a Blochian "concrete utopia," to be precise) without going there mentally, at least the extra mile.[74] Utopia-infused hope is missing from the formula.

A wager, no matter how revolutionary it purports to be, is rational judgment that has yet to make a leap of faith. Hope is not a strategy or an "ingredient" in operational planning, to be calculated into a plan. It can be calculated only externally (after the fact, not in advance). Yet no will or "kairotic" talent in the world can get out of bed in the morning without hope. It lies in the logic of the bet, moreover, to run everything through the dualism of winners and losers, all or nothing. In a true utopian myth, which activates hope, there is meanwhile no room for losers. If we win, everyone will. And if we lose the future, we won't have lost anything.

Not revolution then, not for us. But why utopia? Because the conditions for a better, less defective, less dominated life are something nearly everyone would take if offered them. That is a universal minimum. And most of us recognize that a better life is worth some degree of commitment if, in the end, it can be secured. Fewer are willing to take the risk of such a commitment without guarantees. How much hope is enough, and when? The commitment of hope is inimical to any such calculation. The exact formula escapes us, and that may be for the best. The left was good at chemistry, but never at alchemy; we do not know how to transmute hope into gold, or where to look for "the gold of time."[75]

What has been lost of the immanent proletarian experience of politics acquired in more than a century of struggle can be regained by the renewed utopian promise from the left. It is no use wishing that the working class, precarious and fragmented, would put itself back together again. But proletarian experience is still recognizable by its "fettered or distorted needs, wishes or imaginary formations evoking another society"—in other words, by the collective dream of utopia.[76] Social dreams thus continue to speak to the working class, atomized though it may be. The shared dreamworlds of mass utopia may have given way to private ones proffered by capitalism,[77] but these in turn have disappointed with runaway economic inequality, as wealth has failed to stop poverty from spreading.[78] With its competition in the realm of social dreaming disqualified, left utopia wins in a walkover.

Among the distorted needs, unrecognized as such until quite recently, has been relief from manual labor. Its gospel is automation.[79] The twentieth century dreamed of the manual laborer released from what Marx called the realm of necessity into that of freedom. The saviors then were machines. But, as Marilynne Robinson soberly predicts, "human labor will in effect be eliminated as a cost, or, to put it another way, as a claimant on some portion of collective wealth, once grudgingly allotted to him or her on the grounds that workers were needed."[80] What will this inoperative proletariat do with itself? Dispossessed and disposable, will it continue to know how to hope and dream?

One hopes; but social critique must become its supple companion: intertwined, myth and criticism must strike together. Of course, it is this whole business of myth (and, consequently, of utopia as a myth) that myth-hunting critical theorists are likeliest to find problematic. Transcended as bearer of historical reason (G. W. F. Hegel), theorized as the ineliminable, antitheological, if potentially politically noxious, companion to reason (Blumenberg),[81] exposed as the reversal or perversion of reason, rather than as logos's pure opposite (Horkheimer and Adorno),[82] demystified as the depoliticized fruit of right-leaning bourgeois, and especially petit-bourgeois, ideology (Barthes), myth has been thoroughly assimilated to the archaic, the primitive, the irrational, the distorted, the illusory, and the oppressive. In a largely disenchanted world, in which "truth" counts for everything, "myth," seen as its contrary, is suspect and undesirable.

Yet it is the repeated call for a "new mythology," beginning with Romanticism (Friedrich Schlegel and Novalis) and Idealism (Schelling and Hegel), that constitutes the ambivalent character of modernity, its affective revolt or defense against domination by reason and capture in the iron cage of instrumental rationality. Utopian socialism, whose crowning jewel was Fourier's mythology of Harmony, is a direct expression of revolutionary Romanticism. Sorel, for whom social myths were "expressions of a will to act," merely theorized the imaginative core of revolutionary politics.[83] His myth of the general strike was a counter-myth unifying class struggle, transcending contemporary divisions in the proletariat created by antisemitism (e.g., the Dreyfus affair). Surrealism, its internationalism and unconditional support for individual and collective emancipation now mostly overlooked, anchored its subversive attitude and new social myth in, among others, indigenous myths from Australia to the Americas. It saw the elaboration of such a modern collective myth as imperative, and to the question *"How can man be saved?"* replied proleptically with another: "In what measure can we choose or adopt, and *impose*, a myth fostering the society that we judge to be desirable?"[84]

Revolutionary utopian politics, action oriented by radical social change, tends to posit a special relationship to time, such as a deep temporal attunement or an arrest. The new myth of telos, befitting social critique, belongs to Gaston Bachelard's immanent, *vertical* time, which, unlike its transitive, horizontal counterpart, rejects the expectation, displacement, and postponement characteristic of determinate "blueprint" utopias—and of bets. The creative imagination is first and foremost the faculty of *deforming* existing images.[85] Concentrating the will, the experience of time's verticality in the present instant (allowing for the superimposition or layering of multiple durations at once) is that of decisive, critical invention causing a radical temporal rupture.[86] Only that "time of the self"—that line perpendicular to the temporal axis of life, of history, of the world, and of matter—"gives consciousness of the present the means to flee and escape, to expand and deepen," to break and to oppose.[87] Vertical time, discontinuous, is the birthplace of the person.[88] "Even 'in' time, humans remain upright," noted Alexandre Marc of the intellect's "vertical dimension."[89]

The Bachelardian conception of the creative moment of freedom, applicable to revolutionary time, was a critique of Henri Bergson's idea of *duration* as the intuitive continuity or *a priori* homogeneous flow of lived life. The latter, as it happens, had been adapted by Sorel to theorize the mythic general strike and "catastrophic" socialist revolution.[90] "To act freely," or creatively, Bergson wrote, "is to recover possession of oneself, and to get back into pure duration."[91] This direct experience of the undivided unity of time became for Sorel inseparable from the unswerving determination of revolutionary thought.

Bachelard, meanwhile, understood duration as a *temporal dialectic* of used, effective time, "consolidated into duration," and refused time, perceived as multiple "disparate instants." By moving vertically between instants, we constitute perceived time as continuous, with different durations. The "intuition of disorder in the mind" shows psychic continuity to be artificial and belated, an impression due to a "paralysis of action"; the primary temporal experience is one of discontinuity. The mind's "speculative function" and "negating powers" (both features associated with utopia) belong to the present instant, "mak[ing] time flow back upon itself so as to bring about renewals of being." The instant is fertile, *fécond*: "instants are distinct because they are fertile. And they are fertile not by virtue of the memories they can actualize, but by the fact that a temporal novelty is added at that point, a temporal novelty suitably adapted to the rhythm of progress" (aesthetic, moral, or religious). From the perspective of the instant, the future is here and now. Apart from things, what endures of the past is what has reasons for beginning again; Bachelard calls this "duration through reason." Ridding the mind of "all false permanence" would cure souls "suffering the pain of time and of despair."[92] Seen in this light, the telos myth and revolutionary action, their groundwork in social analysis, are instances of the mind's recalibration for a deeper, more harmonious and dialectical, well-ordered relationship to time while aiming for happy repose.

In the past, time itself seemed propitious and reality pregnant with change on a utopian scale. That sense of real possibility is today at an all-time low, from which it can only rise, or disappear altogether. For the time being, the world going from bad to worse is the sole intellectually honest prediction. The desired turnaround now would appear supernatural, miraculous. Utopian desire has reason to come back to us as myth. Confronted by the magnitude of the climate crisis and its likely toll on human society, the left has a moral responsibility to concentrate utopian energies for a future whose very existence science rightly throws into doubt. Rather than bicker over these energies' exact colors on the ideological spectrum, the left must attract, to their mutual edification, *any and all* expressions of desire for social utopia. A tall order indeed, requiring the suspension of disbelief for the telos myth to be useful. We must assume that utopia is possible, reachable, and lies somewhere ahead, even if reality points the other way. This is not a strategic assumption, but an anthropological and ethical one: based on our penchant for storytelling and for justice. It is the hypothesis without which there can be no future, let alone politics in a tragicomic and maybe even a comic key (for a change).[93] A hypothesis, unlike a wager, does not assume that there is a good chance of things working out and falling into place one day. No one here is committing a teleological fallacy in recognizing that elements of past utopias have been realized. The utopian hypothesis merely supposes that, with concerted human effort and a renewed, firm belief in utopia, our history might still end better than it started. Only then will we have left behind the horror.

CHAPTER 2

The Emancipation of Desire

Preludes and Postludes of May '68

THE LAST CENTURY was one of utopian promises, broken and renewed. Moving away from the generic concept of utopia as a telos or end-state based on a totalizing sociopolitical blueprint or system, thinkers such as Karl Mannheim, Bloch, Abensour, and Levitas made a strong case for utopia's ubiquity, and its open-ended, self-reflexive, provisional, and processual character. The bridge to this new, exploratory conception of utopia was *desire* and, more specifically, *educated desire*—extending Blochian *educated hope* for social transformation.[1] In Abensour's formulation, it was desire that has been taught "to desire, to desire better, to desire more, and above all to desire otherwise."[2]

This idea of desire as emancipated through critical education, aspiring to and anticipating a utopian future, stands in sharp contrast to desire as morally disciplined consistent with the status quo or with a predetermined program for change that reproduces existing relations of domination. It is, in other words, diametrically opposed to most classical utopias built on the inhibition of the passions for the sake of a particular version of the common good, the change coming about through some or all of the following: a radically different system of education, effective laws, collective spiritual enlightenment, and pioneering scientific experimentation. The implicit assumption in these models, of which book 2 of More's *Utopia* is the best known example, is that under ameliorated social conditions, desire ceases to be transgressive, no longer circumvents obstacles to its expression and realization, and falls into line. The antipodal vision of the good society would, meanwhile, consist in permitting the greatest possible fulfillment of desire, whose capacity to evolve in a socially beneficial direction (given favorable material and pedagogical conditions) is finally recognized.

The nexus of desire and utopia, with its discursive high point in France in 1968, has a long and dialectical history. Well ahead of More's canonical 1516 work, it continued against the grain of the tradition he inaugurated. Rather than carry on the legacy of Utopia's architect by reconciling moral discipline and natural law within sundry rationalist and collectivist, state-based social designs, the utopia of desire tempts, instead, with images of a stateless society organized around the free pursuit of pleasure. This desire-driven body utopia found literary expression in the popular medieval mythology of a land of natural general abundance, leisure, and sensuous enjoyment, known to European cultures as the land of Cockaigne.[3] This last—if we tell utopia by its level of freedom, its libertarian charge—deserves to be placed well above anything dreamed up by More, Henri de Saint-Simon, or Edward Bellamy.[4] Yet those who support utopian thinking and still, *malgré eux*, want a positive, potentially workable plan (otherwise it has too little to offer) might object that the "pastoralism" of Cockaigne is unrealistic, utopian in a pejorative sense, and that its rediscovery is part of a tendency to idealize social simplicity at a time when the march of history is so obviously toward complexity (the gist of Raymond Williams's critique of William Morris).[5] Their criticism, I think, misses the point. By tacitly equating all utopias with their most recognizable subset, that is, with social blueprints, they dismiss utopia as myth. Cockaigne, which is not man-made, is a speculative myth; an affirmative, normative project it is not, and never was.[6]

A second and related charge against any utopia of limitless plenty is, of course, its irresponsibility and incompatibility with the climate crisis. The refrain of climate action is belt-tightening and major lifestyle changes among the world's richest. The imaginary country where no one lifts a finger to work, enjoys greater leisure, or rules, but which (not being man-made) does not inscribe itself in human history properly speaking, surely merits preserving. It is a placeholder to keep us from falling into Spartan or ascetic moralism—more or less inevitable if we continue with current, pronatalist policies in all their forms—making of frugality a cult that will disproportionately impact the global poor, subjecting the powerless to the management of scarcity. Cockaigne helps us aim beyond it. Of course, it seems counterintuitive (contrary to anticapitalist logic), given the very real limits of our resources, renewable or not. Yet Cockaigne's vision does not situate itself in capitalism's productivist optic and reminds us that another optic is necessary. As a social myth of abundance, born from a precapitalist critical spirit, it must be defended in noncapitalist terms.

The basic folk motif of imaginary effortless pleasure and plenty, festivity, and freedom from labor encapsulated by Cockaigne has resurfaced time and again, in tension with statist, city-utopian visions. In the last one hundred years alone, one can isolate three distinct scenes of such resurgence. The first is the rediscovery of the corporal utopia of Fourier by the Surrealists circa 1945. The second is the project of a revolution of everyday life launched by the Situationists in the mid- to late 1950s. The third instance is the cultural ferment in France around 1968, which was followed by a radical narrowing of the utopian horizon of corporal desire.[7] Watching the wave of desire's real liberation and its popularity as the core of utopia break upon the shores of affluent consumer society, critical voices saw that the fetishism of desire, especially in the realm of sexual practices, coopted and commoditized a weapon, turning it into an economically well-adjusted lifestyle choice. The disembodiment of utopian theory is understandable in this context:

the retreat from the sovereignty of sensual pleasure was a response to "emancipated" desire's capture and pacification by capitalism.

The three twentieth-century episodes of body utopianism just named represented different ways of disposing the body for total personal and social freedom. They targeted the body's social oppression, which is to say, the repression of the pleasure instincts and the impoverishment, alienated solicitation, and excitement of all the senses, instead of the emancipation sought by Fourier and Marx.[8] All three took the view of this-worldly, embodied desire as central to the utopian imagination. Each situated body utopia within a particular social-revolutionary movement. Together, they raised questions germane to any critical project aiming for social happiness.

Scene I: A Country Where Desire Was King

Looking backward from the year 1980 at the first half of the twentieth century, Jürgen Habermas (relying on Adorno's *Aesthetic Theory*) described Surrealism as modernity's "doomed" rebellion against the autonomous articulation of art. This rebellion was to make good on art's as-yet-unfulfilled *promise of happiness*: its promise of utopian social transformation. The Surrealists, sentimental and uncritical, attempted to "reconcile" art with life by sacrificing art to life.[9] According to Habermas, this path to the universal emancipation of desire was aberrant, aporetic, fundamentally mistaken. Artistic sublimation is necessary to any such emancipation; the content of art bereft of artistic form loses its emancipatory potential. Art is art precisely because it is not life. In art, desire is sublimated and free. Desublimated, desire perpetuates the very domination to which it is a reaction. It is, moreover, one-sided to attribute to art alone—to the aesthetic, and thus sensuous, expression of experience—the capacity to cure life of its reification.

But Habermas's exclusive focus on how Surrealism as a whole let itself down risks missing the movement's local effects in transforming its many adherents' everyday experience, which in turn fed into their artistic practice—giving art the spontaneity of life, and life the inspiration of art. There was no question of desublimation.[10] He does not note that it marked an effective resistance to the bourgeois containment of artistic energies in a quasi-sacralized sphere, the better to commodify them. Surrealist manifestoes were inseparable from Surrealist actions: already in 1929, Benjamin, the only thinker in the Frankfurt School orbit to grasp Surrealism's revolutionary, meta-aesthetic potential, credited it with reviving a "radical concept of freedom," which was to be enjoyed "unrestrictedly," unconditionally, and with joining this anarchic ecstasy to a "poetic politics." In his view, Surrealism's "technological interpenetration of body [*physis*] and image" brought about a "collective bodily innervation" that could lead to a "revolutionary discharge," making good on the promise of *The Communist Manifesto*.[11] Also worth recalling in this context is the movement's enormous international appeal as early as 1935–36. In a letter from the field, founder André Breton recorded their "triumphal" reception in Prague: "five photographers at the station, banquet and exhibition 'in our honor,' gifts of paintings, etc.," a conference with seven hundred attendees, meetings with the Left Front, students, the German community; in short, he concluded, "a success without precedent."[12] To forget this real and international crescendo of enthusiasm and to dwell on Surrealism's failure to reach its more holistically revolutionary Enlightenment goals obscures the movement's epochal role in renewing the bodily current of the utopian tradition.

The first of the three moments I want to highlight comes, however, a bit later, at the end of World War II. Breton, then in exile in New York, is rediscovering the writings of Fourier, who figured in *The Communist Manifesto* as a revolutionary visionary of "critical-utopian socialism."[13] His *Ode à Charles Fourier*, begun about then, would come out in 1947, in Paris. Breton had already been in contact with Fourier's ideas in the group Contre-Attaque, which he cofounded with Georges Bataille, Claude Cahun, Pierre Klossowski, and others in 1935—the same year he definitively broke with the French Communist Party. In Fourier, he finds a total world and its evolution premised on unrepressed desire.

Between 1959 and 1967, the Surrealists helped lift Fourier out of the selective oblivion into which he had fallen. Thanks to their exhibitions and publications, building on the work of Simone Debout-Oleszkiewicz, the complete text of *Le Nouveau monde amoureux* (The New Amorous World; written 1808–29), the most elaborate body utopia ever committed to paper, saw the light of day.[14] The simultaneous interest in Fourier in Germany can be traced to the Paris-based German doctoral student Elisabeth Lenk: it was while supervising her dissertation in sociology on Breton and Surrealism that Adorno edited a translation of Fourier's *Théorie des quatre mouvements et des destinées générales* (Theory of the Four Movements, 1808), published in 1966 with an introduction by Lenk. Adorno's correspondence with Lenk did not alter the fact that he had a poor grasp of the principles, stakes, and sociopolitical critique practiced by the Surrealist movement.[15]

For Fourier, the harmonious organization of unrepressed passions was humanity's universal destiny. Notwithstanding his cyclical cosmology and history and his disdain for so-called progress and civilization, he looked ahead with optimism to a future free of asceticism and of nostalgia for a Golden Age (the *fin-de-siècle* utopian medievalism of a William Morris is retrograde by comparison). Once society did away with its artifices, the consumption of natural abundance would commence. Reflecting on the enormity of human failure, including the disappointed Enlightenment hopes and promises, Fourier chose the path of absolute doubt, followed by absolute separation (*l'écart absolu*) from history and tradition.[16] Though Breton never shared Fourier's mystical *illuminisme* (he was an atheist and a materialist) or nonegalitarianism (capital and work were his nemeses), he too swore by sensuality and the universal creative power of imagination.

For the visionary left-libertarian socialist, love is right [*a raison*], being "essentially the passion of unreason [*déraison*]." It was no different for the left-libertarian author of *L'Amour fou* (1937) (the titular "mad love" being a union of love's spiritual and carnal forms).[17] Breton took from Fourier the supreme value of desire. Fourier's ideal was not reason, but a balance of reason and desire; their separation leads to no good. The way to achieving such a balance lay in the free expression and immanent development of the passions. Previously destructive passions would then be naturally channeled into play; while this did not eliminate war, it turned it literally into a food fight—a *guerre de pâtés*. *Volupté*, sensual delight, the passional rehabilitation of the flesh, became for Fourier—and later for Breton—the concrete basis for a utopian society. Breton's own projected utopia from the mid-1940s, narrowly predating his *Ode* to Fourier, is permeated by Fourierist ideas on social organization and, in the same vein, features imaginary techno-animal hybrids (a duck-on-wheels, a bottle-dog, and so forth).[18]

Reviving Fourier's dream, Surrealism shone a light on the "region where desire arises unconstrained, a region which is also that where myths take wing."[19] Even before their fateful intellectual encounter, complete self-mastery was, for Breton, "maintain[ing] the body of [one's] desires, daily more formidable, in a state of anarchy."[20] He would later provocatively depict the utopian social revolt at the height of this anarchy in the Second Manifesto:

> It is in fact from the disgusting cauldron of these meaningless mental images that the desire to proceed beyond the insufficient, the absurd, distinction between the beautiful and the ugly, true and false, good and evil, is born and sustained. And, as it is the degree of resistance with which this choice idea meets that determines the more or less certain flight of the mind toward a world at last inhabitable, one can understand why Surrealism was not afraid to make for itself a tenet of total revolt, complete insubordination, of systematic sabotage, and why it still expects nothing save from violence.

The simplest Surrealist act consists of dashing down into the street, pistol in hand, and firing blindly, as fast as you can pull the trigger, into the crowd. Anyone who, at least once in his life, has not dreamed of thus putting an end to the petty system of debasement and cretinization in effect has a well-defined place in that crowd, with his belly at barrel level.[21]

Scene II: Playing in Situ

Fast-forward to 1957, the creation of the Situationist International (SI). From the outset, the group is guided by the idea that "a revolution of everyday life cannot be prepared with asceticism"—that is, with the privation of bodily pleasure.[22] Questioned about the relationship between theory and praxis, its members clarify that their theories are nothing other than a theory of their real life. They "support unconditionally all forms of liberty of *moeurs*, everything . . . called debauchery."[23]

Chronologically speaking, the Situationists were utopian before they were critical: their investigations developed in that order. They were utopian to begin with, in the sense of being concerned with the *construction of situations*. Ivan Chtcheglov's foundational text "Formulaire pour un urbanisme nouveau" (1953) imagines a future civilization, which its author was "not satisfied" with calling "experimental": "I mean that it will be more flexible, more 'playful.'"[24] This was followed by a commitment, on the part of the Lettrist International—SI's immediate precursor—to the "conscious and collective establishment of a new civilization."[25] By 1954, "it [was] time to impose a new human condition." Another collective statement made direct reference to Fourier: "Sovereign attraction, which Charles Fourier discovered in the free play of passions, must be ceaselessly reinvented. We will work to create new desires, and will spare no effort in promoting them."[26]

Constant Nieuwenhuys (known as Constant), an SI member until 1960, had already articulated this dialectic of desire and revolution in 1949, when, as the cofounder of the avant-garde group CoBrA, he proclaimed:

> When we say desire in the twentieth century, we mean the unknown, for all we know of the empire of our desires is that it comes down to one immense desire for freedom . . . Revolution alone will enable us to know our desires this very year, 1949. No definition can replace revolution! Dialectical materialism has taught us that consciousness depends upon social circumstances. And when these prevent us from being satisfied, *it is our needs that push us to discover our desires.*[27]

For Constant, utopian blueprints went hand in hand with critique.[28] The fruit of this double commitment was his design of the postrevolutionary city of New Babylon, applying what he called *unitary urbanism*, a critique of urbanism that married theory to practice. The city of the future is anticapitalist and populated by *homo ludens*: turned into a playground for life organized by leisure, the pursuit of new sensations and, of course, physical pleasure, individual and collective.[29] The practice of *dérive*, or psychogeographic drift, in existing cities was itself a step in the construction of the utopian city.[30] Debord's psychogeographic guide to Paris, *Discours sur les passions de l'amour* (1957), and the SI's subsequent repurposing of the *Carte du pays de Tendre*, Madeleine de Scudéry's map of the imaginary Land of Feelings (conceived as a female social game in the mid-seventeenth century), put romantic desire at the heart of utopia.[31] The juxtaposition of a 1656 version of the map with an aerial photograph of central Amsterdam anticipated the group's experimental "research and project" on the passions undertaken through urban adventure, and the free reconstruction, by such postartistic affective acts, of urban space.[32]

Suffice it to say, ludic practices of this kind were already a part of the Surrealist everyday life. If, just prior to his Situationist days, Debord decried Surrealism for its "senility," at the end of his life he freely acknowledged his admiration for and debt to

Breton.³³ The Surrealists, for their part, would later—in the 1980s and 1990s—embrace Debord's critical theory of capitalist society as spectacle. The Situationist utopia of *homo ludens*—of generalized creativity in all domains of activity—was also concurrently envisioned on the other side of the Atlantic, by Marcuse, whose exploration of *play* joined those of Johan Huizinga and Bataille.³⁴

Clearly, play was in the air. It could be sensed in the prodromes of '68. For the rebellious students of Strasbourg, "proletarian revolutions will be festivals or nothing, for festivity is the very keynote of the life they announce. Play is the ultimate principle of this festival, and the only rules it can recognize are to live without dead time and to enjoy without restraints."³⁵ But in the SI microsociety, utopia and revolution had long played together:

> Utopian practice makes sense, however, only if it is closely linked to the practice of revolutionary struggle. The latter, in its turn, cannot do without such utopianism without being condemned to sterility. Those seeking an experimental culture cannot hope to realize it without the triumph of the revolutionary movement, while the latter cannot itself establish authentic revolutionary conditions without resuming the efforts of the cultural avant-garde toward the critique of everyday life and its free reconstruction.
>
> This temporary, historical utopianism is legitimate; and it is necessary because it serves to incubate the projection of desires without which free life would be empty of content.³⁶

Scene III: Pleasure Demands the Whole World

We are in 1967. Debord's *The Society of the Spectacle* appears alongside SI member Raoul Vaneigem's ironically titled *Traité de savoir-vivre à l'usage des jeunes générations* (known to English readers as *The Revolution of Everyday Life*). Vaneigem's message to the "young generations" warns of those who leave living, desiring bodies out of the revolutionary equation: "People who talk about revolution and class struggle without referring explicitly to everyday life, without understanding what is subversive about love and what is positive in the refusal of constraints, such people have a corpse in their mouth."[37] Central to Vaneigem's argument is a radical reconceptualization of intersubjective, experientially rich communication within situations constructed outside reified capitalist modes of social interaction. No ordinary political program, this, but a social one, entailing the refinement of pleasure in noncommodified, nonalienated forms. For "a truly revolutionary slogan" to go with it, Vaneigem turns to Breton: "Lovers, give one another greater and greater pleasure."[38]

The Situationists' emphasis on "radical subjectivity," in an age in which "high technology bars the road to Utopia," was explicitly bound to utopian hope. For "there is no one who does not cling with all his might to the hope of [utopia] . . . Many, of course, lose their grip on this hope—but they put as much desperate energy into falling as into hanging on." The map of utopia was to be drawn bodily in everyday life: "The semi-barbarity of our bodies, our needs, and our spontaneity . . . give us secret access to places never discovered by centuries of aristocratic rule, and never so much as dreamt of by the bourgeoisie." The nostalgic figure of childhood as a source of such transcendence presides over these reflections, as "from the wild depths of the past which is still close to us, and in a sense still unfulfilled, emerges a new topography of the passions."[39]

By the time Vaneigem wrote these words, Marcuse had published a new edition of *Eros and Civilization,* where a decade earlier he had presented his utopian hypothesis of the future unrepression of desire and sublimation of sensuousness (sublimation not in the Freudian sense of issuing from sexual repression, but as the refinement of sensuousness). The influence of Marcuse's theories specifically on the events of March and May '68 in France was, however, nonexistent.[40] The impact of the Situationists, in contrast, was crucial: the handful of "Enragés" who in January of that year sparked the student movement at the University of Nanterre had read Debord and knew by heart the 1966 pamphlet *On the Poverty of Student Life*, written by Situationist Mustapha Khayati. One response to this "economic, political, sexual, psychological and . . . intellectual" poverty diagnosed in the student milieu came in the form of slogans shot through with utopian hope, desire, *jouissance*—phrases like "The restrictions imposed on pleasure arouse the pleasure of living without restrictions," or like "I take my desires for reality because I believe in the reality of my desires." A good number of them were actually invented by members of the SI or taken directly from Surrealist texts. They announced a preference: "*Plutôt la vie!*" choosing life over survival. They spoke of lived experience. As Lola Miesseroff, a '68 participant, remembers it, "We indulged ourselves."[41] The poet Jean-Christophe Bailly recalls "joy outweigh[ing] all the rest."[42]

The events around "Mai '68" were thus in step with the theoretical tendency to put desire at the forefront of social revolution. Already on May 5, 1968, the Paris Surrealists pledged their support "to students for all practical actions meant to create a revolutionary situation in this country."[43] It is true, within a year, internal conflicts following Breton's death led to the movement's official dissolution.[44] And not long afterward, in 1972, the Situationist International ceased operations—despite or, rather, because of massive interest in its brand of activism and Debord's disinclination to turn it into a political party. That same year, however, Deleuze and Guattari offered the French public *Anti-Oedipus*, their critique of Freud and Lacan combined with a posthumanist vision of the free production of desire as an intrinsically revolutionary social force fit to challenge capitalism—a *pavé* widely considered to be the most substantial theoretical contribution to the "micropolitics of desire," which "questions all situations."[45] The influence of Surrealism on Deleuze and Guattari was no secret: the book's title came from René Crevel, the idea of "celibate machines" was borrowed from Marcel Duchamp and Michel Carrouges. Finally, in 1973—the last in this series of theoretical developments to foreground—Abensour completed his PhD thesis on "the forms of socialist-communist utopia," finding in the fiction of the late nineteenth-century English anarcho-socialist William Morris an image of utopia as "the education of desire" (or "need"), obtained by keeping it, to use Bloch's words, "trained unerringly, usefully, on what is right."[46] Morrisian utopia rejects finality in human progress: it does not "assign 'true' or 'just' goals to desire," but only stimulates, awakens, and "open[s] a path for it."[47]

In a 1976 postscript to his biography of Morris, published two decades earlier, E. P. Thompson embraced Abensour's reading and approach to utopia, and imported it into the Anglosphere.[48] Thus, Morris taught and encouraged his readers to desire, and do so better, more, and, especially, differently. It is in desiring a better life that their desires themselves would be altered, augmented, and expanded. The content, the "what," of educated desire remains open and subject to critique. "There are disciplined and undisciplined ways of 'dreaming,'" explained Thompson, "but the discipline is of the imagination and not of [Marxist] science."[49] Emancipation happens *through* utopia, which is therefore not an end or telos; the imaginary utopian voyage has an interrogative, critical function.

The Abensourian, desire-based conception of utopian thinking was a far cry from Vaneigem's emancipation of corporal desire—emancipation through learning one's own and others' boundaries in the act of self-expression, for example, in orgies. This is not to say that Abensour was unsympathetic to the SI; to the contrary. Like the Situationists, who, in 1969—in homage to the barricades of May '68—illegally replaced the statue of Fourier melted down in 1941 on the orders of the German occupier, Abensour also recognized that, in Fourier's New Amorous and Industrial Worlds, utopia "made a leap from need (lack) to desire (the expansion of being)," and became joined to politics as a "politics of desire."[50] Fourier's own method was inspired by the failure of the French Revolution. "After the catastrophe of 1793," he wrote, "illusions were dispelled and modern political sciences were irrevocably stigmatised and discredited," "social movement [driven] into regression." "Excess of political . . . [and] commercial freedom" plunged Europe again into barbarism and feudalism. Instead of founding what "the spirit of the century called for"—a sect promoting sensual pleasure—philosophers came to "side unreservedly with nature and the voluptuous passions," such as "amorous servitude," instead of countering them with a "religion of love."[51] These insights, *mutatis mutandis*, are applicable to the postludes of '68. Fourier's *écart*, departure from history, was as epic as the postrevolutionary moment that prompted it was disastrous.

Commenting in 1980 on Thompson's affinity for Abensour, Perry Anderson saw his countryman as having been seduced by the "irrationalism" of "disillusioned" Parisian revolutionaries.[52] Both Anderson and Habermas, in their synchronized criticisms of the proclamations of somatic happiness as the path to utopia, were obviously deaf to the recurrence, in the revolutionary artistic and intellectual movements of the twentieth century, of body utopia—a resurgence that attests not just to the appeal of such social-critical visions, but to their vitality.

Three Questions

The three scenes just described—and the history of hope of which they are a part—raise at least three questions worth considering five decades on.

Question the first: *What are the costs of neglecting bodily desire in emancipatory utopian thought*? Answering it would require confronting the historical horrors of applied utopias on the left of the political spectrum. So-called communist regimes, vowing to create a secular New Man, sacrificed the body's creative power and physical-aesthetic enjoyment to an ultra-machinist, Stakhanovite conception of human productive capacity to meet material needs. Theirs was a perversion of the socialist utopia of social labor, the latter proceeding from the egalitarian potential of free productive activity and the emancipation of labor. Happiness was defined by the collective effort to raise society above subsistence level. Its liberal individualistic counterpart in the West, meanwhile, equated happiness with material comfort and health, coming closer in this sense to body utopia.

Second question: *Can a utopian "education of desire" for social transformation dispense with the immanent social critique of need and desire, and if not, what might such a critique look like?* As Adorno states in the all-too-brief "Theses on Need," critique must "latch on to . . . not any pre-given hierarchy of values and needs," but need's contradiction with itself, given the mediation of needs in capitalist society and their fulfillment that cheats subjects out of this very fulfillment. It is, then, a question of distinguishing, not basic from superficial, natural from social, or legitimate from illegitimate needs, but urgent from nonurgent ones.[53] Organizing production for the unconditional, unrestricted elimination of immediate lack would indeed relieve a great deal of suffering and, as needs are not static, the relation between need and satisfaction would be transformed.[54] Need and desire must cease being differentiated by the choosiness of the latter. For that, we need to move away from the lack-based notion of need satisfaction, whereby need is treated materially like a hole to be plugged up with crap (crap air, crap water, crap food, crap shelter, crap education, crap social life, crap freedom, to say nothing of the quality of self-actualization). Opposing need to desire perpetuates the assumption that, to fulfill a need, anything is better than nothing, lowering the standard by sanctioning mediocrity, and justifying an indiscriminate, rather than personalized, approach to need satisfaction as sufficient, good enough for most, who cannot afford better. The same opposition also maintains survival as "bare life," incapable of imagination or cultivated desires and "higher" needs (making their satisfaction virtually irrelevant).

The critique of (socially mediated) desire only makes sense if undertaken in tandem with this emancipatory project. Here we can effectively follow in the footsteps of radical critiques of market-driven prodigality from the 1940s (Karl Polanyi) onward.⁵⁵ We know that the genuinely revolutionary removal or easing of ethical constraints around embodied desire, constraints productive of transgression, has gone hand in hand with desire's capture by economic forces. As avid consumers, buying into the ideology of hedonism, we have been spurred on to desire more (quantitatively) and anew—rather than more (intensely), better, and differently—and to take pleasure as much in the *pursuit* of compensatory satisfaction (that is, in the material acquisition of the means to it) as in the actual *fulfillment* (a fulfillment that everyday social competitiveness locates in mass-produced complexity, extreme experiences, extravagance, and luxury with a price tag). We spend less time creatively enjoying what is (still) free of charge, what we do not have to afford. This socioeconomic model, as Jackson Lears has argued, disembodies desire, distracts and diverts it to ever new commodities, away from any concentrated fulfillment.⁵⁶ Our horizon of expectation thus becomes circumscribed by what capitalism can produce for our amusement. At the same time, desire and pleasure are subject to eclectic ethical controls, indexed to the reality of our material need, as when chastising excess and likewise curbing our expectations, spiritualizing them. The free market and religion—each of these two mutually complementary orders succeeds on its own terms precisely where it fails to wrest control of desire from the other one; each fails to keep its own utopian promise to desire—the promise of the latter's virtuous liberation—instead merely capturing it for its particular libidinal economy, which also sustains the economy of its rival. Given this double constraint, an immanent desire-critique must have at least two interlocking parts: a critique of capitalist society and a critique of religious ideology, which also means of top-down political and economic theology.

Finally, the third question: *Can utopian thinking be rebooted by drawing attention to the bodily roots of desire for emancipation?* This one is about the future of utopian social imagination, which by definition must go beyond so-called "real utopias," or pockets of economic innovation understood as concrete, feasible alternatives to capitalist social relations, on the one hand, and techno-scientific dreams of freedom from labor, of bioenhancement, and of the indefinite extension of human life, on the other hand. And that is because the first of these two options rummages for models of a viable, actionable socialist alternative in the attic of where we presently live; focused on political economy, it is partial, not radical and holistic enough in envisioning the transformation of the totality of human relations as well as categories, hence also social conditions. The second option, meanwhile, vests its utopian hopes in cutting-edge technology; it conceives of transhumanism, eugenics, and life extension as quasi-transcendental emancipation. It does so not only by deferring the fulfillment of corporal desires here and now, limited to the somatic makeup of our species, but also by ignoring emancipation's ethical, political, and economic dimensions. In its current forms, desire for immortality has been written by the history of domination. It resolves into a desire to escape—rather than eliminate—moral, political, and economic oppression.

Desire and Survival

One of the conversations shaping the body-utopian landscape in the 1960s and early 1970s concerned the relationship of desire to survival. The wholly negative concept of survival was shared with the rest of society by the utopian movements I discussed. Among the Situationists, Vaneigem not only elaborated a somatic utopianism where Debord held back; he was also the most outspoken critic of modern life reduced to survival by capitalism. There was, for him as for Debord—who would denounce contemporary "life" as "augmented survival" rather than "true life" (*vraie vie*)—no contradiction between survival and the material abundance of the "new wealth" surrounding it.[57]

Life concerned with the satisfaction of needs even beyond the basic ones was no richer if this meant the repression of desire. Like Marcuse before them, the Situationists picked up on this "new poverty." The apparent shift from "an economy of profit" to one of "needs" boded ill for *an economy of desires*, defined as "technological society plus the imagination of what could be done with it." An economy organized around need satisfaction is "directly geared to the fabrication of habits" and hastens the degradation of fulfilled desire into need through the natural process of inurement. The indulgence of desires is opposed to engagement in habits, though in any given activity the passage from one to the other can be almost imperceptible.[58] In a life taken over by habit, when all that one can legitimately pursue is maintaining one's habitual existence, even if the needs it satisfies have been expanded relative to preindustrial times, this pursuit becomes all the more desperate, qualifying as augmented survival.

Vaneigem took on survival in 1962–63, in the programmatic essay "Banalités de base" (Basic Banalities). The dialectic of life and survival, he argued there, needed to be revived—life being defined by the SI qualitatively as "movement and totality," and survival quantitatively as equivalent to social alienation.[59] The present had reached a crisis point, such that further survival, or complacent, "two-dimensional" (economic and biological) life reduced to the satisfaction of basic needs, had become impossible to accept, and the moment had finally come to start living.[60] Vaneigem envisaged two possible outcomes, presented as a choice between revolution and suicide: "Either the specific forces the SI has counted on will make possible the supersession of these contraries, reuniting space and time in the construction of everyday life; or life and survival will become locked in an antagonism growing weaker and weaker until the point of ultimate confusion and ultimate poverty is reached."[61]

The argument against survival turns on the ideology of voluntary self-sacrifice, a mythical value across the economic spectrum, uniting those who sacrifice themselves for their own sake with those who sacrifice themselves for the sake of others and, in the process, accumulate prestige for the comparative magnitude of their sacrifice. They share the condition of survival, either "mere physical survival or survival as a privileged being." A revolutionary project to abolish sacrifice and the reign of survival must reckon with being itself mediated by this total negativity of social life: its initiators "must survive as antisurvivors," before a world in which work is "the blackmail of survival" and needs are "determined by power" can be changed. Survival is compatible only with a vision of the future as a "mechanical extension" of what came before; the key to unlocking an alternate possibility, the enabler of everyone's revolutionary power of direct action, was play, and the social game to be played was none other than "the moving order of the future."[62]

It was not until four years later, in the *Traité*, that Vaneigem acknowledged the redeeming, indeed utopianizing, side of survival, showing (at least theoretically) that "the supersession of these contraries" envisioned several years earlier might be at hand.

> The man of survival is a man ground up in the machinery of hierarchical power, caught in a net of interferences, a chaos of oppressive techniques whose ordering only awaits patient programming by programmed experts. The man of survival, however, is also the self-united man, the man of absolute refusal. Not a moment passes without each one of us experiencing, on every level of reality, the contradiction between oppression and freedom; without each one of us being caught up and weirdly twisted by two antagonistic perspectives simultaneously: the perspective of power and the perspective of transcendence.[63]

In other words, "the poverty of daily life [made] intolerable in view of the increasing wealth of technical possibilities" was survival "demystified" by capitalism, rather than survival as such. From its frustrated, crushed, and destructive perspective, life was what was lacking and simply too good to live. The reverse side of the "passion for destroying and letting oneself be destroyed" was, however, "the passion for life . . . as a biological need."[64]

It would not be much longer before the integration of survival into the ethos of revolt. The American analogue of a practical guide for rebellious youth, Abbie Hoffman's countercultural classic *Steal This Book* (1971), kicked off with the summons to "Survive!" followed by "Fight!" and "Liberate!" Survival as something endured, as an oppressed, alienated condition, had thus given way to survival as something to be taken up, a set of skills and tricks that became part of activist struggle and radical refusal of illusory "life" under domination. For many, commitment to political subversion meant choosing a life of survival (getting by on little or nothing) over that of membership in the workforce. That choice was what coupled survival with desire.

In mid-1968, trying to solve the social crisis, the Grenelle agreements boosted the purchasing power of the working class. Yet, as the Situationists saw, the society of galloping consumerism that became France in the late 1960s masked an existential poverty that, by higher—that is, utopian—standards, defeated the purpose of plenty. By the end of the decade, others were on to the damage done to desire by capitalism's revolutionary advance into intimate life. In bookstores, one came across such now-forgotten countercultural critiques as Marc Pierret's *Utopies et perversions*, hot off the press in early 1969 (partial censorship prevented the book from being displayed in shop windows). Pierret's target was not, as might be expected, the patriarchal oppressiveness of the old society. Rather, it was desire without a politics, degenerating into a liberal lifestyle, losing itself in the freedom of sexual expression. The "unlimited experience of desire," of taboo-breaking perversions in a purely instinctual revolt, lent itself to exploitation. Such overt hedonism was complicit in reification, diminishing the aptitude for pleasure and promoting erotic spectacle at the cost of political consciousness. "Desublimated," libidinal energy became neutralized, losing much of its possibility for subversion. "Anti-puritanism" proved "a new morality." Emancipation in the so-called sexual revolution, the vanguard of reformist ideology, hid actual "sexual misery."[65]

Before the era was out, another title managed to combine a critique of the new sexuality with a positive conception of survival, citing both Situationist authors and German social theorists Bloch and Adorno (the latter having homed in on the reification and "neutralization of sex" by its alleged liberation in the sex industry in the early 1960s).[66] Published in 1974 in Italy and translated into French in 1981, Giorgio Cesarano's *Manuale di sopravvivenza* (Survival Manual) was determined to get to the heart of capitalism's "short-circuiting" of transgression and how one might extricate oneself from its grasp. It was an answer that incorporated the SI critique while criticizing Vaneigem's hedonism and moral aversion to survival, and claiming to be more radically dialectical than its predecessors. For Cesarano, survival, in all its horror, was "the starting point" of the "fight for survival," the struggle to avoid death, rather than the pursuit of an illusory liberated existence. "To have the origin for a destination is henceforth among the most realistic 'programs.'"[67]

Cesarano's response to the nihilistic fatalism of the post-'68 era was radical optimism. At the same time, he rejected the "ideologies" of hope and utopia (the ideas of material hope and of utopian desire stemming from lack), explicitly targeting Blochian *concrete utopia* for feeding on defeated utopian projects and becoming an annex of capitalism, hence inseparable from the disappointment that drives consumption ("When the social imperative is 'depress yourself,' everyone is constrained to 'see' the possible and the desirable in what they have not"). The last of such concrete utopias to be overcome was that of counterrevolution, the realization of "self-critical capitalism."[68] For the *capital-utopia* to overcome itself, it needed only to be armed with "the certainty of its latent actuality," of its "corporality in the process of becoming." The objective of "all desire and all passion" was to realize the true, subjective human community (transcended as hypothesis and utopia).[69] This coming community already enjoys an "underground" existence. As for the spell of nostalgia, invoking past insurrections so as to exorcise confusion and despair, it is but fetishism and a degraded, betrayed hope, itself a breakdown of certitude.

Passion was central to Cesarano's project (utopian despite refusing the label), insofar as the sole defense against the "fall" of desire, reduced to a "mere appetite" and disarmed in the shift from forbidden to purportedly liberated and in fact obligatory sexuality, was a passionate one. Transformative desire and action—Cesarano's "erotic insurrection," or "eroticization of relations"—could only arise in a condition of imprisonment. The supra-individual impulse to freedom in love and ecstasy arose in "the prison of the couple" and, more fundamentally, "the prison of the self." Love (understood as neither a means nor an end) was the "Trojan horse" whereby subversion was "introduced into the necrotic continuum of survival." Cesarano approached Vaneigem's position in the *Traité* when he took ecstasy, amorous passion, focused self-transcending desire, to spontaneously entail the will to radically transform all human relations.[70] He subscribed wholly to the dialectic of sexual communication envisioned by Vaneigem, as long as it was actively lived through others:

> - the more I detach myself from the object of my desire and the more objective strength I give to my desire, the more carefree my desire becomes towards its object;
>
> - the more I detach myself from my desire, insofar as it is an object, and the more objective strength I give to the object of my desire, the more my desire finds its *raison d'être* in the loved person.
>
> ... To love only oneself through other people, to be loved by others through the love they owe themselves. This is what the passion of love teaches, and what the conditions of authentic communication require.[71]

Vaneigem's conclusion here represents both an alternative to the overspiritualized utopia of educated desire proposed by Abensour and the polar opposite of the Habermasian utopia of rational communication. The pleasure principle was to be permanently strengthened in an effort to extend into social life the moment of total enjoyment. Vaneigem's rationale being that bodily pleasure is a communicative and free activity in the world, an activity whose associative role is summarized in the simple formula: "Pleasure is the principle of unification; love is desire for unity in a common *moment*; friendship, desire for unity in a common *project*."[72]

For Cesarano, the collective experience of revolt was similarly formative for vital transformation: "Is there a radical who, at least as of '68, has not 'left their self,' by obeying nothing but their own heart, when, in the heat of a riot, they joined, in an undeniably real, corporal, and totalizing way, their particular destiny to the generality of destinies?" Both experiences—love and revolution—brought to light the concrete possibility of true, nonnostalgic communism. "*The revolution starts from the body*: from the corporality of desire that knows itself as materially possible" and that *crosses* somatic boundaries; it is, in this sense, biological, life-affirming, defying the death of the individual, and "beyond segregation in the animal or 'mechanical' dimension of the *bios*" (*al di là della segregazione nella dimensione animale e "meccanica" del* bios).[73]

The *Manuale di sopravvivenza*, then, built its utopian project upon emotion and a vision of emancipated desire. *Need* presupposed a symmetry between the organism and its environment, and belonged to the animal order; meanwhile, desire and value were co-constitutive, the former being what moves humankind "toward (and against) the universe." Echoing Adorno, Cesarano recognized the indicative function of lack: "What we lack shows us the way. Mutilations are so many signs." The utopian future was not reducible to the elimination of lack, but it was lack that "ripened plenitude," as (in a Bataillean vein) human life aspired to prodigality. The path to the total human community lay in "the real dialectic of life as the anxious experience of *lack* and as struggle . . . against stasis," against fatality.⁷⁴ The book's most poignant expression of this dialectics—and a sanguine version of the "paradox" with which Mannheim concluded his sociological history of utopia—is the image of the world as immediate possibility taking shape upon a dying world, and the emergence, from a dying species, of a species as a totality in being.⁷⁵

The dialectical view of survival as both the antithesis and the spur to utopian critique was reflected in the birth of environmentalism in France.⁷⁶ Buoyed up by the wave of contestation two years earlier, the effort to raise general ecological consciousness "from below" coalesced in the summer of 1970 around the journal *Survivre* (Survive), published by a militant internationalist movement setting out to bridge the gap between science and life, scientists and the general public. Vulgarization went hand in hand with self-education; the push for science instruction, especially in ecology, was linked to a fundamental rethinking of scientific values. In the first instance, the movement mobilized against research in the military applications of nuclear technology, taking a hard-line antimilitarist stance. Its fight for the survival of the species aimed at reestablishing environmental equilibrium—in theory and practice (e.g., boycotts). Between 1971 and 1973, the journal's critical register was utopian, expanding its critique of scientism and the scientific profession (its ethics, elitism, specialization, centralization) to the condemnation of technocratic forms of ecological and social control.⁷⁷ Its ethical and vital currents were still intertwined in denunciatory critique and hope for an ecological future.

But the young scientist-activists who first brought to public attention the radical disequilibrium in mankind's relationship with the natural environment would soon fall out over the question of desire. A period of self-critique led to an internal split into, on the one hand, supporters of the original aims (including the group's cofounder, the mathematician Alexandre Grothendieck) and, on the other, those who emphasized Bataillean *excess*. The schism, owing to the latter's left-libertarian swerve and break with ecology (for being tied to moderation), was made definite by the departure, in 1973, of two of the founding figures, Grothendieck and Pierre Samuel, signaling their opposition to the "ideology of desire" on the grounds that some repression was socially necessary (from the Marcusian distinction between necessary and surplus repression).[78] Samuel's denunciation of Vaneigem's futuristic dream of a society of masters with mechanical slaves targeted an undialectical Marxist optimism. Automation was not liberation, and ecology must defend society against technolatry and technocratic hubris and the associated individualistic cult of desire. Necessary for averting a self-centered individualism was a dialectic of desire and society, whereby an individual's desires were connected with those of others and formed by a concern for them. Such an expansion of libidinal relations was not to be confused with the total, indiscriminate liberation of desire.[79]

Following the scission, during 1973–75, the movement's critical register and orientation would shift to desire and the formation of alliances with, among others, certain post-Situationist and anarchist groups and individuals.[80] The vital current, taken in the direction of affirming individual desire, became "orthogonal" to the moral current, and the emphasis on *vivre* (the journal had been renamed *Survivre . . . et vivre* [Survive . . . and Live] in mid-1971, breaking with its earlier catastrophism) virtually antithetical to the much-maligned *survivre*, reflecting the growing proximity to the SI.[81] The acts of survival in response to social and ecological crises would change life: renew, augment, and enrich it—"sometimes exuberantly."[82] Survival was to be valorized as sur-vival: no longer thought of as resignation to an existence "mutilated by multiple 'pollutants' [*nuisances*]" or held to a "hygiene" prescribed by the media.[83] The critique of "health fascism"—with life reduced to not being dead—dates from this time.[84] The final period of *Survivre et vivre*'s activity, before its dissolution in 1975, was devoted to the creation of local autonomous affinity groups, communitarian experimentation with new forms of life on the way to reinventing the world.[85]

The journal's last word proved also its most radical. The group went on not only to denounce the local "parallel networks" of alternative economies, advertised as revolutionary or utopian so long as they remained unrealized; it went further still, calling for the "end of the economy"[86]—which is to say, for going beyond the state, beyond its reformist-utopian and thoroughly capitalist "ecofascism," beyond also Marx's communism of the future and the cyclical primitivistic solution inspired by the anthropologist Pierre Clastres.[87] Both of these latter were paradigms of productivity. In subscribing to the dichotomy of socially necessary labor and leisure, Marx remained within the economic horizon. While sustaining a nonautonomized economy, material production in Neolithic societies was organized on cyclical time, rendering them immobile, at odds with the nomadism of modern life. The suggested "beyond" of the economy and the state was not another utopian vision, but "the unimaginable," which might not be as pretty.[88] The movement thus ended with an iconoclastic utopian gesture.

The subversive strand of popular utopianism in this period dissociated abundance from capitalist production, conspicuous consumption, and private appropriation. It wanted abundance to be attuned to the autonomous, free play of the passions; an abundance, above all, of sensory and aesthetic pleasure. In the postwar prosperity of the *trente glorieuses*, meanwhile, consumption for its own sake was rampant and the way to it led, for the vast majority, through alienated work with scheduled leisure time. The mainstream notion of utopia was still that of a rational order, putting the ethos of community into contradiction with the pursuit of individual fulfillment. Keeping things relatively chaste, moderate, and traditional as regards gender roles was to guarantee social reproduction and eliminate conflict, justifying a cap on the individual imagination and initiative in the exploration and satisfaction of desire. Abundance here was the product of a system of constraints. In body utopias, by contrast, material luxury was the byproduct of sensory indulgence, and not its goad or prop. Huxley's *Island* (1962) embodies these contrasting approaches to abundance: beside commercially fed materialistic avarice, it envisions a world in which desire is experienced as arising from within, rather than in response to a stimulus, the market pressure to enjoy. In capitalist society, the body is slave to its passions, abused by overstimulation. Thus, when a life takes its biological functions, such as eating and procreating, for its "sole and ultimate aims," these functions become "animal," and the life in question assimilable to the negative category of survival.[89] In a utopian context, meanwhile, desire emancipated from profit has no limits other than its own satisfaction, because its bodily source is fully attended to. Libidinal relations between individuals expand naturally. To get there, desire must be assumed with lucidity, and revolt become both instinctual and political.[90]

As for the abundance generated by capitalism, one of the cornerstones of the liberal utopia of human rights after its amalgamation with humanitarianism—that watchdog serving the economy against misbehaving states on behalf of well-behaved states (without attacking the state as such)—has been the promise of redistribution to the world's neediest and most oppressed (human rights signifying, in its earliest, wartime, idealistic phase, a combination of internationalism and redistributive socialism).[91] The idea that only advanced capitalist societies are capable of delivering wealth to everyone rests on the definition of wealth as private accumulation, the implicitly moral dichotomy of *advanced* versus *primitive* social organization, and the attribution to the latter of a subsistence-level existence, limited to the struggle for biological survival—notwithstanding ample evidence of the production of wealth and its equitable distribution in tribal societies. In the 1960s, this classical (both liberal and Marxist), lack-based anthropological model was coming under scrutiny, the effect of which was to decenter Western conceptions of life worthy of the name. In 1968, Marshall Sahlins recast Paleolithic hunter-gatherers as members of "the original affluent societies," given a fuller substantivist treatment in his *Stone Age Economics* (1972) (rendered in French as *Âge de pierre, âge d'abondance*, 1976).[92] Following one of the two paths to affluence, the hunters easily satisfied all their material wants by "desiring little"; they enjoyed both material plenty and leisure (which Western criteria translate into a low standard of living or poverty), and even engaged in prodigal behavior, consuming their surplus, which demonstrated reasoned unconcern for material scarcity.[93] Sahlins's "iconoclastic and salutary" account was followed, in 1974, by Clastres's kindred study of "political economy" in surviving Neolithic hunter-gatherer societies, which refused to "allow work and production to engulf them."[94] Thanks to their transvaluations of the "economy of survival," belying the claims of economic progress, body utopia scored a major victory in the court of history.

Yet, in painting the two sides of survival—as actual poverty and as potential abundance—and redefining survival in the process, the postludes of '68 also anticipated the predicament that will soon be ours: desire for a utopia equal to the globalized condition of survival in which both rich and poor shall find themselves. Long the highest conceivable price for individual survival, causing the death of another has been surpassed by a price whose payment is spread out over many installments. These come in the form of everyday actions whose causal link to environmental devastation has been demonstrated beyond all reasonable doubt. In an economic system that locks us into habits of consumption without offering sufficient or accessible ecologically prudent alternatives, the individual determined to live on survives by paying the price that, cumulatively and past the tipping point, entails untold ills and deaths, possibly including their very own. The vicissitudes of climate change, the increasingly blatant indifference of nature to privilege and merit, will eventually undo many habits as survival is scaled back to the basics. For the time being, however, it is from living the condition of survival that we can expect to see the most radical expressions yet of desire for a better life.

CHAPTER 3

The Utopia of Survival

Critical Theory against the State

MOVING BEYOND THE STATE is among the main and oldest legacies of critical theory ecumenically understood. The origins of this theoretical tendency can be traced at least as far back as the radical critique of the modern state written during the French Revolution by the young Hegel (possibly with Hölderlin and Schelling). More recent, broadly neo- and post-Marxist thinkers have come around to the view that human biological and cultural survival depends on a dual—critical and utopian—approach to conceiving a different world, against and beyond states and empires. Research into the viability of a nonstatist, antistatist, poststatist, or anarchist society has given rise to one of the most vital strands of political and social theory of the past fifty years, represented by such figures as Hannah Arendt, Debord, Murray Bookchin, Clastres, Abensour, Giorgio Agamben, and David Graeber.

Grist to the mill of this heterogeneous theoretical project has been the multiplication of resonant, experimental forms of political engagement involving, at times, nonstate or extrastate actors and challenging states' monopoly on legitimate, specialized politics. By their oppositionality to, and incommensurability with, democratic state sovereignty, social movements such as the Yellow Vests not only question the very form of the state as a representative and administrative apparatus; they also, implicitly, undercut high politics. Ethnographically informed reflection on these irregular, infra- or im-political alternatives capable of transcending the political itself is one of the most promising directions for critical theory.

Contemporary theory's vision of politics, notes Étienne Balibar, tends toward a self-destructive biopolitics, "mak[ing] 'bare life' the horizon of all subjection to power." From Balibar's perspective, the process of "de-democratization" diagnosed by Wendy Brown looks a lot like "Marx's nightmare"—which is to say, like an apocalyptic vision of "the extinction of politics, a constitutive dimension of past history, produced as the result of a pure economic logic pushed to its extreme"; like a defeat of "proletarian politics" and the loss of "any prospect of revolutionary organization," "necessitat[ing] a return to the alternative of a disappearance of politics or a messianic solution arising from the very destruction of the conditions of politics."[1]

But such postrevolutionary apocalypticism clearly does not apply to critical theory across the board. Running counter to leftwing melancholy and the fear of a (nonutopian) "end" of politics as we know it is theorists' increasing recognition of the political and social emancipatory potential of what menaces state-based politics. Interviewed in 1977, having just defined politics as an inquiry into the desirability of revolution, Michel Foucault found himself speculating about the possible disappearance of politics—and its reinvention: "It would be necessary to invent another one or something else as a substitute for it. We are perhaps experiencing the end of politics. For politics is a field that has been opened by the existence of the revolution, and if the question of the revolution can no longer be posed in these terms, then politics is in danger of disappearing."[2] Not content with diagnosing popular depoliticization, theorists today are paying closer attention to the phenomenon of contestations featuring the vulnerable, living body as a political tool adapted to the biopolitical status quo and risked in mass public assembly and the occupation of public space. This phenomenon, as manifold as it is unprecedented, and which I discuss here under the heading of *politics of survival*, is reinventing politics by renewing the question of revolution.

Persistence of Utopia

At first glance, survival and utopia seem separated by an unbridgeable gap. The utopian imaginary was articulated as the historical telos of social progress, then, from the mid-eighteenth century onward, as a reformist or revolutionary program that broke with the earlier secular social dream in aiming well beyond the satisfaction of vital needs for all. The second, radically egalitarian Declaration of the Rights of Man and of the Citizen (1793) concluded with a duty to popular insurrection against an abusive republican government. The ground was, thus, laid for a critique of the state as such, as a potentially rigid, dehumanizing mechanism, and for subsequent, overtly political-utopian programs for moving past it: its abolition, as would soon be envisioned in the "Oldest Systematic Program of German Idealism" (1796–97), or its dismantling or withering away—all three later proposed by either Marx or Engels, or both.[3] The utopian, metapolitical, an-archic words of the "Program" would come close to being echoed by Marx. As he wrote in the first draft of *The Civil War in France* (1871), the Paris Commune "was a Revolution against the *State* itself, . . . a resumption by the people for the people of its own social life. It was not a Revolution to transfer it from one fraction of the ruling classes to the other, but a Revolution to break down this horrid machinery of class domination itself."[4] The conceptual polarization between utopia, nature, and body, on the one hand, and state and man-made mechanisms of oppression, on the other hand, was well established by Marx's day.

I have argued that the popular, body-oriented utopianism advanced in the first half of the nineteenth century by Fourier matched the entry of the masses onto the political stage. More than merely bearing the trace of collective want and physical-existential vulnerability, utopian expressions of desire for breaking free of domination by nature, by felt need, were *transformations* of that experience of deprivation and exposure. Fourier's vision of harmonious social life starts from the uninhibited satisfaction of desires, rather than from abstract principles of freedom and equality. It thus breaks with the fixed, regimented, ascetic character of the classic city utopia (a political dream whose instantiation—the plague-stricken town subject to absolute discipline—Foucault so vividly sketched in his chapter on panopticism). Marx's recognition of the critical value of Fourier's utopia of passional freedom and harmony with nature was consistent with his own idea that "the true realm of freedom, the development of human powers as an end in itself, begins beyond it, though it can flourish only with *this realm of necessity as its basis*."[5] Marx shared the *political* recognition of biological survival—"life" being contingent on self-preservation (with the realm of natural necessity expanding, for a civilized humanity, together with the development of productive forces).[6] Without *living on*, no living: no freedom, dignity, or happiness. Security, above all food and shelter, can free us from wretchedness and free up time to think and go about making improvements, but it cannot deliver us from bodily urges, needs, illness, and infirmity.

Biopolitics and Body Politics

Contemporary bodily political contestation on this basic plane of vital necessities reflects the condition of the majority under biopolitical regimes. The apparatus of biopolitical governmentality both produces physical vulnerability and masks its exploitation.[7] Deepening and overlapping crises generalize the psychology of survival. Survival appears as the antithesis of life against an integrated ideological backdrop made up of illusions of individual participation in representative democracy or national sovereignty, promises of pleasure and growth through constant stimulation and commodity consumption, liberal fantasies of bodily optimization, and the rationality of care and security. Consistent with it, corporal political radicalization arises from and amplifies the discontent with life reduced to survival, to a daily struggle to keep the proverbial wolf from the door.

At the same time, between mass migrations and ecological crises, the radicalization of the last few decades turns survival into an ethos of making a virtue of vital necessity—indeed into an active, political form of life. While utopian visions in our century are not articulated with nearly the frequency and fervor they were in the past, we are seeing a rise in political intrastate experiments in alternative living and social organization affected by the environmental degradation and precarity they are designed to address. Examples of what Roberto Esposito calls *politics of ascesis*,[8] they are prefigurations, partial active embodiments, of the desired nonstate society scaled to the urgencies of their historical moment. Suffice it to name the social-revolutionary and emancipatory processes in neo-Zapatism,[9] communalist Rojava,[10] ecologically minded zadism (*zones à défendre*, or ZADs), and the direct democratic participation (*assembléisme*) of an important segment of the Yellow Vests—these last decrying their own condition in the slogan, "Marre de survivre, nous voulons vivre!" (Sick of surviving, we want living!).[11]

Arendt narrates the preoccupation with basic necessities during the French Revolution as follows:

> Liberty now had come to mean first of all "dress and food and the reproduction of the species," as the sans-culottes consciously distinguished their own rights from the lofty and, to them, meaningless language of the proclamation of the Rights of Man and of the Citizen. Compared to the urgency of their demands, all deliberations about the best form of government suddenly appeared irrelevant and futile.[12]

Whether or not she was right in attributing the downfall of the Revolution to this basic unfreedom from want—thus, in her view, unfreedom *of* action and unfreedom *for* politics—the urgency of demands for basic necessities draws back the curtain on biological survival as a possible foundation of any (and not just republican) politics, and as "humankind's first fundamental right" (to be distinguished from both the right to life and the right to an adequate standard of living).[13]

The priorities of those who participate in politics yet are unconcerned with the necessities of life necessarily differ from the priorities of those who are compelled to struggle to stay alive and make ends meet. Anytime real needs are not met, political engagement (if it manifests itself at all) assumes one among the many disparate forms of a politics of survival—a politics whose emotional force, possible gains in momentum and provisions, and concomitant changes in priorities can take it from revolt to, *pace* Arendt, a full-blown revolution. Politics of this sort typically weaponizes the bodies of its practitioners; it is a concrete body politics of resistance conspicuous in acts of "sextremism" (in the style of Femen), die-ins (such as that of the Extinction Rebellion), hunger strikes and lip-sewing protests by migrants to the EU, and self-immolation the world over.[14] Esposito has it right: "A politics *of* life always comes as a reaction to a politics focused *on* life. The human body is central to this conflict. While it is the object of control and exploitation, since all forms of power produce resistance, it is also the subject of revolt."[15] In every such desperate bodily revolt against biopolitical state power, state-based politics loses some vital ground.

Finally, these practices, whose social import is clear, ought to be understood as utopianizing political statements about such things as social injustice. One's biological survival may be endangered not only—or not even—by lacking basic material necessities, but by lacking a purpose, or by being humiliated, denied dignity or rights. Psychological suffering caused principally or solely by this sort of "higher" deprivation can be somatized to the point of self-negligence or willful self-harm terminating in death. Cases when self-destruction is performed as an act of protest, a statement, exemplify the individual impossibility of survival on just the most elementary material terms. The vital necessities demanded are of another sort, but no less vital for that. The struggle to get by operates here in a different register from the demand for daily bread.

Survival and Politics

Survival is the struggle for survival. Politics, political struggle in some form, can continue where biological survival is a minimal (rather than maximal) purpose for individuals and collectivities. Closely preceded by Sahlins, Clastres set out to correct the misconception of "primitive" societies as single-mindedly concerned with self-preservation alone. Such societies also do not lack a political dimension, though this last is not expressed as an individual, central coercive power (since political power lies outside of chieftainship). Their antistate character—refusal of the law of the state—which preserves their acephalous social order, is nonetheless inseparable from their economy. Long consigned to subsistence-level status in the ethnocentric, state-obsessed, productivity-addicted West, the tribal way of life of "archaic" societies, for which survival as well as limited surplus food accumulation remains a daily—albeit not exclusive—preoccupation, ensures their typically small demographic size, essential in preventing state formation.[16]

In Western, Greco-Roman civilization, it was Thomas Hobbes who squarely linked politics to survival: fear of certain death in the prepolitical state of nature becomes the basis for the social contract and the constitution of a polity, a body politic. It falls to the sovereign so constituted to secure release from an existence of self-preservation under the sign of perpetual war of all against all. The sphere of human public activity known as politics thus comes into being as a solution to the problem of survival, protecting against the arbitrariness of a fatal blow dealt by a human hand. The voluntary entry into the political from the extrapolitical realm of experience is therefore wholly motivated by survival as something both lived and desired in a superior, peaceable form. For Hobbes, the shape of the good life is already discernible from within this "brutish" yet free, presocial existence; a conception of felicity arises inside a condition of misery. "The Passions that encline men to Peace, are Feare of Death; Desire of such things as are necessary to commodious living; and a Hope by their Industry to obtain them. And Reason suggesteth convenient Articles of Peace . . ."[17] In civil society, or state order, where demise is an avoidable possibility, "commodious living" finally becomes possible.

Whether we accept human concern with survival as necessary for politics depends on how far we can keep at bay normative, value-loaded questions that have defined Western politics since at least the eighteenth century: does "anything go," or do only those forms of public contestation count as political that advance "lofty" values, such as human dignity, freedom, equality, and so on? Answers to this question have long cast doubt on the ontological status, moral value, and political neutrality of survival. In his "Critique of Violence," Walter Benjamin opposed the "dogma" of the sacredness of "mere [bodily] life for its own sake," in all its vulnerability to injury. This elevation of "being alive" *above* "a just existence"[18] demanding human sacrifice and oppression is refigured by such theorists as Didier Fassin, Judith Butler, and Ewa Plonowska-Ziarek into an ethical-political principle,[19] with survival as the structure of existence *positively* understood.[20] Their recent efforts are motivated by ethical concerns over the vulnerability to politics of life devalued as "mere survival"—a life deemed not really lived, hence disposable. The aim here is to close the gap and undo the hierarchy between the good life and plain life—a gap crucial to Benjamin's 1921 critique—and to imbue survival with political agency, with the power of resistance.

On the other end of the critical spectrum, inspired by Benjamin's critique of Carl Schmitt and by Foucault's biopolitical framework, survival has been theorized as "bare life" (*la nuda vita*), or *zoē*—natural, reproductive life, "exposed to death," as distinct from *bios* (qualified, political form of life, life lived in the *polis*). In Agamben's view, "the [exclusive] inclusion of bare life in the political realm constitutes the original—if concealed—nucleus of sovereign power"—to the point that "*the production of a biopolitical body is [its] original activity.*"²¹ Survival appears here as depoliticized vulnerability whose constitution and dialectical relationship to the law are the transhistorical foundation of political life, or biosovereignty. Life and the community can be redeemed only outside politics.²²

Across this theoretical spectrum, the fluctuating meaning and value of "life"—what it is and what makes it worth living—is linked to power's legitimacy to intervene in and control lives. Similarly, "survival" and "life itself" are exposed as effects of ideological framing, a function and product of power.

An important recent contribution on the question of the *political* valence of survival, Banu Bargu's *Starve and Immolate* contests "the equation of [biological] vulnerability with [political] powerlessness."²³ To this Agambenian claim, her book offers a "counterpoint." As Bargu explains,

> the assertion of a politicized life over and against survival and the prioritization of political causes and ideological convictions over biological existence do not only challenge the foundations of the existing order but also force us to reconsider the turn taken in the biopolitical approach that uses the category of bare life rather indiscriminately and uncritically and, worse, that assumes it to be a matter of fact rather than a biosovereign fantasy.²⁴

Bargu theorizes what she calls *necroresistance*, a form of radical "counterconduct" that reverses the "politics of life" (biological life) into a "politics of death." Necroresistance targets survival as the sovereign means of biopolitical domination. (Bargu's difference from, but also debt to, Achille Mbembe, for whom necropolitics and biopolitics are two sides of one coin, lies in giving a theoretical and empirical account of a necropolitical form of resistance. Mbembe's focus is on bare life as abject "death-in-life," or "living death," created in the zones of exception by the nexus of sovereignty, disciplinary power, and biopower, where, "under conditions of necropower, the lines between resistance and suicide, sacrifice and redemption, martyrdom and freedom are blurred." Following Agamben's dystopian account prevents him from offering more than a glimpse of martyrdom as a counter-logic to the "logic of survival.")[25] In Bargu's analysis, the actor's refusal, by an act of self-destruction, of their individual self-preservation effectively pushes back against biopoliticized sovereignty, or biosovereignty—defined by her as a neoliberal regime of power surfacing "at the intersection of" sovereignty and biopolitics, of the power to kill and the power to regulate life. In asserting politics over survival, necroresistance thus opposes biosovereignty's "power *of* life [and death]" as well as its "power *over* life, including the power over the definition of life."[26] The practices of self-starvation and self-immolation Bargu takes as exemplary of necroresistance strike at what she terms "state monopsony" on political sacrifice. These practices, in other words, challenge the status quo wherein the state is the only legitimate recipient of such sacrifice.

As can be seen, survival figures in such practices only negatively, as a political dead end. Too often their acutely felt starting point, biological survival is not just undesirable but becomes impossible in the presence of psychological anguish due to the lack of purpose, dignity, justice, and rights. *Starve and Immolate* calls attention to problems with theories of politicized survival, be they the new "vitalism"[27] or "affirmative biopolitics,"[28] that detect potential for emancipation in the biopolitical multitude.[29] Such radical "politics of living on" participates, in Bargu's view, in reproducing the very power regime to which it is a reaction. Indeed, Bargu's work is a cogent response not just to the Agambenian thesis—the depoliticization of survival-as-bare-life—but also to positions that, in her words, dwell on the totalizing narrative of governmentality, penetrating and molding ever more spheres of life, [that forecloses the] . . . potential for resistance . . . and . . . theorize[s] resistance as a residual, fragmentary, localized, and restricted response to power relations. At best, resistance has been tied to an affirmation of life as the object of biopolitics, which functions by making claims for greater rights, welfare, and recognition, mimicking the nature of power relations in their contestation.[30]

That said, she leaves open the question, do acts of necroresistance themselves not, in the end, "conform to and reproduce biosovereignty, in their own political structures and communities, discourses and practices, even as they attempt to go beyond it?"[31] If they do conform, they end up not only recuperated in the service of life as the sovereign means of biopolitical domination and of the state form; they also reinforce the view of survival as a political-anthropological constant. At the same time, Bargu's theorization of radical-political sacrifice shows how present-day practices of resistance complicate the orthodox, biological understanding of survival; rather than the physical survival of individuals or groups, these practices demonstrate a commitment to the survival of political resistance *as praxis*.

Politics of Survival

If politics is survival by other means, then any historical development in politics, grounded as it is in survival, must be a development in those means. One such development, as I have suggested, concerns the wagering of bodies. The politics of survival (including practices of "contra-survival") taken up in recent critical theory describes radical struggle with diverse modalities of bodily mobilization that responds specifically to the biopoliticization of sovereignty, to that "politics of life" that is the counter-historical "postevolutionist theme of the struggle for existence" Foucault saw as developing in the nineteenth century.[32] For while the public, ideological face of liberalism revolved around individual freedom, the managerial backside of the state brought out ever more sophisticated tools to process, manage, subdue, and optimize entire populations with only a nominal regard for individual difference. The tightening of this ideological ruse—human rights and governmentality, for short—gave rise to its negation: to the radical-political form of survival, which put groups and, more recently, nonhuman entities, to one side of civil society and the self-possessed, self-interested individual. Fassin, Hardt and Negri, Esposito, Rosi Braidotti,[33] Miguel Vatter, and others, typically drawing on Foucault and Deleuze, are among the theorists of this vitalist, affirmative, emancipatory, and agonistic or antagonistic politics of survival. In this particular cultural gestalt, the *figure* of politics threatens to disappear into its now risen *ground* that is biological survival, stoking fears of the disappearance of politics.

The politics of survival—by making biological survival (as the ground, the condition of possibility, of politics) the prime political emancipatory *stake*, i.e., that which marks one's political presence and acts as its pivot—puts the biopolitical figure of politics itself into question (in reaction to the putting-into-question of biological existence by politics as biopower, as noted by Foucault). The politics of survival thus *appears* as a (temporary? aporetic?) suspension of politics in the name of politics, while contending with the contemporary conjuncture: the "coexistence of sovereignty, discipline, and security"[34] that seems increasingly postnational. The radical "politics of living on" and, even more so, the "politics of death" alluded to by Mbembe and developed, as *thanatopolitics* or *necroresistance*, by Stuart J. Murray[35] and, especially, Bargu is fit for a time in which state-based politics is undergoing transformation and redefinition.

Bargu shows how the "*biopoliticization of sovereignty* meets the *necropoliticization of resistance.*" Co-present with the new power regime of biosovereignty (as she defines the term), necroresistance "defies instrumentality through its disruption of the means-ends relation." It represents, as she puts elsewhere, an "*embodied* form of radical critique."³⁶ In the repertoire of sensate forms of resistance that arise directly from a condition of survival and a sense of political impotence, it may be the unlikely complement of exposed, anti-authoritarian prefigurative praxis, which picks up where embattled digital activism runs aground. I am inclined to answer in the affirmative Bargu's question whether those who in this way "oppose the biosovereign assemblage and express a desire for nondomination and nonoppression . . . call into being another form of community founded on premises and power relations that are substantially different than those that characterize the present."³⁷

Bargu's contribution to our understanding of the "politics of self-sacrifice"—politics asserted *over* survival—exposes the capitalist hegemony of survival as the legitimation of the biopolitical apparatus and as, precisely, the target of some of the most radical politics of our time. Given the sacrificial and utopianizing character of such politics, her intervention supplies a strong argument for jettisoning the struggle for biological, solitary or collective, survival as the condition of possibility of politics, unless only in the most self-evident, trivial (if always debatable) sense of the impossibility of politics in the absence of living human beings who practice it. Taking a long view of (biological) survival—not as the anthropological ground and anchor of politics but, instead, as its cultural-historical continuation and transformation—is unlikely to allay fears of the exhaustion or death of politics.

In the last century, survival has gone from an individual question to a human one, necessitating a reorientation toward what Marc Abélès terms a global *politics of survivance* (rather than of "survival," *survie*). Whereas in the age of what he calls the *politics of coexistence* (*convivance*), bound to the state form and oriented toward harmony, expressed by a social contract, politics and the pursuit of the good life had all but obscured individual survival, in the age of survivance—an age of enormous technological promise combined with natural scarcity, economic precarity, political insecurity, in short, uncertainty about the future—survival serves as the main political orientation. Abélès locates the discursive "turning point," "break[ing] with the philosophies centered on convivance," in Benjamin's "Theses on History."[38] Survivance describes, for Abélès, a new relationship of the individual to politics focused on the anxious anticipation of threats that nation-states cannot preempt or eliminate. Though, in theorizing this new episteme, Abélès means to update biopolitics to evoke governmentality beyond the state as "a rupture with the idea of a bright future," such *prospectively* structured concern about survival (in contrast to Elias Canetti's retrospective construction, relative to what one has outlived) "is far from being incompatible with a utopian vision."[39] The associated diametrical transformation of politics and the political imaginary determines, in Abélès's view, a much more general, "dual displacement . . . in both governmentality and resistance" (here he cites "alter-globalization," *altermondialisme*); it is their "redirection" to a transnational stage of governing institutions, now developing alongside states and poised to outlive them.[40]

In this climate, political acts arising from the lived experience of need, vulnerability, and disempowerment, acts weaponizing the body rather than preserving it intact at all costs, have an advantage over the functioning of government institutions and the effectiveness of policies. The latter have acted more to create than to solve the problem of sustainable human perpetuation. But the utopianizing, frequently antistate, potentially revolutionary acts and movements of what I have been calling the politics of survival—unlike state-based "politics of life"—have virtually no record of endangering the survival of the world, and of all those who live in it.

At this point, the reader might be keen to raise questions and objections to the views just presented. The following imaginary Q&A does not so much anticipate possible challenges as pull them from actual discussions I have had.

The acts you identify do not produce social change but are limited to ensuring survival. They seem, paradoxically, to suspend politics in the name of politics. How exactly are they political?

The objection relies on a basic notion of survival that I want to complicate. A broader conception of survival would include politics, as well as precarity. Survival is dependent not just on material conditions, but also on ideational material and values. It may consist in living on despite our life being judged by others or by ourselves as not worth living (as in cases of ostracism or social death). This does not equate biological with cultural survival, though it may give rise to cultures of survival, which evolve their own poetics.

The individuals acting in concert to form ZADs to survive capitalism do so in opposition to the state, still appeal to a political community, and withdraw from conventional politics only. Demonstrations and the bodily occupation of outdoor public space effectively shift the space of politics from the halls and chambers of political elites to squares, streets, and (for the Yellow Vests) provincial roundabouts. They can draw politicians outside and make space for demonstrators at the table. Crucial here is that the collective, grassroots investment in a politics of survival affects the public's understanding of what can be done, by whom, and to whom. One of the most salient episodes in history that bears this out is the October March on Versailles of 1789. Nowadays, such popular formations benefit from the lateral, real-time dissemination of information and a widespread distrust of leaders and agitators monopolizing public speech. Complementing the soapbox and the podium, the human microphone (the repetition-amplification of an individual's message done by those around them) embodies this spirit of horizontality, pluralism, and tolerance.

The political character of such practices is not measured based on the political change they bring about, that is, on the short- or long-term effectiveness of such clashes and dialogue to satisfy popular demands durably and institutionalize their gains. They are more than social resistance because of their opposition to the violence constitutive of the state and because of their public nature, expressing a need for visibility and political change. Social change is presupposed in political change. Despite their apparent indeterminacy, their prefigurative aspects are mingled with political aims, which remind us that utopia is still relatively far away.

You condone necroresistance?

My approach to political anthropology is descriptive. I am not endorsing suicide for a revolutionary cause, let alone thinking along the lines suggested by Franco "Bifo" Berardi when he blindly states: "Since September 11th, 2001[,] suicide is the decisive political act of our times. When human life is worthless, humiliation grows until it becomes intolerable and explosive. Perhaps hope can only come from suicides."[41] Necroresistance is, in any case, not instrumentalized for mass murder. It is not itself revolutionary, though it can sometimes stoke revolutionary fervor, be part of an insurrection (which, as Wolfgang Streeck points out, "may be the last remaining mode of political expression for those devoid of market power" in countries where "democracy as we know it is effectively suspended").[42] Revolution ends as soon as sacrifice for it becomes necessary. The calculus of laying down one's life or that of a group is alien to the spontaneous risk of life and limb in the passion and necessity of lived struggle. Sacrifice and risk-taking are very different.

How is necroresistance democratic?

Necroresistance may be a public expression of desire for democratic change in an oppressive situation, whatever the nature of the regime: bureaucratic or authoritarian, as in the hunger strike by thousands of Kurds in support of their leader Abdullah Öcalan (serving a life sentence in Turkey), or democratic, as during the 1981 Irish hunger strike by republican inmates of Her Majesty's Prison Maze to obtain the status of political prisoners from a representative democracy. It can be an example of what Abensour calls utopianized, radicalized, *insurgent democracy*, a democracy against state domination, with politics directed against the state and processes of *étatisation*, or state formation.

How is a politics of survival a politics of the good life, a utopian politics?

The politics of survival is utopianizing when it points beyond the condition of survival from which it springs. Theories of agency in necroresistance point beyond the (biopolitical) state without developing a postpolitical vision of society, and even resisting such visions. The acts just mentioned articulate or claim public spaces of freedom. In other forms of the politics of survival I brought up, actors may partly "leave the state" to organically reconstitute a society. Those who take to TAZes[43] and ZADs are in tension with state institutions and refuse to be fully governed by them. They are utopian, without being utopias.

EPILOGUE

The Displaced Imagination

UTOPIAS RELY ON BODIES to dream and to fill them. Unless a utopia can be built in a day, its condition of possibility is the corporal prefiguration of social harmony. Prefigurative practice does not want for ideal conditions; it can be inspired by the experience of collective survival and arise within it, starting from bare life where the body's wants are acutely felt and their fulfillment is paramount, altering desires. The dream of utopia, in such a case, is obviously not just a dream of survival, not a dream of mere life, but a dream of something higher. Survival is simultaneously taken for granted in it and abolished, utopia being essentially that imaginary place where the struggle for existence is no longer necessary. What is more, the utopian existence hinted at by Agamben reconciles the two spheres of bodily being in advanced societies. In his words, "only if, beyond the split between public and private, political and biographical, *zoè* and *bios*, it is possible to delineate the contours of a form of life and of a common use of bodies, will politics be able to escape from its muteness and individual biography from its idiocy."[1] The more we come to experience survival collectively, the more we will dream of such a common use of bodies beyond the biopolitical state taking care of us, whose rational bureaucratic apparatus works to expel, separate, and isolate them, deciding who gets to live and reproduce, who vegetates, and who is left to expire to reduce the risks (economic, political, sanitary) to the rest of the population. Plato may have already dreamed of this body-commonwealth when, in book 5 of the *Laws*, he mused on the absolute best *polis*, in which, according to the Pythagorean maxim *koina ta philōn*, the things belonging to friends really are common:

> Whether this happens anywhere these days, or whether it ever will—that wives are common, that children are common, that all property is common—and whether every possible contrivance has been used to bring about the total eradication of what is called private from every corner of our life, and things have as far as possible been so contrived that even what is by nature private somehow or other comes to be common, in the way eyes and ears and hands seem to see and hear and do things for the body as a whole, and that, within reason, everybody is at one in what they approve or find fault with, getting enjoyment and pain from the same things—well, if you have laws so far as you can which make the city as much of a unity as it reasonably can be, then as far as promoting human goodness is concerned, no one is ever going to lay down a more correct or a better definition of law than that.
>
> A city of that kind—I don't know if its inhabitants are gods or a number of sons of gods, but if that is how they pass their days, then they live lives of great happiness. In our search for a social and political system, we need look no further than this for a model; we should keep a firm hold of it, and do everything we can to find one as like it as possible.[2]

A fusional community of the sort Plato envisioned would, of course, stand above all known constitutions and bear scarcely any resemblance to historical states. Were such symbiosis of its members to become possible, structures comprising the state would fall away in a body.

Where does such speculation leave us, today? Our ethical ideal and pragmatic goal is climate neutrality, leaving no terrestrial "footprint," a striving that entangles us in survival. Fully fledged utopian worlds, if we project them at all, are likelier to find more hospitable outer space. These distant nowheres will be the responsibility of survivors who made their escape. In the meantime, desire will still be moralized, certain pleasures penalized and punished, and enjoyment, taken as before or newly and differently, defended as a right. In the thick of the struggle to survive, some will continue to resist moralism and politicism with their poor, ascetic utopias controlling passions and disciplining bodies.[3] Already gaining traction, the Faustianism of terraforming Earth—since solar geoengineering to combat the greenhouse effect is just that—will attempt lab-tested fixes on a planetary scale, under the pretense of buying us time to get to the root of the problem. Relying on technocratic capital not to touch the tatters of the social fabric or the ruins of political structures already in place, it will tempt us with promises that life can go on as complacently as ever, complete with "happiness hacks" and the imposture of "utopias for one" as (at least) attainable.

On the verge of anthropogenic climate catastrophe, the natural first stop on the way to utopia would seem to be a radical global reduction in consumption. There are fortunes to be made selling guilt-ridden consumers on the pursuit of minimalism-by-gadgets. There is a special kind of irony reserved for those who claim self-sufficiency and opt for "less stuff" while clinging to modernity. ("To foster 'voluntary simplicity' amidst mindless opulence is to taint the entire ecological project in a manner that renders the ecological crisis unresolvable," notes Bookchin.)[4] Yet, despite these compromising contradictions, theirs is a utopianizing ethos. Experimenting in voluntary personal divestment—discovering, as Socrates did in the marketplace, "How many things I can do without!"—becomes a gauge of superfluity.[5] A still more radical attitude is obviously secession from consumerism. It might come across as poverty to those used to a modern standard of living, but the jury-rigging improvisation by which anticonsumerism can (but needn't, as shown in the simple living of Plain people) manifest itself bespeaks an active imagination oriented by hope toward a new horizon.

Impoverished multitudes require no such nudging or coaching on how to do with less. If it heightens precariousness—felt lack and existential, bodily vulnerability—then precarity, defined by political and socioeconomic marginality, is assimilable to survival.[6] "Survivability is a function of a frail and brokered sociality," writes Butler.[7] The precariat has been suspected as a political wildcard, susceptible to extremism and conceivably kept from mischief only by a "proudly" if "mildly utopian" "politics of paradise" in a progressive statist vision of the "Good Society of the twenty-first century."[8] But in the wake of mass protests by the same precariat in France (where it was unjustly vilified as a violent, populist, antisemitic grievance-spewing mob), some were obliged to recognize its condition as a source of agency and a utopianizing force of nature, conceding, as did Vaneigem, that "the will to better living springs from the precarity of existences."[9] This praiseworthy will, cut off from any hope that at one point, in relative comfort and security, may have tethered it to the status quo, cuts itself loose from a passive hopefulness in reduced circumstances.

Economic precarity was also the state from which the visionary poet Charles Baudelaire incited his readers to take the utopian voyage. "Imagine how sweet / To go live there together! / . . . / There, all is order and beauty, / Luxury, calm, and pleasure" ("Songe à la douceur / D'aller là-bas vivre ensemble! / . . . / Là, tout n'est qu'ordre et beauté, / Luxe, calme et volupté").[10] The lines name facets of felicity, completing or competing with justice, equality, and liberty as principles structuring the good society. While we agree that some, if not all, of these compose an ideal life, the culture that forms us does not always offer occasions for their experience. The "oriental splendor" brought in to gratify the "least desire" and among the sources of sensory and aesthetic delight sketched by the poet may seem dated to us (not to mention, ethically problematic). The "rare flowers," amber, and "lustrous furniture" might do nothing for us. Yet we cannot assume that equal or greater satisfaction and enhancement of life can be found in other things. They will be different pleasures, afforded by and associated with different objects. Countless kinds of happiness have been and will be lost, not just to death or genocide, not just with the extinction of archaic humans, the Neanderthals and the Denisovans, or the demise of pre-Columbian civilizations, but also due to the collapse of ecosystems, precarity, and human migration.

The modern imagination, including the utopian, was aroused and shaped by unattainable, actually existing or fictional "other" places promising fulfillment unavailable at home. Rare were the adventurers who tried their fortune in setting out for these heterotopias. By contrast, the human condition in the twenty-first century is overwhelmingly one of displacement. Those nowadays dreaming of life somewhere else are likelier than ever to find the means to reach their destination. Once there, their imagination is liable to displace itself elsewhere again, or back whence it came, as it is drawn into the vortex of nostalgic memories; and, as so often happens, their body follows suit.

In certain regions of the world, "dystopias" and "utopias" are mapped within one and the same national boundary, an ambivalence producing imaginary and physical, desire-driven displacements. According to the Congolese sociologist and anthropologist Joseph Tonda, modern society is subject to what he calls postcolonial capitalism's *éblouissements*, or amazements. Tonda's original critique of global imperialism, and especially of the symbolic violence of sexualized corporal imagery projected on screens, targets its unconscious workings especially in Central African society. Africans, he argues, are colonized—and active participants in their own colonization—by the amazing mirage of a utopia on the other side of the Mediterranean. The African continent, conversely, figures as dystopia, albeit with utopian evolutionary potential whose actualization is hindered by economic logic.[11] The European utopian dream is powerful enough to act as a physical magnet, inspiring migration that too often ends in misery and disappointment, sometimes death. Indeed, the precarious nomadism of economic migrants differs radically from the nomadisms of leisure or business (combined in the sham dream-come-true of do-it-anywhere tele-work). In the one as in the other, however, imagination must adapt to a greater or lesser degree to where it happens to go.

Rounding out this picture of imaginative displacement is the everyday avalanche of information, a vehicle of travel in its own right. Through the medium, less of imported sense-ravishing commodities—the stuff of Baudelairean fantasies—abstracted from their material conditions of production, and more of data on distant realities and events soliciting our empathy and attention, our imagination is ceaselessly on the move.

Since its inception, utopia has distinguished itself as the transcendence of existing conditions and historical tendencies either through their direct critique or through its own partial realization. The globalized twenty-first century's heaven on earth is unavoidably a universal *terra beata*, a mythic totality, merging mythos with logos. As such, it is imaginable solely as the dialectical sublation of hell on earth—as a comprehensive geography where ever-present danger, suffering, and death under all their guises have been overcome (human life transcending its absolute limit). The myths of decay and demise to which we presently subscribe could thus give way to myths of birth and harmony.

The utopian imagination does not need more elaborate positive visions. We steer by utopia in dreaming socially and debunking what we dream. If anything, we ought to remain resolutely iconoclastic. Turned outward, then inward, iconoclasm is the story of utopia. In the twentieth century, its iconoclasm went structural, either in the form of the provisionality of its substantive images or in the formalism of its regulative ideas of the good life—utopia's lack of determinate content safeguarding against iconolatry and fetishism. We have reason to think that group solidarity and egalitarianism within the close-knit bands of migrating humans in prehistory depended on the deflation of egos.[12] You will find hardly any depictions of people, singly or together, in the animal-dominated Paleolithic rupestrian art. Throughout the fifty-five hundred or so years of recorded time, in contrast, the visual representation of humans, tending to inflate the self-worth of our species, has only spread and multiplied. Capitalism has driven the cult of one's image and image-based self-recognition to new heights. The utopian *future*—for we are not fools enough to believe it is present and know the past too well to be lured by it—can be about humans only insofar as it is about nonhuman nature. This need not be a utopia in pictures, unless they be of what nature-friendly humans and human-friendly nature *should* look like. With due deference to Margaret Mead's claim that we need utopias to be less "pallid," their "blank white space" wants no filling once the explanation for their insipidity—namely, that "the prefiguration of [individual] bliss lies in the womb, where the child has no chance to use its distance receptors, and so the feeling remains one of undifferentiated and unspecified ecstasy" (an explanation she finds compelling)—is extended to our species as a whole.[13]

The times are propitious, say historians of utopianism: crises, upheavals are fertile soil for mythic utopian imagination and speculation. For the "myth of telos" to return, we should cease to rely on intellectual abstraction and, instead, let hope take root in both individual and social soil, given their interdependence. "New utopias," Frye ventured in the mid-1960s, "would have to derive their form from the shifting and dissolving movement of society . . . They would be rooted in the body as well as in the mind, in the unconscious as well as the conscious, in forests and deserts as well as in highways and buildings, in bed as well as in the symposium."[14]

Bodies are our utopian cue; the rest is imagination. But the latter cannot activate while ignoring the former if the goal is prefigurative, respecting bodily limits. More than any other figure I have engaged with, Adorno saw the dialectical link between the body and utopia. On the one hand, he observed, "he alone who could situate utopia in blind somatic pleasure, which, satisfying the ultimate intention, is intentionless, has a stable and valid idea of truth."[15] On the other hand, "the incarnate moment," the consciousness of disquiet, "registers the cognition that suffering ought not to be, that things should be different"—that what is, is false.[16] Greater attention to the "corporeality of thought," to one's physicality and range of somatic experience, pleasure and pain, need and desire, and their rhythms and intensities, is crucial.[17] The same holds on the societal level, where collective desire for excess and waste is helpless against its economic capture and conversion into commodity consumption (including in the name of frugality). It need not be so.

Considering its double heritage in Marxism and Freudian psychoanalysis, Critical Theory's interest in utopia was far from obvious. While the first of its two tributary currents was critical of social utopian blueprints as "recipes for the cookbooks of the future" (if not for disaster), the second promoted the *reality principle* and aimed only to replace, in Freud's famously modest formulation, "hysterical misery" with "ordinary unhappiness." Utopia's negativist theorization by the first generation of Critical Theorists, notably Adorno, owes much to the tension in both Marxism and psychoanalysis with the collective and individual aims of, respectively, communism and therapy. Both of these tributaries, however, took dictation from the suffering and desiring bodies of their contemporaries. Both, separately and together, have been championed as revolutionary or as preparatory for revolution.[18]

There is reason to cautiously rejoice in the rediscovery of Critical Theory's utopian heritage, not as material for academic commentary, but as living theory.[19] The alternatives are nowhere near as promising. Between praise for historical utopia, vague gestures of fraternal support for "real utopias," and shrill cheers for popular uprisings or "ecological Leninism" loud enough to wake the dead,

Jacobin, a leading platform for the socialist left in America, spouts a defeated utopianism, a hope without ambition.[20] In its pages, "cribbing from Freud, and drawing from my own anti-utopian utopianism," Corey Robin tells us that "the point of socialism is to convert hysterical misery into ordinary unhappiness"—adding, "God, that would be so great."[21] We will need to do better than such mushy invocations. "Anti-utopian utopianism," straining for a sophisticated, Marxian ambivalence over a vulgar Marxist stance on utopia, is a position inadequately thought through.[22] (As Jameson points out, to anti-utopians "utopia is a transparent synonym for socialism itself, and the enemies of Utopia sooner or later turn out to be the enemies of socialism.")[23] It is as if, these days, the only sensible, defensible utopist is a conflicted, defeatist one. The unstated assumption is that utopia is naïve, so that, to avoid making oneself an easy target, self-consciousness or a critical, semi-ironic distance must modulate (and erode) any meaningful commitment. Meanwhile, among the options available to those who are not quite done with utopia but not always comfortable admitting it outright—being "only too wary of the motives of its critics, yet no less conscious of Utopia's structural ambiguities ... [and] mindful of the very real political function of the idea and the program of Utopia in our time"—Jameson-style double-negative "anti-anti-utopianism" sounds like the canniest choice.[24] A commitment of the second degree instead of a ruse, it has the markings of intellectual progress. That it should be nothing more than the start of making up one's mind about where one stands on the issue of human survival, its chances and conditions and their possible improvement, goes without saying. When utopia passes into myth, one will no longer feel obligated to qualify it and turn it into a posture or position.

In his one-year anniversary study of the Yellow Vests, among the new social movements relocating politics, French sociologist Laurent Jeanpierre catches a glimpse of "real and local utopias," a category that contains kibbutzim, the Chiapas of the Zapatistas, and, more recently, Rojava's democratic confederalism, inspired by the communalist theory of Bookchin. Radical politics, in Jeanpierre's account, is moving away from its traditional, working class-concentrated commonplaces (factories and cities, workers' councils and communes) and taking itself elsewhere, a shift that corresponds to the contemporary fragmentation of the *demos*.[25] The unease about utopian speculation in this analysis is palpable; too much abstract description of popular risings and one risks foreclosing immanent possibilities on the ground. The reluctance may also be due to the influence of Erik Olin Wright's concept of "real utopia."[26] The true socialist utopia emerging from the American Marxist sociologist's opus magnum is a hybrid, evolutionary beast, assembled out of alternative social arrangements, successes in the practical "erosion" of capitalism, proposals treated as if they were the actual building blocks of a desirable society, rather than mere "interstitial" gaps or cracks or "symbiotic" scaffolding to the social edifice still standing that cannot fundamentally weaken its capitalist economy.[27] To take, as Wright did, Wikipedia as an example of a "real utopia" (of collective, supposedly anticapitalist self-organization, egalitarian ethos, and direct deliberative voluntary contribution) shows just how low his expectations of human striving and flourishing had sunk.[28] Instead of cheering us up, this version of dry scientific utopianism depresses. With utopia as a gold star attached to qualifying social phenomena by this or that academic, independent scholar, or participant, we are as far from myth as we have ever been. And that goes for the myth of revolution as well as of telos.

My unwillingness to call existing communal experiments engaged on the utopian front "utopias" is, in a way, poetic. To identify utopia with what already exists, in the form of enclaves partly integrated into and thus voluntarily benefiting what should be gone beyond, is to adopt austerity in the realm of the imagination, compromising on dreams when acting on them proves too difficult. My other basis for objecting to "real utopia" (or any other notion of a partial concretization of utopia) is moral, and none too complicated. The experiments labeled as such are compromised from the start, for no other reason than because they are taken to be viable alternatives, which is to say, fairly integrated into the status quo. Their very viability in a bad totality, which may or may not directly profit from them, is the problem; it discredits them. They are, for the most part, reformist rather than revolutionary (a distinction which we would do well to hold on to for future use). But neither are living experiments that are truly revolutionary, like Chiapas or Rojava, "real utopias," qualifying instead as what Joël Gayraud calls "historical windows," openings onto human historicity and thus the possibility of transcending present social conditions—their utopian horizon.[29] While theoretically informed, they grow out of, not the abstract templates of speculative fiction, but bodily and mental affordances and extensions of hope into politics. Nonetheless, we are liable to lose from view the open horizon when cultivating our gardens in intentional communities or the marginal microsocieties Yona Friedman dubbed "realizable utopias," regardless of how commendable their principles and the felicity of their members.[30] Such communities are the experimental counterpart of the utopia of social labor, a version of the myth that has had its day. They sink if they remain insular: metaphoric islands. Doggedly small-scale, local utopian thinking suffers from myopia and is a dead end for the myth. (Enclosure has dogged utopia ever since the beginning.) The nowhere, long projected somewhere, must now extend everywhere.

The myth of utopia such as we might see revived in our lifetime will be neither an abstract ideal nor a sociopolitical order realized in miniature. The plethora of "lost horizons" testifying to the myth's past vitality, on the one hand, and the fiascoes or impasses of utopian history, on the other, while they do enrich its story, are not in themselves enough for a new version, or versions, of the myth. It would be difficult to renew that myth without them, and even as their traces float through my memory, I am uplifted by past utopias, if less by their content than by their very survival. Utopia does not die of its own too much; it is nourished by it. Yet to see the myth of telos as nothing more than a summation would only do for a culture of defeat. Far from ignoring this melancholy history, utopian thinking involves a social learning process whose telos is universal eudaemonia. It finds inspiration in all egalitarian projects, including those not meant in earnest (such as Cockaigne), while elaborating on their critiques and, in turn, critiquing them. The thrust of bygone determinate visions and experiments is the reason of the myth. It is not necessary for utopia to present a historically united front against the dying "utopian capitalism," in which the market, and not moral or political agents bound by a social contract, assures social harmony.[31] History teaches that there can be multiple reworkings of the same fundamental myth. The individual and collective advantages of the diversity of utopias are many, as long as things do not devolve into a competition for first place. Luckily, utopists have no equivalent of that institution, the Poet Laureate—though their ranks are full of poets. We the living are not good judges of what in us exceeds our reality. A reconstructed Enlightenment must make room for still greater utopian plurality. The point is not choice between these utopias, but the whetting of will. Political will likes incentives in the form of agreement and competition. In a global community, part real and part imaginary, social dreams can be shared, and their limits debated. The public sphere is not just a clearinghouse for facts and policy.

Utopian dreams are always relative, and the social gains we now take for granted could well be the dreams of tomorrow. Extreme constraints on survival are bound to affect ever more of the earth's inhabitants, ushering in a crisis of conscience and the creative imagination. The more humanity courts disaster, making existence increasingly untenable and sending survivalists and collapsologues into ecstasy, the greater the utopian thrust of fantasy.[32] The scenario is one of extremes: the doomsday mood liberating or utterly stifling our capacity to envision a common future. The visionaries will not be free of nostalgia, which keeps vivid in their mind's eye what segments of humanity, in their most enlightened moments, have aspired to beyond self-interest, but hardly managed to realize. Beside the utopians, in the same nightmarish boat—set adrift at capacity like a ship of fools without port of call or shipwreck to cast it on utopia's shores—there will be nostalgists *purs et durs*, who, instead of facing the present, re-create in their minds the world as it once was: imperfect but habitable. Neither party will be the engineers of the future. But our future doesn't need any more engineers.

Where survival is guaranteed, it is not desirable per se. With the loss of that guarantee in the coming decades, the value of "merely" living will grow as we recognize its utopian propensity. What we have long relegated to "survival," as beneath human dignity, will again be appreciated, and not just for rebooting utopia. The more our common survival depends upon putting our heads together to imagine radical social alternatives, the more convergence we can expect to see in such images, under pressure from a rapidly mutating material environment. Whether the boat is rocked from inside or from outside, there is no avoiding accidents. Workable ideas for saving humanity will oblige us to draw on and recognize competencies hitherto marginalized or invisible, rendering ever more seductive the dream of a society built on empathic inclusivity rather than on mutual mistrust, hatred, and every-man-for-himself refugeeism.

It is not that, in extreme circumstances, bringing into view our common welfare will result in a flawless social model on which we can all agree. But, as a creative expression of human desire for survival contingent on a radical transformation of our life as an Earth-bound species, the myth of telos, and the circulation and contest of its versions, can keep us focused on our purpose. Utopia's time comes when survival is at stake. The alternative is a path of least resistance ending, sooner or later, in the greatest mass grave in history. Without utopia, our consciousness is not up to "what is to be done." While we cannot will ourselves utopian, we must be willing to choose the myth—if only at the eleventh hour—over falling headlong into that abyss.

POSTSCRIPT

STAY HOME. STAY SAFE. BE HAPPY. Of the slogans of 2020, this one, in the window of a North American bakery, combined all the elements of the zeitgeist minus the leaven. Here was an expression of civil compliance and civic-mindedness with which the individual voluntarily sealed their alienated condition. It communicated trust in the government's decision to impose a set of measures consistent with the state of sanitary emergency. At first glance, the statement seemed to have little or nothing to do with ephemeral writing as described by Blanchot in 1968:

> Tracts, posters, bulletins, words of the streets, infinite words—it is not through a concern for effectiveness that they become imperative. Effective or not, they belong to the decision of the instant. They appear, and they disappear. They do not say everything; on the contrary, they ruin everything; they are outside of everything . . . Like words on the wall, they are written in insecurity, received under threat; they carry the danger themselves and then pass with the passerby who transmits, loses, or forgets them.[1]

The bakery's sign, by contrast, looked to be written from a position of relative security. It was received by passersby not as an order but as a friendly memo. It "carried the danger," all right. But its ultra-simple advice, miming principles of the good life, also carried a promise. Its first two sentences acted as conditions to the third, with staying home guaranteeing staying safe and, consequently, being happy. Displayed in the window, the words reminded one of a live social obligation (public safety) by appealing to presumed shared interests (personal safety and happiness) intimately tied to the former duty. Finally, they also represented the author's commitment or pledge to follow prudential rules as stated, projecting a sense of contentment in all its banality. The writer's exemplariness was implied in the message. All this was meant to exert a positive, encouraging influence on passersby.

With life confined indoors during the worst of the pandemic, proclamatory slogans like the one that struck me could be interpreted in diametrically opposite ways: as a retreat from public life or as a move toward it. The initially mild lockdown measures adopted in Canada made conformity seem less than onerous and the public's readiness to conform relatively harmless. The intensity of liberticidal restrictions in a pestilential world varies, to be sure, from state to state and area to area. To cite another Western example, the extended, blanket stay-at-home order in France required of all the production of an *attestation de déplacement dérogatoire* (declaration of permitted reason for being in public outside one's domicile) every time they left the house, no matter the duration, but for no more than an hour a day and within a one-kilometer radius, in town and country alike. The reasons for thus curbing the freedom of movement make only imperfect sense outside the context of recent history: the hebdomadal expressions of justified *colère* by the Yellow Vests still fresh in the French government's memory. The six-month stretch of intense Saturday demonstrations resulted in reinforced police presence even in smaller municipalities. The top-down imperative to carry a valid *attestation* or else risk fines suggests that the fear of illness and death is an insufficient deterrent to social and mass gatherings, let alone protests over the leadership's gross incompetence, should a trigger be present. The authorities have learned their lesson. Without the unstated hazard of insurrection, the rationale for the restriction does not alone justify its severity. It is painfully obvious that such exceptional paternalistic, *soi-disant* humanitarian surveillance and biopolitical techniques as contact tracing, quarantines, and curfews need little to normalize them and make them authoritarian. If we accept this extension of what Deleuze called *the society of control*, it should be with the full consciousness that it might not be in our best interest, insofar as staying home and staying safe do not actually guarantee happiness.[2]

It is remarkable to watch how fear migrates, moving between crises as if looking for them, rarely contracting, chiefly swelling and spreading. Its causes may be major or very minor, from acts of terrorism to police brutality to viruses to nuclear threats. Downplayed or blown out of proportion by misinformation, by the risk or fact of public panic, by enforced prolonged social isolation, and by other circumstances beyond our control, they mix and morph, their contours changing. Fear takes on a life of its own; it can take hold of us even when we court distraction and reach for technologies made to alleviate tedium and loneliness. These tools reduce direct physical contact and wean us off it, furthering under the guise of enhanced "distimacy" ever greater social atomization and anomie. In the global division of labor, the illusion of self-sufficiency has no ground to stand on; fear of the other is there to prop it up.

The cliché that crises bring out the best and the worst in us gains by being joined with the truism that crises come in many shapes and sizes. The quality of ethical response brought out in those affected had a lot to do with the pandemic's perceived magnitude and profile. The worst will always be the unjustified use of lethal force. And the best? Could that be personal happiness, whether it stems from responsible social distancing or actively aiding those in need? Are not hope and a social vision from which apprehension, deception, and suffering have been all but eliminated, in some ways, better? Whether dreamed silently in the safety of one's home or vocally in the streets, utopias trump individual virtue and fulfillment when it comes to what is *critically* best. They provide the mental frame in which altruism and care of the other can flourish.

If the pandemic menaces individual survival globally, climate change menaces humanity collectively. The outbreak of the novel coronavirus merits no more than this to describe it: tip of the iceberg. In 2020, the news finally hit home, in between commercials: a catastrophe is upon us. It is true that the world in 1968–69, during the most recent influenza pandemic of comparable magnitude, not to mention in 1918–20, which had the Spanish flu, exhibited a higher threshold for disruption. Answers to this escalation in sensitivity must be sought in increased risks to infrastructure and investments, in rising social expectations as the number of the living continues to climb, and in greater connectedness and knowledge of events as they happen, stoking anxiety and defensiveness.

Nevertheless, to some, the pandemic has given hope. It began with the dramatic drop in air pollution from fine particles and nitrogen dioxide. As countries began relaxing stringent lockdown measures, air quality predictably worsened, demonstrating that such positive effects of the economic downturn due to COVID-19 cannot be sustained. The confinement-related rise in residential energy demand for such activities as online streaming, for example, is on track to counteract falling power use in air traffic. If global energy demand, fossil fuel consumption, and carbon dioxide emissions registered a sharp overall decline in the first quarter of 2020 on a scale not seen since World War II, the gradual rebound in cumulative emissions of greenhouse gases is expected to more than make up for this. With the environmental benefits from stunted economic growth worldwide apt to be temporary, cleaner skies and gradual ecosystem recovery—symbolized by the return of wild animals to largely deserted urban areas—have the makings of a mirage. "The good life beyond growth"—or, for that matter, degrowth—still awaits broad-based support.[3] Will the slump precipitated by a mutating viral agent take on the interwar proportions finally capable of "shaking the parameters of the current consensus"?[4]

In the wake of the pandemic's first great wave, social revolt brought hope where it did not frighten, with open conflict engendered by long-simmering economic and racial tensions. The struggle for survival in the face of state violence became compounded by a sanitary disaster itself exacerbated by ignorance and poverty. The list of associated social ills is long: food shortages, mass unemployment, evictions, reduction in non-COVID-related medical care, the crippling of essential travel, the petty economy of small businesses brought to its knees, a global recession, and ongoing habitat loss through inattention or indifference. These were just some of the knock-on consequences. Meanwhile, the US federal administration spent itself in damage control and desperately saving face by shirking accountability. Sooner or later, public dissatisfaction will again boil right over, as it has in Chile, Iran, and Hong Kong. With frustration and unrest mounting left, right, and center, there is plenty of hope for change. In such situations, critical lucidity always competes with indignation and outrage as mere reflexes. We can only hope that it carries the day.

Reactions to the public health crisis confirm as much as they give a preview of the human responses that can be expected in the event of any large-scale disaster, be it the result of war operations, environmental decline, or the exhaustion of natural resources. The reactions fall between and, as a situation deteriorates, tend toward two extremes. On one side is the radical individualist or social-bubble mentality, whose hallmark is naked self-preservation (forfeiting its prefix, as Adorno would say), stockpiling everything from food to weapons.[5] On the other stands the altruist, whose reason for existence is serving the weak, the sick, and the wounded, bringing social assistance. Exactly midway between these extremes, we find the hermetic intentional community, which thinks itself utopian by following best practices among its members—an enlightened, hyperconnected, bourgeois version of Boccaccio's Florentine plague refugees in the *Decameron*, one foot in the e-economy, the other in a rented garden.

In the COVID-19 fight, the extremes, like the point of their apparent reconciliation, are fertile ground for utopian dreaming. To maximize our chances of survival, we have simultaneously grown more attuned and attentive to bodies. Under the regime of social distancing, testing, and self-monitoring, the sense of one's bodily needs has become more acute, and the need for physical contact, hitherto taken for granted, more pronounced. This holds for the entire gamut of such contact: from exchanging glances and smiles with strangers, to listening to voices without technological mediation, to touching in the context of play and sexual intimacy.

The superrich in their artificial paradises in New Zealand and on private islands are neither representative nor promising in this respect. But a page from the anarchist playbook is. One radical guide to surviving the virus outlines safe practices of resistance and, contra survivalists, calls for the creation of affinity groups and networks of mutual aid:

> Despite the models of safety that are represented by the bourgeois dream of nuclear family home ownership and the US foreign policy that reflects it, togetherness and care are much more important than the kind of security that depends on fencing out the whole world . . . It is our bonds with others that keep us safe, not our protection from them or our power over them. Preppers who have focused on building up a private stockpile of food, gear, and weapons are putting the pieces in place for an each-against-all apocalypse. If you put all your energy into individual solutions, leaving everyone around you to fight for survival on their own, your only hope is to outgun the competition. And even if you do—when there's no one else to turn those guns on, you'll be the last one left, and that gun will be the last tool at your disposal.[6]

The survival the guide's authors have in mind, though it avails itself of such tactics as rent, labor, and transit strikes along with prison revolts, does not reach for the vocabulary of heroism so widespread in the pandemic-stricken public sphere. For mainstream media coverage and advertising purposes, we are all "heroes" for being responsible survivors, looking out for others and ourselves. The title of "superhero" is spontaneously bestowed—no questions asked—on anyone who shows up for work when others, who can afford to stay home, are fearful of so much as poking their head outside. There is solace in this, no doubt: the world is not irredeemably dystopian. But the incessant clapping, cheering, outpourings of gratitude, and self-congratulation, while they may alleviate our conscience, do little fundamentally to change the rules of the "hunger game," in which we are all actual or potential participants. Appreciation for the bravery of those who often have no choice but to be exposed to risk so as to assist others and, in the process, to endanger the lives of those closest to them does not replace anger at democratically elected governments that, despite ample warning, failed to be proactive, to cooperate, and to plan for emergencies by establishing appropriate protocols and ensuring safe working conditions for essential workers. Similarly, no amount of vocal anger, indignation, and dissent can replace the decision, followed by action, to oppose state tyranny on its own terrain. And, lastly, politics as we know it is no substitute for open revolt.

Barring mass infertility, a man-made nuclear cataclysm, or a cosmic one, natality will continue to outstrip mortality for the foreseeable future. Yet most of us who pay attention see only death and the risk of death everywhere we look. As the global human population numbers keep rising, we are confronted with the prospect—nay, the reality—of a sixth mass extinction. Though it would take nothing less than a cosmic wrecking ball for humans to drop off the planet, worse-than-worst-case scenarios of an uninhabitable earth or the ultimate pandemic feed morbid fantasies of the end of humanity. Like it or not, survival, if only for smaller numbers, will long remain possible.

Faced with the prospect of a protracted degeneration of our situation—rather than the upward trajectory we have been used to seeing as our destiny—we might at last be willing to admit that life without the social dream and the slimmest hope of its realization would be meaningless and hardly worth living. "I do not want to survive the hope of the happiness I expected," says the sage Idamas, conversant with world history, in Grainville's *The Last Man* (1805), the first in a line of "dying earth" fiction.[7] (In the novel, humanity meets its maker and the world comes to an end.) We, too, must not accept the possibility of outliving utopian dreams. And even if we could survive them, we ought not, unless that day dawns when, at last, we can ascertain: THIS IS UTOPIA. Only then, and not a day sooner, should we rest.

Oscar Wilde, in his wonderful essay "The Soul of Man under Socialism" (1891), pictures a restless humanity: as soon as it lands on a utopia it has dreamed up in advance—an arrival that indicates progress, since "progress is the realization of utopias"—as soon as humanity realizes one dream, it looks out and sees, which is to say envisions, a still better place to go and sets sail for it.[8] That is the optimistic side of things.

The pessimistic side is that, as soon as we set sail for another utopia of our dreams, we are pursued and eventually joined by the profit motive, the capitalistic mentality. It keeps us company not as a mere stowaway, but at the helm. And when we arrive at our new destination, we realize that we have been diverted, reoriented, distracted. We notice that something is missing as regards happiness. We sense, and perhaps—knowing ourselves and our capacity for boredom, curiosity, and enjoyment—we assume, that a greater happiness is possible, only elsewhere. Some of us, obstinately, keep imagining other places to go. We imagine new utopias to escape those false or partial ones that we have landed on, which we have already peopled with our greed and savagery. We depart again to escape the cooption of our dreams by a system to which, as a society, we are bound hand and foot.

Worrywarts might object that a pandemic is not the time to think about utopias and dream big. Yet what better time is there for this than a period of confinement, when thinking is among the few pleasures we have left? What better moment than when thousands upon thousands perish in full view, while rulers throw up their hands or tighten their grip on power over us, revealing the system's fragility? In those hoping to recover, desire to survive lives on to the very last breath. This hope of survival is our supreme right, since it drives us to demand a qualitatively better existence.

The natural experiment into which the pandemic has plunged us is also, we mustn't forget, an unprecedented social experiment. Its range of responses to a global health emergency speaks volumes about a society's general emergency preparedness: infrastructure resilience, capacity for bipartisan cooperation, individual self-sacrifice, and (last, but not least) self-interest. State competition in weathering the crisis is good for virtually everything save nationalism if it stops at leadership in testing, vaccine R&D, or super-fast construction to address hospital bed shortages that should not have been allowed in the first place. States' taking credit for action under pressure distracts from the role they and their citizens play in a world economy responsible for taking the virus on a *tour du monde*. It remains to be seen what we will learn about ourselves from the pandemic as we wake up from reassuring air quality indexes and virtual socials to the sputtering of engines, ubiquitous screens, and seas of disposable, nonbiodegradable masks, gloves, and other plastics, which did so much to assuage our giant or little terrors.

One thing, however, is certain: there is plenty to learn to keep us busy. We would do better to keep our distance from those who jump to groundless conclusions or are called upon to dispense buoyant messages to the masses. Take Bruno Latour giving us the pandemic's "first lesson," to cite just one prominent example of such misleading punditry: "we have actually proven that it is possible, in a few weeks, to put an economic system on hold everywhere in the world and at the same time, a system that we were told it was impossible to slow down or redirect."[9] The "we" who showed that pausing the world's economy is within our reach refers presumably to humans, collectively. The assumption is that, since we did it together once, we can do it again. Only, I am not aware of such a wholesale systemic suspension, just of evidence to the contrary: from the boom in business for American multinational corporations like Amazon and illicit profiteering, to no more than economic depression in Korea, to the unstoppable economy of China, the alleged cradle of the crisis. Or look to Brazil, whose federal government refuses to get with the program and turns a blind eye on the ongoing illegal resource extraction from the land of Amazonian Indigenous communities, some so isolated as to be without "immunological memory," hence at a greater risk of infection from invaders and losing resilience as the virus wipes out their "living libraries," the elder keepers of tribal cultural memory. We are ill served at present by the gospel of human potential, by cloudy impressions delivered in upbeat rhetoric out of touch with economic facts. Whatever of value we do end up drawing from the plague, our only hope as a species on this lonely abode of ours is that its lessons will benefit universally, everyone.

And, just as an afterthought, there is no reason to confine utopia to a humanistic enterprise. What if we have been wrong all along? What if we went about things differently? What if utopia is not principally about us, but about saving the planet on which we happen to live?

ACKNOWLEDGMENTS

I am deeply indebted to my main critical interlocutors, James D. Ingram and Joël Gayraud, for their support and generous feedback on drafts of parts of this book. Special thanks go to my editor, Faith Wilson Stein, and my anonymous reviewers for Stanford University Press, whose comments led to significant improvements in the text. I wish also to thank Maude Trottier for her assistance with preparing the manuscript for publication.

Chapter 2, "The Emancipation of Desire: Preludes and Postludes of May '68" had its start as a paper delivered at the Emancipation Conference at Humboldt-Universität zu Berlin in May 2018. Chapter 3, "The Utopia of Survival: Critical Theory against the State," began as a presentation at a Manchester Centre for Political Theory workshop, "The Value of Survival," in September 2015, and was later expanded for the Critical Theory and Political Modernity Conference held at the Hamburg Institute for Social Research in May 2019. I am very grateful to the organizers of these events for inviting me to speak.

NOTES

Prologue

1. *Utopia* (nonplace, imaginary nonexistent place) is used here in the common sense of *(e)utopia*, or *good* nonplace, as the obverse of *dystopia*, or negative utopia. As a *place*, utopia has rectified what critique had exposed. As a discursive *genre*, it blends with critique and even social theory. It might then give rise to a political and social *program*, which acts on the critique to get to the place.

2. Consider, for instance, Thomas Hobbes's worry in *Leviathan*: "I fear that this writing of mine will be numbered with Plato's *Republic*, [Thomas More's] *Utopia*, [Francis Bacon's *New*] *Atlantis*, and similar amusements of the mind." Thomas Hobbes, *Leviathan: With Selected Variants from the Latin Edition of 1668*, ed. Edwin Curley (Indianapolis: Hackett, 1994), 244n15, translation modified. (The reference to More and Bacon is absent in the first, English edition of 1651.) Or the way Baruch Spinoza illustrates a lack of realism plaguing political philosophy: "Philosophers . . . conceive men not as they are, but as they want them to be. That's why for the most part they've written Satire instead of Ethics, and why they've never conceived a Politics which could be put to any practical application, but only one which would be thought a Fantasy, possible only in Utopia, or in the golden age of the Poets, where there'd be absolutely no need for it. In all the sciences [that] have a practical application, Theory is believed to be out of harmony with Practice. But this is especially true in Politics.

No men are thought less suitable to guide Public Affairs than Theorists, *or* Philosophers." Benedictus de Spinoza, "Political Treatise" (1677), in *The Collected Works of Spinoza*, ed. and trans. Edwin Curley, vol. 2 (Princeton, NJ: Princeton University Press, 2016), 503–4. Jean-Jacques Rousseau likewise recites the "usual suspects" to highlight the realism of his *Social Contract* (1762), "taking men as they are, and laws as they can be": "Since there was a Government existing upon my model, I thus did not tend toward destroying all those that existed. What! Sir; if I had only made a System, you can be sure that they would have said nothing. They would have been content to relegate the *Social Contract* along with the *Republic* of Plato, *Utopia* [of More], and *Sevarambes* [of Denis Vairasse] into the land of the chimeras." Jean-Jacques Rousseau, *The Social Contract*, trans. Christopher Betts (Oxford: Oxford University Press, 1994), 45, trans. mod.; Jean-Jacques Rousseau, "Letters Written from the Mountain," in *The Collected Writings of Rousseau*, vol. 9: Letter to Beaumont, Letters Written from the Mountain *and Related Writings*, ed. Christopher Kelly and Eve Grace, trans. Christopher Kelly and Judith R. Bush (Hanover, NH: University Press of New England, 2001), 233–34.

3. I draw no systematic distinction between *utopia* and *utopianism*.

4. Auguste Blanqui, *Oeuvres complètes*, vol. 1: *Écrits sur la révolution: Textes politiques et lettres de prison*, ed. Arno Münster (Paris: Galilée, 1977), 257. Where not otherwise noted, English translations are my own.

5. Karl Marx and Friedrich Engels, *The Communist Manifesto*, trans. Samuel Moore (London: Pluto, 2008), 31 (part 3, sec. 3, "Critical-Utopian Socialism and Communism").

6. Ernst Bloch, *The Principle of Hope*, trans. Neville Plaice, Stephen Plaice, and Paul Knight (Cambridge, MA: MIT Press, 1995), 583. The work was written in the United States in 1938–47, revised in 1953 and 1959, and published in 1954–59.

7. Isaiah Berlin, "The Sense of Reality" (c. 1953), in Berlin, *The Sense of Reality: Studies in Ideas and Their History*, ed. Henry Hardy (New York: Farrar, Straus & Giroux, 1996), 36.

8. Isaiah Berlin, "Political Judgment," in Berlin, *The Sense of Reality*, 53.

9. Michel Foucault and Pierre Boulez, "Contemporary Music and the Public" (1983), trans. John Rahn, in Foucault, *Politics, Philosophy, Culture: Interviews and Other Writings, 1977–1984*, ed. Lawrence D. Kritzman (New York: Routledge, 1988), 317.

10. "A Blueprint for Survival" was the title of a reformist manifesto for radical social restructuring, first published as an issue of *The Ecologist* in 1972, in advance of the United Nations Conference on the Human Environment held that same year. It was coauthored by the journal's editors (Edward Goldsmith et al.) and announced the formation of the initially national Movement for Survival (MS), on whose eventual internationalization the authors staked their hopes. *The Ecologist* 2, no. 1 (1972): 1, 23.

11. Ruth Levitas, *Utopia as Method: The Imaginary Reconstitution of Society* (London: Palgrave Macmillan, 2013), xiii. See also chap. 8, "Future Perfect: Retheorising Utopia," in Levitas, *The Concept of Utopia* (1990) (Witney, UK: Peter Lang, 2011), 207–31.

12. Levitas, *Utopia as Method*, xviii.

13. Darko Suvin, "Locus, Horizon, and Orientation: The Concept of Possible Worlds as a Key to Utopian Studies," in Jamie Owen Daniel and Tom Moylan, eds., *Not Yet: Reconsidering Ernst Bloch* (London: Verso, 1997), 122–37; Suvin, "Erkenntnis: Keystones for an Epistemology (11 Theses and 1 Indication)," version 8 (2012), https://darkosuvin.com/2015/05/23/erkenntnis-keystones-for-an-epistemology-11-theses-and-1-indication/.

14. This is the distinction between *sperare* (hope or expecting) and *optare* (desire or wishing) at the end of More's *Utopia*, where the author's fictional stand-in, Morus, concludes: "I freely confess that in the Utopian commonwealth there are very many features that in our own societies I would wish rather than expect to see" (*quae in nostris civitatibus optarim verius, quam sperarim*). Thomas More, *Utopia*, ed. George M. Logan and R. M. Adams, trans. Robert M. Adams, rev. ed. (Cambridge: Cambridge University Press, 2002), 107; Thomas More, *Utopia: Latin Text and English Translation*, ed. George M. Logan, Robert M. Adams, and Clarence H. Miller (Cambridge: Cambridge University Press, 2006), 248.

15. Benedict de Spinoza, "Ethics" (1677), in *A Spinoza Reader: The Ethics and Other Works*, ed. and trans. Edwin Curley (Princeton, NJ: Princeton University Press, 1994), 225 (II/246, P47). The relevant passages are on 228 (II/250, P54), 161–62 (II/150, P12, P13).

16. Raoul Vaneigem, *The Revolution of Everyday Life* (1967), trans. Donald Nicholson-Smith (London: Rebel, 2001), 58.

17. Eugène Minkowski, *Lived Time: Phenomenological and Psychopathological Studies* (1933), trans. Nancy Metzel (Evanston, IL: Northwestern University Press, 1970), 94–96, 100.

18. Minkowski, *Lived Time*, 101.

19. David Graeber, *Revolutions in Reverse: Essays on Politics, Violence, Art, and Imagination* (London: Minor Compositions, 2011), 31–32.

20. Thomas Piketty, *Capital in the Twenty-First Century*, trans. Arthur Goldhammer (Cambridge, MA: Belknap Press of Harvard University Press, 2014), 515.

21. Benjamin Kunkel, *Utopia or Bust: A Guide to the Present Crisis* (New York: Verso, 2014), 16; Rutger Bregman, *Utopia for Realists: And How We Can Get There* (2016), trans. Elizabeth Manton (London: Bloomsbury, 2018) (subtitles of other English editions: *How We Can Build the Ideal World* and *The Case for a Universal Basic Income, Open Borders, and a 15-Hour Workweek*).

22. Kai Heron and Jodi Dean, "Revolution or Ruin," *e-flux* 110 (2020).

23. E.g., David Schweickart, *After Capitalism* (Lanham, MD: Rowman & Littlefield, 2002); Gar Alperovitz, "America beyond Capitalism: Reclaiming Our Wealth, Our Liberty, and Our Democracy," *Philosophy and Public Policy Quarterly* 25, nos. 1–2 (2005): 25–35; and Alperovitz, *What Then Must We Do? Straight Talk about the Next American Revolution* (White River Junction, VT: Chelsea Green, 2013); Peter Frase, *Four Futures: Visions of the World After Capitalism* (London: Verso, 2016); Paul Mason, *Postcapitalism: A Guide to Our Future* (London: Allen Lane, 2015).

24. Barack Obama, transcript of Keynote Address, 2004 Democratic National Convention, Fleet Center, Boston, MA, Tuesday, July 27, 2004, http://p2004.org/demconv04/obama072704spt.html.

25. Obama, transcript of Keynote Address, 2004 Democratic National Convention.

26. Anarchist Uri Gordon identifies anxiety-based forms of hope operative in the prefigurative politics (stressing means-ends unity) of contemporary social movements in response to environmental collapse in a toxic, no longer revolutionary, future. Gordon, "Prefigurative Politics between Ethical Practice and Absent Promise," *Political Studies* 66, no. 2 (2018): 521–37. For more on *prefiguration* in this sense, see also note 32, below.

27. Levitas, *Concept of Utopia*, 230–31.

28. The "hope" in "hopepunk" is "hope as resistance, hope as the antidote to apathy, hope as a motivating force to inspire action in the face of overwhelming odds." Its fans see hopepunk—a creative protest and a welcome positive alternative to both climate-apocalyptic science fiction and technological dystopia—as a potent destresser and a public service. Rebecca Diem, "Hopepunk and the New Science of Stress," *Tor.com*, March 2, 2020; Aja Romano, "Hopepunk, the Latest Storytelling Trend, Is All about Weaponized Optimism," *Vox*, December 27, 2018.

29. This is not to be confused with utopian social theory, one of the three faces of utopianism, or *social dreaming*, identified and discussed by Lyman Tower Sargent in "The Three Faces of Utopianism Revisited," *Utopian Studies* 5, no. 1 (1994): 21–28. His first attempt at classification divided utopianism into utopian thought or philosophy, utopian literature, and communitarian movements or experiments. Sargent, "The Three Faces of Utopianism," *Minnesota Review* 7, no. 3 (1967): 222.

30. Compare Elias Canetti's classic conception of the logic of survival: "each man is the enemy of every other." Canetti, *Crowds and Power*, trans. Carol Stewart (New York: Continuum, 1981), 227–80.

31. S. D. Chrostowska, "Coda: Utopia, Alibi," in Chrostowska and James D. Ingram, eds., *Political Uses of Utopia: New Marxist, Anarchist, and Radical Democratic Perspectives* (New York: Columbia University Press, 2017), 269–310.

32. I have previously noted the convergence of utopia and politics in such practices (see, again, my "Coda: Utopia, Alibi"). *Prefiguration* refers to the utopian dimension of anarchism and of other forms of nonviolent communitarian direct action. Rather than the anticipation of a predetermined end, it stresses the consistency of means and ends in radical political practice. The term was originally defined by Carl Boggs with reference to a tradition spanning nineteenth-century anarchist, syndicalist, council communist, and New Left forms of radicalism as "the embodiment, within the ongoing political practice of a movement, of those forms of social relations, decision-making, culture, and human experience that are the ultimate goal." Boggs, "Marxism, Prefigurative Communism, and the Problem of Workers' Control," *Radical America* 11, no. 6/12, no. 1 (1977–78): 100. Winifred Breines described prefiguration in New Left politics and (from 1965 on) the mass student

movement in the United States as "the effort to build community, to create and prefigure in lived action and behavior the desired society, the emphasis on means and not ends." This comprised "the spontaneous and utopian experiments that developed in the midst of action while working toward the ultimate goal of a free and democratic society"—exemplary experiments that grew in theoretical sophistication and defied the labels "apolitical" and "expressive" politics (i.e., uncompromisingly idealistic, irrational and chaotic, extremist and nihilistic). Wini Breines, *Community and Organization in the New Left, 1962–1968: The Great Refusal* (New Brunswick, NJ: Rutgers University Press, 1989), xiv, 6, 47, 3; see also 46–52. As Andrew Boyd sums up the purpose of prefiguration in a manual for activists in the twenty-first century: "To give a glimpse of the Utopia we're working for; to show how the world could be; to make such a world feel not just possible, but irresistible." Boyd, "Tactic: Prefigurative Intervention," in Boyd and Dave Oswald Mitchell, eds., *Beautiful Trouble: A Toolbox for Revolution* (New York: OR, 2012), 82. Beyond articulating ultimate social desiderata as immediate guidelines to present praxis meant to embody them in microcosmic "foreshadowings," *prefiguration* designates physical attraction *here and now* to a better world—and not *after* a piecemeal social revolution, when systematic planning would have created the right conditions. Rather than "ends-guided"—that is, positing beforehand "remote and long-distance ends which are to be either achieved or lived up to"—it is "ends-effacing," to the extent that its ends emerge from practice and are understood as provisional, evolving. Dan Swain, "Not Not But Not Yet: Present and Future in Prefigurative Politics," *Political Studies* 67, no. 1 (2019): 57. For an alternative conceptual analysis, associating prefiguration, on one end of its contemporary spectrum, with negativity and dystopianism, see Ruth Kinna, "Utopianism and Prefiguration," in Chrostowska and Ingram, eds., *Political Uses of Utopia*, 198–215.

33. S. D. Chrostowska, "The Flesh Is *Not* Sad: Returns of the Body in the Utopian Tradition," *diacritics* 46, no. 3 (2018): 4–30.

34. A. L. Morton, *The English Utopia* (London: Lawrence & Wishart, 1952), 21.

35. Morton, *English Utopia*, 14. "It may be argued," Morton adds, "that in these fantasies, Cokaygne dreams and symbolic festivals, this revolutionary feeling was canalised, diverted and rendered harmless. It

would be truer to say that this was a period in which revolution was not objectively possible though popular riots were, of course, frequent, and that they were the means of keeping alive hopes and aspirations that might otherwise have died away, and which at a later date would prove of immense value" (23).

36. For a definition of *body utopia*, see chap. 2, note 3, below.

37. Bloch, *Principle of Hope*, 1369.

38. For an endorsement of this view, central to what she terms *transgressive utopianism* and anchored in a critique of liberal private property relations, see Lucy Sargisson, *Utopian Bodies and the Politics of Transgression* (New York: Routledge, 2000); and Sargisson, *Fool's Gold? Utopianism in the Twenty-First Century* (Basingstoke, UK: Palgrave Macmillan, 2012). David Harvey's proviso bears recalling here: "We have to find a path between 'body reductionism' ["the idea that the body is the *only* foundational concept we can trust in looking for alternative politics"] on the one hand and merely falling back into what Benton (1993, 144) calls 'the liberal illusion' about political rights . . . on the other"; that middle way is the "relational" view of the body "as a nexus through which the possibilities for emancipatory politics can be approached." David Harvey, *Spaces of Hope* (Edinburgh: Edinburgh University Press, 2000), 119, 130.

39. Slavoj Žižek in the documentaries *Žižek!* dir. Astra Taylor (Hidden Driver Productions, Documentary Campaign, US, 2005) and *Slavoj Žižek: The Reality of the Virtual*, dir. Ben Wright (Ben Wright Film Production, UK, 2004). This is practical, "Real utopia" in the Lacanian sense of "Real."

40. The thinkers of utopia and interlocutors to whom I directly owe the development of my present position in this area are cited here, albeit not exhaustively. My other contributions to utopian studies, extending and deepening some of these engagements, can help fill in what might be perceived as gaps or even glaring omissions. They are noted at the end of this book, in the bibliography.

Chapter 1: The Utopian Hypothesis

1. Theodor W. Adorno, *Minima Moralia: Reflections on a Damaged Life*, trans. E. F. N. Jephcott (New York: Verso, 2005), 152.

2. Accordingly, "the local [political] issue"—for example, the fight for certain forms of sexual liberation—"is meaningful and desirable in

and of itself, but is also at *one and the same time* taken as the *figure* for Utopia in general, and for the systemic revolutionary transformation of society as a whole," the aim being to invent "ways of uniting the here-and-now of the immediate situation with the totalizing logic of the global or Utopian one. So a given economic demand must always be in some sense a figure for a more total revolutionary transformation, unless it is to fall back into economism." Fredric Jameson, "Pleasure: A Political Issue" (1983), in Jameson, *The Ideologies of Theory*, rev. ed. (London: Verso, 2008), 384.

3. The case for the compatibility of utopia with political realism is elegantly made in Raymond Geuss's 2010 article "Realism, Wishful Thinking, Utopia," in S. D. Chrostowska and James D. Ingram, eds., *Political Uses of Utopia: New Marxist, Anarchist, and Radical Democratic Perspectives* (New York: Columbia University Press, 2017), 233–47. Both utopianism and realist political theory must guard against unreflective illusion (wishful thinking, ideology, purportedly self-evident unities). Benjamin L. McKean offers a more vigorous defense of utopia's value for politics—utopian thinking as a source of orientation in political interests—concluding that, "if political thinking and political action are to be productively linked, both realism and utopia are essential today." According to McKean, Geuss's at best "measured appreciation" of utopianism assumes that prioritizing—as utopias "and other ideal theories" do—particular normative, nonpolitical values "leads directly to an orientation to politics as an application of those values." McKean, "What Makes a Utopia Inconvenient? On the *Advantages and Disadvantages* of a Realist Orientation to Politics," American Political Science Review 110, no. 4 (2016): 887, 881, 876, 881. But what about those utopias that cloud their own normativity? Do they also risk disorienting us? Mathias Thaler argues for political realism and certain utopian fiction (e.g., the ambiguous utopia of Ursula K. Le Guin's *The Dispossessed*) as potentially each other's productive complements. Such fiction "exhibit[s] precisely those features that Geuss foregrounds as the critical and antinomian elements of 'content-based' utopianism." Thaler, "Hope Abjuring Hope: On the Place of Utopia in Realist Political Theory." *Political Theory* 46, no. 5 (2018): 682. As Antonio Y. Vázquez-Arroyo notes about the balancing act involved in this broadly Geussian position, a realism that "refuses to relinquish Utopia . . . resists any accommodation to the ruling

powers, as it relentlessly debunks the quest for silver linings," making the realism-utopia dialectic "indispensable for responsible political action in all its modalities." Vázquez-Arroyo, *Political Responsibility: Responding to Predicaments of Power* (New York: Columbia University Press, 2016), 255, 254. For the limits of Geuss's conception of utopia's place in realist Critical Theory, see my "Serious, Not All That Serious: Utopia beyond Realism and Normativity in Contemporary Critical Theory," *Constellations* 26, no. 2 (2019): 330–43. The case for utopian fiction (and utopian thought more generally) as supplying a much-needed orientation to political theory (and through it, to politics) needs to be made wherever utopia is not already mixed or overlapping with political or social theory (Rousseau's *The Social Contract* is an example of such a fusion, as is Michael Hardt and Antonio Negri's trilogy, *Empire* [2000], *Multitude* [2004], and *Commonwealth* [2009]).

4. Frederick Engels, "Anti-Dühring," in Karl Marx and Engels, *Collected Works*, vol. 25: *Frederick Engels:* Anti-Dühring, Dialectics of Nature (New York: International, 1975), 268.

5. Vaneigem "commemorates" the bad past in just this way in his own utopia, the City of Desire named Oaristys (Greek for "familiar conversation" and "intimate relationship") (n.b., misspelled in the title). Raoul Vaneigem, *Voyage à Oarystis* (Blandain-Tournai: Estuaire, 2005), 47.

6. Aldous Huxley, *Island* (New York: Harper Perennial, 2009).

7. T. J. Clark, "For a Left with No Future," *New Left Review* 74 (2012): 53, 57.

8. Clark, "For a Left with No Future," 73.

9. Walter Benjamin, "Paralipomena to 'On the Concept of History,'" trans. Edmund Jephcott and Howard Eiland, in Benjamin, *Selected Writings*, vol. 4: *1938–1940*, ed. Howard Eiland and Michael W. Jennings (Cambridge, MA: Belknap Press of Harvard University Press, 2003), 403–4 (New Theses C).

10. "Optimism is now a political tonality indissociable from the promises of consumption." Clark, "For a Left with No Future," 72.

11. T. J. Clark, foreword to *Guy Debord* by Anselm Jappe, trans. Donald Nicholson-Smith (Berkeley: University of California Press, 1999), x.

12. Clark, "For a Left with No Future," 69, 67, 72, 75.

13. Clark, "For a Left with No Future," 57, 58, 67, 73.

14. I am referring here to Slavoj Žižek's *The Year of Dreaming Dangerously* (London: Verso, 2012). The book's cover is a photograph of the author against the backdrop of a burning car. In his conclusion ("Signs from the Future"), Žižek sees the "radical emancipatory outbursts" of 2011 as revealing "limited, distorted (sometimes even perverted) fragments of a utopian future that lies dormant in the present as its hidden potential" (128). At the time, the left targeted by Clark had cause for boundless optimism. Bregman's more recent left manifesto, *Utopia for Realists*—a self-help manual for societies already living in the "Land of Plenty"—is still more buoyant, especially when read alongside his 2019 "hopeful history" (his words) of humanity. Its three utopian recipes, while uplifting to many, justify its placement on Amazon.com in the subcategory of Utopian Ideology. Professing a piecemeal utopianism without dogmatism, the author wants oxymoronically to call into being an "anarchist state": "The anarchists want to abolish the state; what I want to do is to make the state think like an anarchist." Rutger Bregman, quoted in George Eaton, "'I Want the State to Think Like an Anarchist': Dutch Historian Rutger Bregman on Why the Left Must Reclaim Utopianism," *New Statesman*, February 19, 2018.

15. Clark, "For a Left with No Future," 68, 54, 71.

16. Enzo Traverso, *Left-Wing Melancholia: Marxism, History, and Memory* (New York: Columbia University Press, 2016), 231, 233–34.

17. Walter Benjamin, "On the Concept of History" (1940), trans. Harry Zohn, in Benjamin, *Selected Writings*, 4:391–92 (sec. VII). The historicist historian is affected by an "indolence of the heart" (*acedia*) that not only "despairs of appropriating the genuine historical image," but causes sadness and identification with history's victors and "current rulers," their heirs (391). He colludes with them by treating as an object of melancholy contemplation, and therefore tacitly accepting, the historical process anointing them. Max Pensky, "Contributions toward a Theory of Storms: Historical Knowing and Historical Progress in Kant and Benjamin," *Philosophical Forum* 41, nos. 1–2 (2010): 172. Earlier on, in the *Trauerspiel* book (1928), Benjamin represents the pensive baroque melancholy of history as mourning and thus reviving an empty world. Walter Benjamin, *The Origin of German Tragic Drama*, trans. John Osborne (London: Verso, 1998), 139. Beneath his pen, melancholy becomes what it was throughout its long history: protean and

polyvalent. The melancholy disparaged in the 1931 essay stands in stark contrast to the "heroic melancholy" of Baudelaire's genius (a temper important for poetic inspiration and intoxication); or, again, to the melancholy beauty of early photographs in the "Work of Art" essay (1935). *Spleen*, "the quintessence of historical experience" in modernity, is also capable of "expos[ing] the isolated experience [*Erlebnis*] in all its nakedness," of drawing attention to a real loss and to the horror of regressing to barbarism, or "a mere state of nature." Benjamin, *Selected Writings*, 4:184, 190, 95–96, 336.

18. Walter Benjamin, "Left-Wing Melancholy," trans. Ben Brewster, in Benjamin, *Selected Writings*, vol. 2: *1927–1934*, ed. Michael W. Jennings, Howard Eiland, and Gary Smith (Cambridge, MA: Belknap Press of Harvard University Press, 1999), 426, 424–25.

19. Wendy Brown, "Resisting Left Melancholy," *boundary 2* 26, no. 3 (1999): 21.

20. Brown, "Resisting Left Melancholy," 26.

21. Traverso, *Left-Wing Melancholia*, 18–19.

22. Traverso, *Left-Wing Melancholia*, 8.

23. The expression is best known from the long title of Paul Signac's utopian canvas, *In the Time of Harmony* (1893–95), which appears to have been inspired by the anarchist Charles Malato. R. L. Herbert, Anne-Marie Rougerie, and Jacques Rougerie, "Les Artistes et l'Anarchisme d'après les lettres inédites de Pissaro, Signac et autres," *Le Mouvement social* 36 (1961): 9n38. Signac likely took it from Malato's "Le Rêve d'Humanus," published in *La Revue anarchiste* in 1893. By then, the idea was already something of a commonplace. It had been employed, for instance, by Edward Bellamy in *Looking Backward, 2000–1887* (1888) ("Postscript: The Rate of the World's Progress"), available in French translation in 1891. Russian satirist Mikhail Saltykov-Shchedrin reached for it when describing the confidence in humankind's destiny emanating from France. But traces of the modernized topos can be found much further back, as for instance in this verse from an obscure English writer: "The Golden Age is not behind / But in the forward, future mind." Edward Youl, "The Golden Age," *Howitt's Journal of Literature and Social Progress* 2 (1847): 118.

24. See Thesis 7 in Benjamin's "On the Concept of History."

25. Emmanuel Levinas, preface to *Utopie et socialisme*, by Martin

Buber, trans. Paul Corset and François Girard (Paris: Aubier Montaigne, 1977), 8.

26. The diagnosis comes from Perry Anderson, "Editorial: Renewals," *New Left Review* n.s. 1 (2000): 1–20.

27. Terry Eagleton, *Hope without Optimism* (Charlottesville: University of Virginia Press, 2015), xi–xii.

28. Eagleton, *Hope*, 40. Another useful argument against conflating hope with optimism can be found in Jonathan Lear's 2006 book *Radical Hope: Ethics in the Face of Cultural Devastation* (Cambridge, MA: Harvard University Press, 2006), 113–17.

29. See part 2 of Hans Blumenberg's *Work on Myth* (1979), trans. Robert M. Wallace (Cambridge, MA: MIT Press, 1988). Rather than being an original myth, the fundamental myth "is varied and transformed by its receptions, in the forms in which it is related to (and has the power of being related to) history," affecting the situations and needs that also, in turn, "work" on it. Imaginatively representing the "historical life-style" associated with an epoch's self-conception, and acting as the synthetic principle of the multiplicity of an epoch's mythical objectifications, it can coincide with a final, or last (*letzter*), myth—that is, a myth to end all myth—this latter, when at its best, setting a standard to be imitated, equaled, or even surpassed. It should be noted that, for Jonas, the hypothesis of a fundamental myth, unlike utopia, is not "a matter of fact . . . found in the history of literature" and competes with dogma (his *Das Prinzip Verantwortung* [The Imperative of Responsibility, 1979] was a critical response to Bloch's *Das Prinzip Hoffnung* [The Principle of Hope]). Blumenberg likewise does not count the literary genre of utopia among myths, which are generated by historical selection (on the analogy with natural selection); he puts it in with dogmas, which originated as "canon[s] by which to exclude heresies." In utopias, the poverty of the imagination is on display. His example: "When it was announced from the walls during May 1968 in Paris that the imagination should and now would come to power, it was immediately clear to the late grandchildren of aesthetic Idealism that this guaranteed that everything would become different and thus better. No one thought they needed to ask—no one would have been permitted to ask—what the imagination had to offer, what it had ever offered." For Blumenberg, Adorno's "restoration by 'negative dialectics' of the pure and empty horizon of possibility" around

this time was an attempt to uphold the imagination's weakness by turning it into a normative standpoint: utopia must be free of all positive description (verbal or iconic), as every such determinate image consolidates the existing state of affairs and "spoils the ideal." Either way, utopia "commands one to think what no man's eye has ever yet seen" (174, 181, 288, 179, 221, 224, 162, 161, 222, 221).

30. Northrop Frye, "Varieties of Literary Utopias," *Daedalus* 94, no. 2 (1965): 323. By contrast, to Robert C. Elliott, Louis Marin, and now Jameson, utopia is the structural inversion of myth. Fredric Jameson, "Of Islands and Trenches: Neutralization and the Production of Utopian Discourse" (1977), in Jameson, *The Ideologies of Theory*, 390.

31. Frye, "Varieties of Literary Utopias," 338, 323, 336.

32. Roland Barthes, *Mythologies* (1957), trans. Annette Lavers (New York: Noonday Press of Farrar, Straus & Giroux, 1972), 8, 144, 128, 132, 142, 150.

33. Barthes, *Mythologies*, 8, 138, 134.

34. Barthes, *Mythologies*, 142–43.

35. Barthes, *Mythologies*, 146–47.

36. Ritually cited by scholars of utopia thereafter, Lamartine's line is quoted by Karl Mannheim in *Ideology and Utopia: An Introduction to the Sociology of Knowledge* (1929), trans. Louis Wirth and Edward Shils (New York: Harcourt, Brace, 1954), 183.

37. Georges Sorel, *Reflections on Violence* (1908), ed. and trans. Jeremy Jennings (Cambridge: Cambridge University Press, 1999), 28.

38. Sorel, *Reflections on Violence*, 28.

39. Sorel, *Reflections on Violence*, 28. See also note 89, below. The *general strike* "embraced all the aspirations of socialism and [gave] to the whole body of revolutionary thought a precision and a rigidity which no other method of thought could have given" (117). For Blumenberg, Sorel's idea of the social myth contains the minimum of what can be called myth, as it tells no story. His *general strike* constitutes a *final myth* (that category of myths "fully exploit[ing], and exhaust[ing], the form") and converges with dogma (again, the category in which Blumenberg puts utopia). It is exclusive, "a canon by which one can always know and will what is not allowed to exist." (Besides this, as he later explains, "since there is only room for one final myth, the rivalry between candidates for that position takes on characteristics of dogmatism.") Blumenberg,

Work on Myth, 224, 288, 224, 289. For Lewis Mumford before him, social myths—Sorel's mobilizing myth of "pure action" aside—could be very hard to distinguish from classic utopias, which they approach "very closely" and, like them, can be divided into *escapist* and *reconstructive* ("myths of escape" and "myths of reconstruction"). Social myths, or "collective utopias"—such as that of political freedom formulated by American revolutionaries, or the proletarian myth (which Mumford would rather have criticism consign to the dustbin of history)—are "the ideal content of the existing order of things, myths which, by being consciously formulated and worked out in thought, tend to perpetuate and perfect that order." This "taint of actuality" notwithstanding, "these idola are scarcely as credible as the Republic and it will help matters a little to realize that we are still within the province of utopia, and may exercise all the utopian privileges." Mumford, *The Story of Utopias* (1922) (New York: Viking, 1962), 194, 193, 194, 196, 300–301.

40. Sorel, *Reflections on Violence*, 116–17, 115, trans. mod.

41. Sorel, *Reflections on Violence*, 115–16, trans. mod.

42. Barthes, *Mythologies*, 147.

43. Barthes, *Mythologies*, 157; Roland Barthes, *Mythologies* (Paris: Seuil, 1996), 230.

44. Barthes, *Mythologies*, 157–58, 148, 157. This and subsequent citations of this work refer to the English translation.

45. Barthes, *Mythologies*, 147–50.

46. Barthes, *Mythologies*, 157.

47. Barthes, *Mythologies*, 158.

48. Barthes, *Mythologies*, 158.

49. Bronislaw Baczko, *Utopian Lights: The Evolution of the Idea of Social Progress*, trans. Judith L. Greenberg (New York: Paragon House, 1989), 315, 321.

50. Baczko, *Utopian Lights*, 322–23.

51. Pierre-Joseph Proudhon, *General Idea of the Revolution in the Nineteenth Century* (1851), trans. John Beverly Robinson (London: Dover, 2003) [unpaginated electronic edition], trans. mod.

52. See Peter Turchin, *Historical Dynamics: Why States Rise and Fall* (Princeton, NJ: Princeton University Press, 2003).

53. Blumenberg, *Work on Myth*, 3 and following.

54. See Maurice Tournier, "'Le Grand Soir,' un mythe de fin de

siècle," *Mots* 19 (1989): 79–94; and Aurélie Carrier, *Le Grand Soir: Voyage dans l'imaginaire révolutionnaire et libertaire de la Belle Époque* (Montreuil: Libertalia, 2017).

55. For a critical history of millenarianism, see Norman Cohn, *The Pursuit of the Millennium: Revolutionary Messianism in Medieval and Reformation Europe and Its Bearing on Modern Totalitarian Movements*, 2d ed. (New York: Harper & Brothers, 1961). Debord counters Cohn's anti-utopianism by seeing in the Reformation-era peasant revolts the first stirrings of the revolutionary impulse: "Modern revolutionary hopes are not irrational continuations of the religious passion of millenarianism, as Norman Cohn thought he had demonstrated in *The Pursuit of the Millennium*. On the contrary, millenarianism, revolutionary class struggle speaking the language of religion for the last time, was already a modern revolutionary tendency, a tendency that lacked only the consciousness that it was a *purely historical movement*. The millenarians were doomed to defeat because they were unable to recognize their revolution as their own undertaking. The fact that they hesitated to act until they had received some external sign of God's will was an ideological corollary to the insurgent peasants' practice of following leaders from outside their own ranks." Guy Debord, *The Society of the Spectacle* (1967), trans. Ken Knabb (Berkeley, CA: Bureau of Public Secrets, 2014), 76 (sec. 138).

56. On the progress myth as secular millennialism, see Ernest Lee Tuveson, *Millennium and Utopia: A Study in the Background of the Idea of Progress* (Berkeley: University of California Press, 1949); and Albert Salomon, "The Religion of Progress," *Social Research* 13, no. 4 (1946): 441–62.

57. Russell Jacoby, *The End of Utopia: Politics and Culture in an Age of Apathy* (New York: Basic, 1999), 181.

58. Jacoby, *End of Utopia*, 181. For the distinction between the *iconoclastic* and the *blueprint* traditions of utopia, see Russell Jacoby, *Picture Imperfect: Utopian Thought for an Anti-Utopian Age* (New York: Columbia University Press, 2005). The utopian blueprint is a prescriptive picture of society, more or less systematic and detailed, complete with its architect's prejudices and restricted by what is possible and imaginable at that historical moment. Iconoclastic utopians resist all such representations.

59. Oskar Negt, *Nur noch Utopien sind realistisch: Politische Interventionen* (Göttingen: Steidl, 2012) [gatefold text].

60. Herbert Marcuse, "The Radical Transformation of Norms, Needs, and Values" (1977), in Marcuse, *Transvaluation of Values and Radical Social Change: Five New Lectures, 1966–1976*, ed. Peter-Erwin Jansen, Sarah Surak, and Charles Reitz (Toronto: International Herbert Marcuse Society, 2017), 55.

61. Marcuse, "Radical Transformation of Norms," 57, 55.

62. Herbert Marcuse, "The End of Utopia" (1967), in Marcuse, *Five Lectures: Psychoanalysis, Politics and Utopia*, trans. Jeremy Shapiro and Shierry M. Weber (Boston: Beacon Press, 1970), 69. See also his *Eros and Civilization: A Philosophical Inquiry into Freud* (1955) (London: Routledge, 1998); and *One-Dimensional Man: Studies in the Ideology of Advanced Industrial Society* (Boston: Beacon Press, 1964), where Marcuse quotes several lines from Blanchot's 1958 article "Refusal," later revised and included in the volume *Friendship* (1971), and reproduced in Maurice Blanchot, *Political Writings, 1953–1993*, trans. Zakir Paul (New York: Fordham University Press, 2010). I include here a slightly longer passage from this brief text: "Refusal is absolute, categorical. It does not discuss or voice its reasons. This is how it remains silent and solitary, even when it affirms itself, as it should, in broad daylight. Those who refuse and who are bound by the force of refusal know that they are not yet together. The time of common affirmation is precisely what has been taken away from them. What they are left with is the irreducible refusal, the friendship of this sure, unshakable, rigorous No that unites them and determines their solidarity . . . What we refuse is not without value or importance. This is precisely why refusal is necessary. There is a kind of reason that we will no longer accept, there is an appearance of wisdom that horrifies us, there is an offer of agreement and compromise that we will not hear. A rupture has occurred. We have been brought back to this frankness that does not tolerate complicity any longer. When we refuse, we refuse with a movement free from contempt and exaltation, one that is as far as possible anonymous, for the power of refusal is accomplished neither by us nor in our name, but from a very poor beginning that belongs first of all to those who cannot speak" (7).

63. Marcuse, "End of Utopia," 62.

64. "As Marx and Engels themselves acknowledged, Fourier was the only one to have made clear this qualitative difference between free and unfree society." Marcuse, "End of Utopia," 68.

65. Barthes, *Mythologies*, 164n29.

66. Kompridis, too, wants Critical Theory *sensu stricto* to resist the exhaustion of utopian energies while avoiding determinate utopias (which foreclose possible futures). Nikolas Kompridis, *Critique and Disclosure: Critical Theory between Past and Future* (Cambridge, MA: MIT Press, 2006), 263.

67. Jameson shares this emancipatory perspective when he states that "it is difficult enough to imagine any radical political programme today without the conception of systemic otherness, of an alternate society, which only the idea of utopia seems to keep alive, however feebly. This clearly does not mean that, even if we succeed in reviving utopia itself, the outlines of a new and effective practical politics for the era of globalization will at once become visible; but only that we will never come to one without it." Fredric Jameson, "The Politics of Utopia," *New Left Review* 25 (2004): 36.

68. Gustav Landauer, "Revolution" (1907), in Landauer, *Revolution and Other Writings*, ed. and trans. Gabriel Kuhn (Oakland, CA: PM, 2010), 114, 113, trans. mod.

69. Landauer, "Revolution," 116, trans. mod.

70. See Shemon, "The Rise of Black Counter-Insurgency," Ill Will Editions, July 30, 2020.

71. The Invisible Committee, *The Coming Insurrection* (2007), trans. anon. (New York: Semiotext[e], 2009); Giorgio Agamben, *The Coming Community* (1990), trans. Michael Hardt (Minneapolis: University of Minnesota Press, 1993), as well as his *Homo Sacer: Sovereign Power and Bare Life* (1995), trans. Daniel Heller-Roazen (Stanford: Stanford University Press, 1998), and *The Use of Bodies: Homo Sacer IV, 2* (2014), trans. Adam Kotsko (Stanford: Stanford University Press, 2016); Raffaele Laudani, *Disobedience in Western Political Thought: A Genealogy* (2011), trans. Jason Francis McGimsey (Cambridge: Cambridge University Press, 2013); Pierre Dardot and Christian Laval, *Commun: Essai sur la révolution au XXIe siècle* (Paris: La Découverte, 2014) (the common is here the first step in a revolution by the left, as the only way out of the present impasse); Judith Butler, *Notes toward a Performative Theory of Assembly*

(Cambridge, MA: Harvard University Press, 2015); Michael Hardt and Antonio Negri, *Assembly* (Oxford: Oxford University Press, 2017).

72. Hardt and Negri, *Assembly*, 258, 274, 240.

73. Traverso, *Left-Wing Melancholia*, 233–34. The Pascalian wager was reinterpreted from a Marxist perspective by Lucien Goldmann in *The Hidden God: A Study of Tragic Vision in the* Pensées *of Pascal and the Tragedies of Racine* (1956), trans. Philip Thody (London: Verso, 2016). The "Marxist wager" on humanity's utopian future was a tragic vision.

74. Bloch's *concrete utopia*, the power of anticipating the future, is "distinct from the utopistic and from merely abstract utopianizing." Contrasted with *abstract utopia*, it consists in what is "future-bearing" within history. "Reality without real possibility is not complete, the world without future-bearing qualities deserves as little regard, art, or science as the world of the philistine (*Spießer*) does. *Concrete utopia stands on the horizon of every reality; real possibility encloses the open dialectical tendency-latency until the very last moment.*" Concrete utopia is "the unfinished forward dream, the *docta spes* [educated hope—S. D. C.] which can only be discredited by the bourgeois . . . : *a methodical organ for the New.*" The unconscious, latent anticipatory "Not-Yet-Conscious" of concrete utopia contrasts with Freud's regressive unconscious. Bloch, *Principle of Hope* trans. Neville Plaice, Stephen Plaice, and Paul Knight (Cambridge, MA: MIT Press, 1995), 157, 223, 157, 137, trans. mod. For in-depth discussions, see Peter Thompson, "What Is Concrete about Ernst Bloch's Concrete Utopia?" in Michael Hviid Jacobsen and Keith Tester, eds., *Utopia: Social Theory and the Future* (Burlington, VT: Ashgate, 2012), 33–46; and Ruth Levitas, "Educated Hope: Ernst Bloch on Abstract and Concrete Utopia," *Utopian Studies* 1, no. 2 (1990): 13–26.

75. André Breton, "Introduction to the Discourse on the Paucity of Reality" (1924, pub. 1927), trans. Bravig Imbs, in Breton, *What Is Surrealism? Selected Writings*, ed. Franklin Rosemont (New York: Pathfinder, 1978), Bk. 2, 28.

76. Oskar Negt, postface to the French edition, *L'Espace public oppositionnel*, trans. Alexander Neumann (Paris: Payot, 2007), 222.

77. See Susan Buck-Morss, *Dreamworld and Catastrophe: The Passing of Mass Utopia in East and West* (Cambridge, MA: MIT Press, 2000).

78. If defined exclusively in terms of income, extreme poverty has been in decline globally, but parts of the world, notably sub-Saharan Africa,

have seen it rise. Poverty, however, is far from eradicated. The picture of overall progress in this domain alone becomes less rosy when the poverty metric is adjusted to include dimensions other than the monetary—such things as clean air, potable water, good nutrition, availability of health care, and quality of education—taking into account pollution levels, environmental degradation, and the depletion of natural resources.

79. For the latest word on the utopian potential of automation, see John Danaher, *Automation and Utopia: Human Flourishing in a World without Work* (Cambridge, MA: Harvard University Press, 2019). To get the upper hand of growing "human obsolescence" in the age of technology and advanced automation, we are invited to retreat to "virtual" worlds—the utopias of video games based on our technological infrastructure. The author admits that, "at first glance, this seems tantamount to giving up, but there are compelling philosophical and practical reasons for favoring this approach." Danaher thus touts the "vast horizon of possible worlds" as "the most stable and pluralistic understanding of the ideal society (in the form of the virtual meta-utopia)." The "virtual meta-utopia," of course, merely transposes the problems of design and implementation of the ideal society onto the virtual plane. Its virtuality, the supposedly unlimited, experimental sandbox-like space to get things right offered by VR, does not guarantee the simulated utopia's eventual reality. It assumes that we will agree and get along in the games we design. When "real utopia" proves too challenging, the "Virtual Utopia" of universal reconciliation will help us cope with the enormity of our failure outside it and (since even thoroughly mediated utopia cannot fail to be addictive) abandon to itself that which we could not change, but which somehow will have arranged itself to make universal gaming possible (how, in a future of automated work, all will have the leisure to play utopia, with technology also providing everything from real food to real climate control for all is not clear). If this "compromise between obtaining the benefits of advanced automation and ensuring that humans can live a flourishing and meaningful life" after having "ced[ed] the cognitive niche" to machines is really the best we can do, then we should not only embrace (as the author suggests we do) but actively hasten our complete obsolescence (133, 270, 156).

80. Marilynne Robinson, "Is Poverty Necessary? An Idea That Won't Go Away," *Harper's Magazine*, June 2019.

81. Blumenberg's study of political, history-making myths, missing from his *Work on Myth*, was published as *Präfiguration: Arbeit am politischen Mythos*, ed. Angus Nicholls and Felix Heidenreich (Berlin: Suhrkamp, 2014). For a rehabilitation of, specifically, political myth, see Chiara Bottici, *A Philosophy of Political Myth* (Cambridge: Cambridge University Press, 2007). Their many similarities (which she goes through) aside, Bottici separates political myth from related concepts—ideology and utopia, if only on a narrow understanding of utopia as a modern literary genre inaugurated by More (196–200).

82. Max Horkheimer and Theodor W. Adorno, *Dialectic of Enlightenment: Philosophical Fragments*, ed. Gunzelin Schmid Noerr, trans. Edmund Jephcott (Stanford: Stanford University Press, 2002).

83. Sorel, *Reflections on Violence*, 28. Myth, based on the accumulated knowledge of past generations, is a mental image for galvanizing the will and transforming individuals into historical actors. Sorel sets myth above reason as a valuable framework for interpreting social reality, myth's antirationalism allowing for the legitimation of revolutionary activity, including proletarian violence, in the face of the status quo.

84. André Breton, "Nonnational Boundaries of Surrealism" (1937) and "Surrealist Comet" (1947), in Breton, *Free Rein (La Clé des champs)* (1953), trans. Michel Parmentier and Jacqueline D'Amboise (Lincoln: University of Nebraska Press, 1995), 14–15, 17, 25, 94–96; Breton, "Prolegomena to a Third Surrealist Manifesto or Not" (1942), in Breton, *Manifestoes of Surrealism*, trans. Richard Seaver and Helen R. Lane (Ann Arbor: University of Michigan Press, 1969), 287–88. Following in the footsteps of Louis Aragon's "Preface to Modern Mythology" (1924; later integrated into his *Paris Peasant* [1926]), Breton spoke of the need for such a myth in 1935 and 1937, to finally, in a collective declaration from 1947, identify "the will to myth" as a force of progress and declare: "The time has come to put forward a new myth able to carry mankind onwards into the next stage of its ultimate destination. This is the enterprise Surrealism has specifically set itself. It is its great rendezvous with history." Breton, "Political Position of Today's Art" (1935), in Breton, *Manifestoes of Surrealism*, 231–32; Paris Surrealist Group, "Inaugural Rupture" (1947), in Michael Richardson and Krzysztof Fijałkowski, eds., *Surrealism against the Current: Tracts and Declarations* (London: Pluto, 2001), 48.

85. Gaston Bachelard, *Air and Dreams: An Essay on the Imagination of Movement* (1943), trans. Edith R. Farrell and C. Frederick Farrell (Dallas: Dallas Institute Publications, 2002), 1.

86. Bachelard developed the idea across his *Intuition of the Instant* (1932), trans. Eileen Rizo-Patron (Evanston, IL: Northwestern University Press, 2013); *The Dialectic of Duration* (1936), trans. Mary McAllester Jones (Manchester: Clinamen, 2000); and "Poetic Instant and Metaphysical Instant," a 1939 essay included in the English edition of *Intuition of the Instant* and republished in French in his posthumous *Le Droit de rêver* (Paris: PUF, 1970), 224–32. To the best of my knowledge, there is as yet no comparative study of Bachelard's theory and Benjamin's concept of "now-time" (*Jetztzeit*), the messianic moment or instant.

87. Bachelard, *Dialectic of Duration*, 105.

88. Bachelard, *Dialectic of Duration*, 109.

89. Quoted in Bachelard, *Dialectic of Duration*, 105.

90. Sorel, *Reflections on Violence*, 26, 63.

91. Henri Bergson, quoted in Sorel, *Reflections on Violence*, 26.

92. Bachelard, *Dialectic of Duration*, 42, 91, 19, 43, 19, 18, 48–49, 20, 21.

93. On the limits of the tragic sensibility that goes with political realism, see Allison McQueen, *Political Realism in Apocalyptic Times* (Cambridge: Cambridge University Press, 2017), 198–200. Susan Watkins also calls on comedy as an alternative to Clark's tragic perspective: its contrary values—multiplicity, coupling and procreation, popular mockery of rulers, "alongside . . . tragic unity[,] . . . death," but also "in place of pity and awe"—are better attuned to the "internationalist, but also irreducibly pluralist," multitonal, and multitemporal reality of present-day struggles. Watkins, "Presentism? Reply to T. J. Clark," *New Left Review* 74 (2012): 101. That comedy placates the masses, distracts them from their misery by instilling upper-class social codes, remains a hazard, but only if the utopian schemes (comic in direction) entertained by or produced for popular consumption are not tempered by a sober realism or laced with social satire (as Watkins herself notes, "insights gleaned from dreamworlds . . . may be precious, but a politics led by them would be heading for disaster" [102]). The advantage of Cockaigne over many a utopia in this regard is its bottom-up comic subversion of social ills, its passional *castigat ridendo mores*.

Chapter 2: The Emancipation of Desire

1. On the distinction between Bloch and Abensour, see Levitas, "Educated Hope: Ernst Bloch on Abstract and Concrete Utopia," *Utopian Studies* 1, no. 2 (1990): 13–26. Central to his materialist ontology, desire appears in Bloch as an existential constant. All the same, his is not a philosophy of corporal desire. *Educated hope* is informed and directed hope that does not "lead astray," because its horizon is defined by a Marxist "*knowledge of realities.*" It "operates on this knowledge as expectant emotion in ratio, as ratio in expectant emotion," or, in other words, as "as a dialectic between reason and passion." Bloch, *Principle of Hope*, trans. Neville Plaice, Stephen Plaice, and Paul Knight, 3 vols. (Cambridge, MA: MIT Press, 1995), 1735, 146, trans. mod.; Levitas, "Educated Hope," 17.

2. Miguel Abensour, "William Morris: The Politics of Romance," trans. Max Blechman, in Blechman, ed., *Revolutionary Romanticism: A Drunken Boat Anthology* (San Francisco: City Lights, 1999), 145–46.

3. *Body utopia* refers to the earliest and simplest form of literary utopianism, which prioritized the gratification of the senses. It is contrasted to *city utopia,* or the utopia of human contrivance and control. Sargent, "The Three Faces of Utopianism Revisited," *Utopian Studies* 5, no. 1 (1994): 4, 10. The main motifs of Cockaigne are found centuries earlier, in Old Attic Comedy (fifth century BCE): drawing on mythic material inherited from oral traditions, the poet Telecleides fantasized about an archaic cornucopian land of peace, health, and corpulence. The more elaborate, medieval body utopia of Cockaigne, however, entertains the real possibility of such a carefree place, though not as a result of a historical process. In this premodern form, somatic utopia is a gift of nature or gods, rather than a human product. The latter, is *city utopia,* the other fundamental tradition of utopian literature: epitomized by More's utopian commonwealth, with classical antecedents in Plato and modern developments in Étienne Cabet and Edward Bellamy, among others. If city utopias are manmade, engineering a flawless human community, the basic "utopian visions of the Middle Ages . . . start from man as he is and seek to fulfil his present desires," with nature spontaneously catering to human needs. František Graus, "Social Utopias in the Middle Ages," trans. Bernard Standring, *Past and Present* 38 (1967): 6.

4. On this basis, Murray Bookchin goes so far as to deny More's Utopia the title of utopia, a category to which, however, he assigns not only Cockaigne, but also Rabelais's Thélème, the Diggers, Fourier's phalanstery, and William Morris's quasi-medieval commune. In them, the tension between society and the individual is removed, "the historic demand for 'happiness' . . . replaced by the more liberatory demand for pleasure," and the realms of freedom and necessity reconciled, "integrated." As much as Bookchin praises the ideal of freedom emanating from these "traditional" utopias, he is against "blueprints" for the future. Instead, everyday life must become central to the revolutionary project of far-reaching social transformation. Bookchin, *Toward an Ecological Society* (Montreal: Black Rose, 1980), 281–84.

5. For Cockaigne as distinct from the pastoral, see Frye's analysis of these forms in Frye, "Varieties of Literary Utopias," *Daedalus* 94, no. 2 (1965): 339. While interested in the introduction of historical discontinuity into utopian fiction by Morris in his pastoral *News from Nowhere* (1890) and by later utopian novelists, such as H. G. Wells, Williams deems the social simplicity that follows this break "untenable." "The extent to which the idea of socialism is attached to that simplicity is counter-productive. It seems to me that the break towards socialism can only be towards an unimaginably greater complexity." Raymond Williams, *Politics and Letters: Interviews with* New Left Review (London: Verso, 2015), 128–29.

6. In recognizing Cockaigne as an "outlawed and furtive" social myth or ideal, rather than the imaginative, speculative, and telic one of utopia proper, whose worked-out literary constructs can contain social ideals but are informed by social analysis, being "less concerned with achieving ends than with visualizing possibilities," Frye delimits the utopian imagination by overrationalizing it and linking the telos myth with the myth of origin (i.e., the social contract, imagining society's origins to offer an explanation, a theory, of present social facts)—both of them social conceptions in fictional form ("Any serious utopia has to assume some kind of contract theory as the complement of itself, if only to explain what is wrong with the state of things the utopia is going to improve. But the vision of something better has to appeal to some contract behind the contract, something which existing society has lost, forfeited, rejected, or violated, and which the utopia itself is to restore"; "utopia . . . in

literature is a relatively minor genre never quite detached from political theory"). Cockaigne does not make the cut since it offers a "fairyland," a "fantasy dream," instead of a desirable "vision" (utopia) buttressed by social analysis; it is, for Frye, incompatible with "the typical utopia." Frye, "Varieties of Literary Utopias," 339–40, 329, 336, 323, 338, 339, 330, 339. Cockaigne's literary brevity and relative concision, however, should not blind us to its significant social-critical content.

7. Michael Löwy's *Morning Star: Surrealism, Marxism, Anarchism, Situationism, Utopia* (Austin: University of Texas Press, 2009) remains unsurpassed in drawing out the "elective affinities" between these currents of thought and practice. Also instructive is Luisa Passerini's reading of the geometry of '68 as a "conceptual triangle": subjectivity—desire—utopia. As she describes the relationship among the three terms, "utopia is innovated by the non-hierarchical conception of subjectivity, while subjectivity is embodied, and translated into intersubjectivity, by desire; at the same time, utopia allows the concrete putting into practice of desire." Passerini subscribes here to the assessment of '68 utopianism as aporetic and mythopoeic: "the intense desire to change was transformed into myth by the lack of political tools, and this mythology was based on a misinterpretation of the simultaneity of various revolts in the world, leading to the self-misunderstanding of revolt as revolution. Therefore '68 was not sufficiently utopian in a positive sense, while it was utopian in a negative way, when it took as already achieved what was only a potentiality, and mistook wishful thinking for actual possibility." Passerini, *Memory and Utopia: The Primacy of Intersubjectivity* (London: Routledge, 2014), 74, 70. Chap. 3, "'Utopia' and Desire," was first published in *Thesis 11* 68, no. 1 (2002): 11–30.

8. Marx diagnoses this poverty in his "Economic and Philosophic Manuscripts of 1844," in Karl Marx and Frederick Engels, *Collected Works*, vol. 3: *1843–1844* (New York: International, 1975), 300.

9. Jürgen Habermas, "Modernity: An Unfinished Project" (1980), trans. Nicholas Walker, in Maurizio Passerin d'Entrèves and Seyla Benhabib, eds., *Habermas and the Unfinished Project of Modernity: Critical Essays on* The Philosophical Discourse of Modernity (Cambridge, MA: MIT Press, 1997), 52, 49. Habermas reiterated his earlier conclusion about the Surrealist revolt's ultimately "false sublation of culture" in "Questions and Counterquestions," in Richard J. Bernstein,

ed., *Habermas and Modernity* (Cambridge, MA: MIT Press, 1985), 202. For Habermas, a correct "mediation of art with the life-world" lies, instead, in incorporating aesthetic experience into individual life histories, making art part of "everyday communicative practice" and "communicat[ing] its impulses to a collective form of life"; art can then "[reach] into our cognitive interpretations and normative expectations and [transform] the totality in which these moments are related to each other. In this respect," he goes on, "modern art harbors a utopia that becomes a reality to the degree that the mimetic powers sublimated in the work of art find resonance in the mimetic relations of a balanced and undistorted intersubjectivity of everyday life. However, this does not require the *liquidation* of an art set off from life in the medium of *appearance*, but rather a *changed constellation* of art and the life-world" (202). In this view, art's realization of its utopian *promesse de bonheur* requires a new social constellation—precisely the goal the Surrealists set themselves!

10. The Surrealists responded to Habermas's statements in 1987, with a text written by Michael Löwy. They denounced, in no uncertain terms, Habermas's misinterpretation of the movement's aims: Surrealism was not about desublimating life, but about using art as a "lever" by which to transform life, reestablishing (contrary to the Dadaist avant-garde) art's magical aura as a means of "'auratic' metamorphosis . . . of *all* the activities of the human mind [*esprit*]" (also: spirit or understanding); it was, then, not at all about "liquidating" art (in Habermas's exact words from the 1984 essay "Questions and Counterquestions": "the liquidation of appearance as the medium of artistic representation . . .[,] a false *Aufhebung* of art into life" [202]), but about truly sublating it—via its "*critique/conservation/transcendence*." Löwy, "Oiseau hermétique: La Réponse des surréalistes à Jürgen Habermas," in Guy Girard, ed., *Insoumission poétique: Tracts, affiches et déclarations du groupe de Paris du mouvement surréaliste 1970–2010* (Paris: Le Temps des Cerises, 2011), 43, 42.

11. Walter Benjamin, "Surrealism: The Last Snapshot of the European Intelligentsia," trans. Edmund Jephcott, in Benjamin, *Selected Writings*, 2:215–18, trans. mod. Jameson's 1971 *Marxism and Form* contains some pertinent observations on the Surrealists' notion of freedom and desire confronting its double in market society. Fredric Jameson, *Marxism and*

Form: Twentieth-Century Dialectical Theories of Literature (Princeton, NJ: Princeton University Press, 1971), 100–102.

12. André Breton, Jacqueline Breton, and Paul Éluard, letter to Benjamin Péret, March 30, 1935, in Breton and Péret, *Correspondance 1920–59* (Paris: Gallimard, 2017), 39.

13. It is to Fourier's credit (as to Saint-Simon's and Robert Owen's, the other two chief representatives of this intellectual current) that his impractical social fantasies were innocent of "inculcating universal asceticism and social levelling in its crudest form," attacking instead "every principle of existing society." Marx and Engels, *The Communist Manifesto*, trans. Samuel Moore (London: Pluto, 2008), 78, 80.

14. See Simone Debout and André Breton, *Simone Debout et André Breton, correspondance 1958–1966*, ed. Florent Perrier (Paris: Claire Paulhan, 2019).

15. *Aesthetic Theory* (1970) describes Surrealism's origin and fate as follows: it "protested against the fetishization of art as a special sphere, yet as art, which after all Surrealism also was, it was driven beyond the pure form of protest. Painters for whom the quality of *peinture* was not a decisive factor, as it was for André Masson, struck a balance between scandal and social reception. Ultimately, Salvador Dalí became a society painter to the second power, the Laszlo or Van Dongen of a generation that liked to think of itself as being 'sophisticated' based on a vague sense of a crisis that had in any case been stabilized for decades. Thus the false afterlife of Surrealism was founded." Theodor W. Adorno, *Aesthetic Theory*, ed. Gretel Adorno and Rolf Tiedemann, trans. Robert Hullot-Kentor (London: Continuum, 2004), 229, trans. mod. Adorno here overlooks Surrealism's real beginnings and continuation in radical nonconformism, revolutionary politics, and the poetics of the "disinterested play of thought," freed from rational control and open to chance. André Breton, "Manifesto of Surrealism" (1924), in Breton, *Manifestoes of Surrealism*, 26. The betrayal of the principles of Surrealism by some of its figures did not mean the movement as such was dead. That those who stayed true to these principles and continued did not seek or find the limelight would have been commendable if it had not simply gone unnoticed. See also note 44, below.

16. See Charles Fourier, *The Theory of the Four Movements*, ed. Gareth Stedman Jones and Ian Patterson, trans. I. Patterson (Cambridge: Cambridge University Press, 1996), 6–9.

17. Charles Fourier, *Oeuvres complètes*, vol. 7: *Le Nouveau monde amoureux* (1967), ed. Simone Debout-Oleszkiewicz (Paris: Anthropos, 1972), 384. I disagree with Löwy's characterization of Breton as a Romantic Marxist. Löwy, *Morning Star*, 22.

18. André Breton, "Projet d'un texte utopique," in Breton, *Oeuvres complètes*, 4 vols. (Paris: Gallimard, 1999), 3:343–45.

19. André Breton, "On Surrealism in Its Living Works" (1953), in Breton, *Manifestoes of Surrealism*, 299.

20. Breton, "Manifesto of Surrealism," 18.

21. André Breton, "Second Manifesto of Surrealism" (1930), in Breton, *Manifestoes of Surrealism*, 125, trans. mod.

22. Internationale situationniste, "Le Questionnaire," *Internationale situationniste: Bulletin central édité par les sections de l'internationale situationniste* 9 (August 1964), reprinted in *Internationale situationniste, 1958–1969* (Amsterdam: Van Gennep, 1972), [26].

23. Internationale situationniste, "Le Questionnaire," [26].

24. Gilles Ivain [Ivan Chtcheglov], "Formulary for a New Urbanism," in Ken Knabb, ed. and trans., *Situationist International Anthology: Revised and Expanded Edition* (Berkeley, CA: Bureau of Public Secrets, 2006), 3–4.

25. The editors' introduction to the first issue of the LI bulletin *Potlatch* (June 22, 1954), reprinted in Internationale lettriste, *Potlatch, 1954–1957* (Paris: Gérard Lebovici, 1985), 11.

26. Internationale lettriste, "Réponse à la question: 'La pensée nous éclaire-t-elle, et nos actes, avec la même indifférence que le soleil, ou quel est notre espoir et quelle est sa valeur?'" [Response to the Question: "Does thought enlighten both us and our actions with the same indifference as the sun, or what is our hope, and what is its value?"], in René Magritte, ed., *La Carte d'après nature* (Brussels: June 1954), [24]; English translation by Nick Tallett at http://www.notbored.org/la-carte.html.

27. Constant, "C'est notre désir qui fait la révolution" [It's Our Desire That Makes Revolution], *Cobra: Organe du front international des artistes expérimentaux d'avant-garde* 4 (1949), reprinted in Cobra, *Cobra 1948–1951* (Paris: Jean-Michel Place, 1980), [3].

28. Internationale situationniste, "L'Urbanisme unitaire à la fin des années 50" [Unitary Urbanism at the End of the 1950s], *Internationale*

situationniste 3 (December 1959), reprinted in *Internationale situationniste, 1958–1969*, [14]; English translation by Paul Hammond at https://www.cddc.vt.edu/sionline/si/unitary.html. Guy Debord, "Premières maquettes pour l'urbanisme nouveau" [First Models for the New Urbanism], *Potlatch* 30 (July 15, 1959), in Gérard Berréby, ed., *Documents relatifs à la fondation de l'Internationale situationniste 1948–1957* (Paris: Allia, 1985), 255; English translation by Gerardo Denis at https://www.cddc.vt.edu/sionline/si/models.html.

29. See Mark Wigley and Constant, *Constant's New Babylon: The Hyper-Architecture of Desire* (Rotterdam: Witte de With Center for Contemporary Art and 010 Publishers, 1998). Constant's "Pour une architecture de situation," a text purportedly published in 1953 and cited by many as "foundational," appears to be a confusion perpetuated by an interview between Kristin Ross and Henri Lefebvre, available online: http://revueperiode.net/sur-les-situationnistes-entretien-inedit-dhenri-lefebvre-avec-kristin-ross/.

30. Guy Debord, "Theory of the Dérive" (1956 in *Les Lèvres nues*; reprinted in 1959 in issue 3 of the SI journal), in Knabb, ed., *Situationist International Anthology*, 62–66. The journal *Les Lèvres nues* was published by Belgian Surrealists.

31. Internationale situationniste, "L'Urbanisme unitaire," [14].

32. Internationale situationniste, "L'Urbanisme unitaire," [12].

33. Guy Debord, "Report on the Construction of Situations and on the Terms of Organization and Action of the International Situationist Tendency" (1957), trans. Tom McDonough, in McDonough, ed., *Guy Debord and the Situationist International: Texts and Documents* (Cambridge, MA: MIT Press, 2002), 35. Debord's diatribe was a way of demarcating his own breakaway avant-garde, the Lettrist International. (Surrealism, incidentally, did not regard itself as an avant-garde movement, but as an exponentiation of Romanticism and Symbolism, stressing heritage over radical innovation.) His one-upmanship with Surrealism continued after the foundation of the Situationist International. Surrealism, which "expected nothing less than the overthrow of the dominant social order," was a "success . . . only in the context of a world that has not been essentially transformed." This success, promoting "multiple degraded repetitions," was "backfiring." Internationale situationniste, "Amère victoire du surréalisme" [Surrealism's Bitter

Victory], *Internationale situationniste* 1 (June 1958), reprinted in *Internationale situationniste, 1958-1969*, [3]; English translation by Reuben Keehan at https://www.cddc.vt.edu/sionline/si/bitter.html. Tensions between the two movements flared up alongside rapprochements: Elisabeth Lenk, for instance, was excluded from the Paris Surrealist Group some months after Breton's death on the grounds of her perceived "Situationist deviation" (her newfound interest in that movement). Lenk, commentary to her letter from October 1966, in Theodor W. Adorno and Lenk, *The Challenge of Surrealism: The Correspondence of Theodor W. Adorno and Elisabeth Lenk*, trans. Susan H. Gillespie (Minneapolis: University of Minnesota Press, 2015), 130. Focused on overarching similarities, Löwy places Debord in the revolutionary-utopian Romantic tradition, along with William Blake, Morris, Fourier, and Breton. Löwy, *Morning Star*, 101. For Debord's praise of Breton, see vols. 6 and 7 of his *Correspondance*.

34. In *Eros and Civilization*, acknowledging the pioneering nature of Surrealism's reading of Freud, Marcuse quotes Breton's 1924 manifesto in support of the thesis that fantasy's critical function lies "in its refusal to accept as final the limitations imposed upon freedom and happiness by the reality principle, in its refusal to forget what *can be*." He also commends Fourier for having come "closer than any other utopian socialist to elucidating the dependence of freedom on non-repressive sublimation," even if he then goes on to criticize "his detailed blueprint for the realization of this idea" as "hand[ing] it over to a giant organization and administration and thus retain[ing] the repressive elements." Herbert Marcuse, *Eros and Civilization: A Philosophical Inquiry into Freud* (London: Routledge, 1998), 149, 218.

35. "On the Poverty of Student Life Considered in Its Economic, Political, Psychological, Sexual, and Especially Intellectual Aspects, With a Modest Proposal for Doing Away with It, by members of the Situationist International and students of Strasbourg University" (1966), in Knabb, ed., *Situationist International Anthology*, 429; French edition: "De la misère en milieu étudiant considérée sous ses aspects économique, politique, psychologique, sexuel et notamment intellectuel, et de quelques moyens pour y remédier," in René Viénet, ed., *Enragés et situationnistes dans le mouvement des occupations* (Paris: Gallimard, 1968), 219-43.

36. Pierre Canjuers [Daniel Blanchard] and Guy Debord, "Preliminaries toward Defining a Unitary Revolutionary Program" (1960), in Knabb, ed., *Situationist International Anthology*, 392.

37. Vaneigem, *The Revolution of Everyday Life*, trans. Donald Nicholson-Smith (London: Rebel, 2001), 26.

38. Vaneigem, *Revolution of Everyday Life*, 254.

39. Vaneigem, *Revolution of Everyday Life*, 244, 219, 223.

40. As the principal actors of '68 themselves wrote at the time, "Nobody among us read Marcuse!" Daniel Cohn-Bendit and Jean-Pierre Duteuil, *La Révolte étudiante: Les Animateurs parlent* (Paris: Seuil, 1968), 70.

41. Public discussion, February 15, 2018. For a synthetic account of the *libertaire* (broadly left-wing) experience of '68, see Lola Miesseroff, *Voyage en outre-gauche* (Montreuil: Libertalia, 2018).

42. Jean-Christophe Bailly, "68, année philosophique?" Episodes 3-4, "Un printemps à Nanterre," *Les nouveaux chemins de la philosophie*, April 25, 2018, Radio France Culture.

43. "Pas de Pasteurs pour cette Rage!" Paris, May 5, 1968, reprinted in José Pierre, ed., *Tracts surréalistes et déclarations collectives, 1922–1969*, vol. 2: *1940–1969* (Paris: Terrain vague, 1982), 276.

44. The dissolution by a fraction, led by Jean Schuster, was not accepted by all members, and the Group exists to this day, alongside numerous groups internationally, most notably in Prague and Chicago.

45. For a discussion of the first term (which appears in several works he coauthored with Deleuze) alongside Foucault's economy of power relations, see Félix Guattari, "Microphysics of Power / Micropolitics of Desire," trans. John Caruana, in *The Guattari Reader*, ed. Gary Genosko (Oxford: Blackwell, 1996), 172–81 Gilles Deleuze and Guattari, *Kafka: Toward a Minor Literature*, trans. Dana Polan (Minneapolis: University of Minnesota Press, 1986), 42.

46. Bloch, *Principle of Hope*, 3.

47. Abensour, "William Morris: The Politics of Romance," 145.

48. Miguel Abensour, "Les Formes de l'utopie socialiste-communiste: Essai sur le communisme critique et l'utopie," PhD diss., Panthéon-Sorbonne, 1973, unpublished; Abensour's argument, developed in his discussion of Morris, resurfaces in his "William Morris, utopie libertaire et novation technique," in [collective], *L'Imaginaire subversif: Interrogations*

sur l'utopie (Geneva: Éditions Noir, 1982), 113–50 (translated as "William Morris: The Politics of Romance").

49. E. P. Thompson, "Postscript: 1976," in Thompson, *William Morris: Romantic to Revolutionary*, rev. ed. (New York: Pantheon, 1977), 793.

50. Miguel Abensour, *L'Histoire de l'utopie et le destin de sa critique: Utopiques 4* (Paris: Sens & Tonka, 2016), 54–55.

51. Fourier, *Theory of the Four Movements*, 6, 269, 195–96.

52. Perry Anderson, "Utopias," in Anderson, *Arguments within English Marxism* (London: Verso, 1980), 161.

53. Theodor W. Adorno, "Theses on Need" (1942), trans. Martin Shuster and Iain Macdonald, *Adorno Studies* 1, no. 1 (2017): 102–4, trans. mod. based on David Fernbach's new translation in *New Left Review* 128 (2021): 79–82.

54. Adorno, "Theses on Need," 104. See also his "Aldous Huxley and Utopia," in Adorno, *Prisms*, trans. Samuel Weber and Shierry Weber (Cambridge, MA: MIT Press, 1981), 95–117.

55. See chap. 9, "Pauperism and Utopia," in Karl Polanyi, *The Great Transformation* (Boston, MA: Beacon Press, 2001), 108–15. Polanyi exposes the liberal principle of laissez-faire capitalism as utopian, with democratic socialism as anti-utopian countermeasure.

56. Jackson Lears, *Fables of Abundance: A Cultural History of Advertising in America* (New York: Basic, 1994).

57. Guy Debord, *The Society of the Spectacle*, trans. Ken Knabb (Berkeley, CA: Bureau of Public Secrets, 2014), 15–16 (sec. 40), 84 (sec. 153); Situationist International, "The Bad Days Will End" (1962), in Knabb, ed., *Situationist International Anthology*, 113.

58. Situationist International, "Bad Days Will End," 113.

59. Raoul Vaneigem, "Basic Banalities" (pts. I and II), in Knabb, ed., *Situationist International Anthology*, 171, 126, 120–21. The text appeared over issues 7 and 8 of *Internationale situationniste*. The original English translation from 1966 by SI member Christopher Gray and Philippe Vissac bore the title "The Totality for Kids."

60. Vaneigem, "Banalities," 168, 121.

61. Vaneigem, "Banalities," 121, 168.

62. Vaneigem, "Banalities," 124, 158–59, 162, 171–72, 157–58, 173.

63. Vaneigem, *Revolution of Everyday Life*, 18.

64. Vaneigem, *Revolution of Everyday Life*, 159, 163.

65. Marc Pierret, *Utopies et perversions: Un dossier ouvert par Marc Pierret* (Paris: Nouvelles Éditions Debresse, 1969), 20, 43, 37–38 (citing Marcuse), 27, 34, 25.

66. As Adorno wrote in 1963, "Pleasure that is either caught or permitted with smiling complaisance is no longer pleasure at all; psychoanalysts would be able to demonstrate without difficulty that in the entire sex industry—monopolistically controlled and standardized as it is, with its ready-made appliqués of film stars—fore-pleasure and ersatz pleasure have surpassed pleasure itself. The neutralization of sex, which has been traced in the disappearance of grand passion, blanches sex even where it believes itself to be unabashedly satisfied." Theodor W. Adorno, "Sexual Taboos and Law Today," in Adorno, *Critical Models*, trans. Henry W. Pickford (New York: Columbia University Press, 2005), 73, trans. mod. Adorno's critique here of the "desexualization of sexuality" precedes the sexual revolution, and the "sex industry" boom he targets should not take away from the later, genuine libidinal emancipation.

67. Giorgio Cesarano, *Manuel de survie*, trans. Benjamin Villari, rev. ed. (Bordeaux: La Tempête, 2019), 52, [preface, unnumbered], 117.

68. Cesarano, *Manuel*, 114, 112–18, 39, 117. See also his unfinished *Critica dell'utopia capitale* (Milan: Colibri, 1993).

69. Cesarano, *Manuel*, 114, 117, 124, 114.

70. Cesarano, *Manuel*, 139, 250, 52, 205, 39, 205, 46, 75 and following, especially 77 and 82.

71. Vaneigem, *Revolution of Everyday Life*, 250–51, 253.

72. Vaneigem, *Revolution of Everyday Life*, 253.

73. Cesarano, *Manuel*, 48, 66, 249, 220, 50; Giorgio Cesarano, *Manuale di sopravvivenza* (Bari: Dedalo libri, 1974), 25.

74. Cesarano, *Manuel*, 86, 243, 246–48.

75. Cesarano, *Manuel*, 116; see Mannheim, *Ideology and Utopia: An Introduction to the Sociology of Knowledge*, trans. Louis Wirth and Edward Shils (New York: Harcourt, Brace, 1954), 236.

76. For a study of the heterodox genesis of political ecology in France, see Alexis Vrignon, *La Naissance de l'écologie politique en France: Une nébuleuse au coeur des années 68* (Rennes: Presses Universitaires de Rennes, 2017). A pivotal contemporary reference is René Dumont's

programmatic *L'Utopie ou la mort!* (1973), which at once issued a realist's warning against mounting threats to human survival and rehabilitated utopian thinking. Survival depended on utopia; nothing short of utopia could prevent catastrophe. The book proposed, "for rich countries, a *general mobilization of survival*, a state of emergency, with a series of 'utopias' paralleling those proposed in countries until now dominated . . . [aiming for lesser injustice and] abundance for *all.*" Dumont, *L'Utopie ou la mort!* (Paris: Seuil, 1974), 6–7.

77. Céline Pessis, ed., *Survivre et vivre: Critique de la science, naissance de l'écologie* (Paris: L'Échappée, 2014), 11.

78. Laurent Samuel, "L'Idéologie du désir, une nouvelle mystification" (1973), in Pessis, ed., *Survivre et vivre*, 306–7.

79. Samuel, "L'Idéologie du désir," 306–7.

80. Pessis, ed., *Survivre et vivre*, 11.

81. Jean-Paul Malrieu, "Un soir de printemps à Survivre et vivre, réflexions à propos d'un départ," in Pessis, ed., *Survivre et vivre*, 442–43.

82. Jean-Pierre Aboulker, "Survivre . . . et vivre" (1971), in Pessis, ed., *Survivre et vivre*, 165.

83. Aboulker, "Survivre . . . et vivre," 166, 165; Vaneigem, *Revolution of Everyday Life*, 161.

84. Anon., "La révolution médicale: Comment la médecine avance en se mordant la queue" (1973), in Pessis, ed., *Survivre et vivre*, 278.

85. Jean-Paul Malrieu, "Si nous sommes raisonnables . . ." (1973), in Pessis, ed., *Survivre et vivre*, 322.

86. The idea, again, seems to have originated with Vaneigem. "The rejection of economic logic (which economises only on life) would of necessity entail the death of economics and carry us beyond the realm of survival." Vaneigem, *Revolution of Everyday Life*, 163.

87. *Pace* Jay Winter, if "major utopians 'see like a state,' in Jim Scott's felicitous phrase," certain "minor utopians" of the '68 moment wanted more than just "partial transformations": both "to rethink what a state is" *and* "to do away with it." Winter, *Dreams of Peace and Freedom: Utopian Moments in the Twentieth Century* (New Haven: Yale University Press, 2006), 208–9. Vaneigem's project of *autogestion généralisée*, of which Winter does not seem to be aware, was an answer to the theory and practice of *autogestion* (local collective self-management, still in the framework of the enterprise and the state; Winter's example of a "minor

utopia" [153]). See Raoul Vaneigem, "Notice to the Civilized concerning Generalized Self-Management," in Knabb, ed., *Situationist International Anthology*, 363–71 (originally published in September 1969, in issue 12 of *Internationale situationniste*).

88. Survivre et vivre, "Fin de l'économie," *Survivre . . . et vivre* 19 (1975): 7.

89. Karl Marx, first manuscript, "Economic and Philosophic Manuscripts of 1844," in Marx and Engels, *Collected Works*, 3:275.

90. Pierret, *Utopies et perversions*, 43.

91. On the history of the international human rights movement, see Samuel Moyn, *The Last Utopia: Human Rights in History* (Cambridge, MA: Harvard University Press, 2010). Moyn frames the movement as a utopian program of international law that took off in the mid-1970s by outliving political and other (both state-based and internationalist) utopian constructs of the 1960s, which "collapsed" or "imploded." Readers looking for insights into the root of this crisis affecting, above all, welfarist and socialist models—namely, the passage from industrial to finance capitalism and the disintegration of the Soviet bloc—will be disappointed. In Moyn's account, human rights, catapulted into first place by the postwar lack of sympathy for *political* utopias and "born of the yearning to transcend politics," have since come to constitute "the core language of a new politics of humanity that has sapped the energy from old ideological contests of left and right" (by "displacing" politics and toning down aspirations for change) and, in the process, became "bound up with the power of the powerful." The legalistic poverty of this "last utopia standing in world affairs," this apparently lone "survivor" on the universalistic battlefield, is in tune with the worldwide persistence of material poverty. In this fundamental respect, the *moral*, suprapolitical utopia of human rights remains "a minimalist utopia of antipolitics, as it was in its era of breakthrough." Given such limitations, and despite its growing cathexis with utopian hope, Moyn rightly concludes, the mass utopianism of human rights will not do as the final, unsurpassable utopian vision ("the last utopia cannot be a moral one") unless it comes with a "new form of maximal politics" of its own (225, 227, 218, 214, 218, 227).

92. Marshall Sahlins, "La Première société d'abondance," *Les Temps modernes* 268 (1968): 641–80. The article is an abbreviated version of chap. 1 in *Stone Age Economics*, though in it Sahlins still holds an

orthodox view of the economy as the need-serving behavior of individuals rather than (as in the book's later essays) as a cultural category and material life process of society. Sahlins, *Stone Age Economics* (London: Routledge, 2017), xxviii.

93. Sahlins, *Stone Age Economics*, 2. The (per capita) increase of labor with the evolution of culture sets off work from leisure. Sahlins sharpens his point further: "if [hunter and gatherer] men lack leisure, it is then in the Enlightenment sense rather than the literal. When Condorcet attributed the hunter's unprogressive condition to want of 'the leisure in which he can indulge in thought and enrich his understanding with new combinations of ideas,' he also recognized that the economy was a 'necessary cycle of extreme activity and total idleness.' Apparently what the hunter needed was the *assured* leisure of an aristocratic *philosophe*" (34).

94. Pierre Clastres, "Primitive Economy," in Clastres, *Archeology of Violence*, trans. Jeanine Herman (New York: Semiotext[e], 1994), 118; Clastres, *Society against the State: Essays in Political Anthropology*, trans. Robert Hurley and Abe Stein (New York: Zone, 1989), 199.

Chapter 3: The Utopia of Survival

1. Balibar, *Equaliberty: Political Essays*, trans. James D. Ingram (Durham, NC: Duke University Press, 2014), 24–25.

2. Michel Foucault and Bernard Henri-Lévy, "Power and Sex" (1977), trans. David J. Parent, in Foucault, *Politics, Philosophy, Culture: Interviews and Other Writings, 1977–1984*, ed. Lawrence D. Kritzman (New York: Routledge, 1988), 122.

3. Likely authored in 1796–97 by Hegel himself and unpublished until 1917, the "Systematic Program" calls for a new, rational mythology to do away with the modern state. See my treatment of this foundational text in "Utopia and Political Theology in the 'Oldest Systematic Program of German Idealism,'" in Kirill Chepurin and Alex Dubilet, eds., *Nothing Absolute: German Idealism and the Question of Political Theology* (New York: Fordham University Press, 2021, 54–72.

4. Karl Marx, "First Outline of *The Civil War in France*," in Marx and Frederick Engels, *On the Paris Commune* (Moscow: Progress, 1971), 152.

5. Karl Marx, *Capital: A Critique of Political Economy*, vol. 3, trans. David Fernbach (London: Penguin, 1991), 959, trans. mod., my italics.

For Marx's views on Fourier, see, for example, (Kibbutz member) Avraham Yassour, "Communism and Utopia: Marx, Engels and Fourier," *Studies in Soviet Thought* 26, no. 3 (1983): 217–27.

6. Marx, *Capital*, 3:959.

7. For a discussion in the context of the migrant crisis of the 2010s, see Luca Mavelli, "Governing Populations through the Humanitarian Government of Refugees: Biopolitical Care and Racism in the European Refugee Crisis," *Review of International Studies* 43, no. 5 (2017): 809–32.

8. The impolitical is "both the final resting place of political thought and . . . its fullest realization." On the outer limits of politics, "impolitical 'politics of ascesis'" in the case of the early Simone Weil renders insubstantial all traditional political categories and vocabulary. Roberto Esposito, *Categories of the Impolitical* (1988, rev. ed. 1999), trans. Connal Parsley (New York: Fordham University Press, 2015), 74, 144. The political is words, words, words. "'Revolution' is a word . . . [that] does not possess any content," and we must be careful about the meaning we give it—for one, by not tying it hopelessly to "the misery of the working condition." "The revolution is a struggle against all that forms an obstacle to life." Simone Weil, "Reflections concerning the Causes of Liberty and Social Oppression" (1934), in Weil, *Oppression and Liberty*, trans. Arthur Wills and John Petrie (London: Routledge, 2001), 53; Weil, "Prerequisite to Dignity of Labour" (1941), in *Simone Weil: An Anthology*, ed. Siân Miles (London: Penguin, 2009), 267; Weil, *Oeuvres complètes*, vol. II, 3: *Écrits historiques et politiques: Vers la guerre (1937–1940)*, ed. André A. Devaux and Florence de Lussy (Paris: Gallimard, 1988), 319, quoted in Esposito, *Categories of the Impolitical*, 156. The contemplative attitude, or exercise of "intuitive attention"—which in principle can transform the working condition, with which it is "compatible," into "supernatural poetry"—is, for Weil (whom David McLellan characterizes as a "utopian pessimist"), a prefiguration of the good life, which can follow it if such attention is applied to all of one's experience. Weil, "Prerequisite to Dignity of Labour," 273, 276, 272.

9. As Sergio Tischler writes, Zapatismo's "communitarian-revolutionary form rejects the idea of politics and the government as a separate field of action that is based on the separation of politics and the economy, of state and civil society." Tischler, "Detotalization and Subject:

On Zapatismo and Critical Theory," *South Atlantic Quarterly* 113, no. 2 (2014): 330. On Zapatista indigenous communities' local ways of limiting, and maintaining a tension with, state power, experimenting with "insurgent universality," see chap. 5, "1994: Zapatistas and the Dispossessed of History," in Massimiliano Tomba, *Insurgent Universality: An Alternative Legacy of Modernity* (New York: Oxford University Press, 2019), 186–222.

10. See Stephen Bouquin, Mireille Court, and Chris Den Hond, eds. and trans., *La Commune du Rojava: L'Alternative kurde à l'état-nation* (Paris: Syllepse, 2017).

11. For example, the Assemblée de Commercy and the Assemblées des Assemblées in Commercy and Saint-Nazaire, convened between January and April 2019, the latter two gatherings partly infiltrated by leftist parties such as the New Anticapitalist Party (NPA). [Source: oral testimony by attendee.] ZADs should not be conflated with utopian intentional communities; the former, though they may constitute relatively isolated counter-societies, are defined principally by their dynamic opposition to capitalist development projects and are either dismantled or fall apart on their own when such opposition becomes untenable. See Charles Reeve, *Le Socialisme sauvage: Essai sur l'auto-organisation et la démocratie directe dans les lutes de 1789 à nos jours* (Paris: L'Échappée, 2018), 245–47.

12. Hannah Arendt, "The Freedom to Be Free," *New England Review* 38, no. 2 (2017): 65.

13. See Furio Cerutti, "Humankind's First Fundamental Right: Survival," *Constellations* 22, no. 1 (2015): 59–67. Judith Butler crucially takes issue with Arendt's confinement of the body to the prepolitical realm of the satisfaction of bare, material necessities, i.e., to survival. For Butler, "the private is not the opposite of the political, but enters into its very definition." Butler here proposes a body politics founded on a critique of the unacknowledged dependency of the political on the purportedly prepolitical sphere, the public on the private; a politics that "can account for the relation between precarity and performativity." Butler, *Notes toward a Performative Theory of Assembly* (Cambridge, MA: Harvard University Press, 2015), 206–7. See also epilogue, note 6.

14. For a study of nonviolent political acts of self-sacrifice (hunger strikes, self-immolation, martyrdom), see K. M. Fierke's *Political*

Self-Sacrifice: Agency, Body and Emotion in International Relations (Cambridge: Cambridge University Press, 2013). Also informative on this score is Nicholas Michelsen's *Politics and Suicide: The Philosophy of Political Self-Destruction* (New York: Routledge, 2016).

15. Roberto Esposito, *Persons and Things: From the Body's Point of View* (2014), trans. Zakiya Hanafi (Cambridge: Polity, 2015), 143.

16. Clastres, *Society against the State: Essays in Political Anthropology*, trans. Robert Hurley and Abe Stein (New York: Zone, 1989), 13–14, 197, 206, 188, 212–13. See also Clastres, "Primitive Economy," in Clastres, *Archeology of Violence*, trans. Jeanine Herman (New York: Semiotext[e], 1994).

17. Thomas Hobbes, *Leviathan: Revised Student Edition*, ed. Richard Tuck (Cambridge: Cambridge University Press, 1996), 89, 90.

18. Walter Benjamin, "Critique of Violence" (1921), trans. Edmund Jephcott, in Benjamin, *Selected Writings*, vol. 1: *1913–1926*, ed. Marcus Bullock and Michael W. Jennings (Cambridge, MA: Belknap Press of Harvard University Press, 1996), 251.

19. See Judith Butler, *Frames of War: When Is Life Grievable?* (New York: Verso, 2009); and Ewa Plonowska-Ziarek, "Bare Life," in Henry Sussman, ed., *Impasses of the Post-Global: Theory in the Era of Climate Change*, vol. 2 (Ann Arbor: Open Humanities Press, 2012), 194–211.

20. Didier Fassin, "Ethics of Survival: A Democratic Approach to the Politics of Life," *Humanity* 1, no. 1 (2010): 81. Compare his earlier critical analysis of Foucault's concept of biopolitics in Fassin, "Another Politics of Life Is Possible," *Theory, Culture and Society* 26, no. 5 (2009): 44–60.

21. Giorgio Agamben, *Homo Sacer: Sovereign Power and Bare Life*, trans. Daniel Heller-Roazen (Stanford: Stanford University Press, 1998), 6.

22. See Agamben, *The Coming Community*, trans. Michael Hardt (Minneapolis: University of Minnesota Press, 1993). The last volume of the Homo Sacer cycle gestures toward a utopian politics of happiness merging *bios* and *zoē*—since "*zoè* and *bios* are today completely pulled apart or have just as completely collapsed into one another, and the historical task of their articulation seems impossible to carry out. The bare life of the *homo sacer* is the irreducible hypostasis that appears between them to testify to the impossibility of their identity as much as their

distinction." Agamben, *The Use of Bodies: Homo Sacer IV, 2*, trans. Adam Kotsko (Stanford: Stanford University Press, 2016), 133.

23. Banu Bargu, *Starve and Immolate: The Politics of Human Weapons* (New York: Columbia University Press, 2014), 82.

24. Bargu, *Starve and Immolate*, 344.

25. Achille Mbembe, "Necropolitics," trans. Libby Meintjes, *Public Culture* 15, no. 1 (2003): 21, 40, 35–36. The original essay became part of his *Politiques de l'inimitié* (Paris: La Découverte, 2016), translated as *Necropolitics* (2019).

26. Bargu, *Starve and Immolate*, 340, 84.

27. See, for instance, Scott Lash, "Life (Vitalism)," *Theory, Culture and Society* 23, nos. 2–3 (2006): 323–49.

28. See, for example, Miguel Vatter, *The Republic of the Living: Biopolitics and the Critique of Civil Society* (New York: Fordham University Press, 2014).

29. For a critical perspective on the "vitalization of politics" as mirroring capitalist fantasies of excess value creation, see Benjamin Noys, "The Poverty of Vitalism (and the Vitalism of Poverty)" (paper, To Have Done with Life: Vitalism and Anti-vitalism in Contemporary Philosophy Conference, June 17–19, 2011, MaMa, Zagreb, Croatia), https://www.academia.edu/689255/The_Poverty_of_Vitalism_and_the_Vitalism_of_ Poverty_.

30. Bargu, *Starve and Immolate*, 339.

31. Bargu, *Starve and Immolate*, 348.

32. Michel Foucault, *"Society Must Be Defended": Lectures at the Collège de France, 1975–1976*, ed. Mauro Bertani and Alessandro Fontana, trans. David Macey (New York: Picador, 2003), 80. For a selection of recent critical perspectives, see Miguel Vatter and Vanessa Lemm, eds., *The Government of Life: Foucault, Biopolitics, and Neoliberalism* (New York: Fordham University Press, 2014).

33. Rosi Braidotti, "Biopower and Necropolitics: Reflections on an Ethics of Sustainability," *Springerin* 13, no. 2 (2007): 18–23.

34. Bargu, *Starve and Immolate*, 339–40.

35. See Stuart J. Murray, "Thanatopolitics: On the Use of Death for Mobilizing Political Life," *Polygraph* 18 (2006): 191–215.

36. Bargu, *Starve and Immolate*, 27, 335; Banu Bargu, "Why Did Bouazizi Burn Himself? The Politics of Fate and Fatal Politics," *Constellations* 23, no. 1 (2016): 33.

37. Bargu, *Starve and Immolate*, 348. Taking a biopolitical lens to Mohamed Bouazizi's self-immolation in Tunis in 2010—a particular instance of the self-destructive weaponization of the body as a political form of resistance—Bargu reads it as "revelatory of a desire to transform collective despair into hope and rekindle the belief in the potential that history may yet hold in store, if only by way of elevating a singular fatal act into an omen of a more equitable and just future." She concludes that Bouazizi's protest "served as a catalyst . . . because the desire to refuse domination, to reject the status of disposability, and to change the precarious conditions of existence, were already there, even though the collective forms of struggle to realize this desire were lacking." Understood symbolically in this way, the act stands for "a desire for justice and a revolutionary temporality—a futurity—that cannot be achieved within the confines of the existing order." Bargu, "Why Did Bouazizi Burn Himself?" 29, 34, 33. Although Bargu herself takes this "more equitable and more just" futurity to be political, I would go further and suggest that the motivating desire here was not only to realize it through collective forms of struggle, but to be forever done with disempowerment, as in a postpolitical world wherein the body would no longer be disposable, abused, or weaponized.

38. Marc Abélès, *The Politics of Survival*, trans. Julie Kleinman (Durham, NC: Duke University Press, 2010), 20.

39. Abélès, *Politics of Survival*, 12–17, 20, 19. See also his *Thinking beyond the State* (2014), trans. Phillip Rousseau and Marie-Claude Haince (Ithaca, NY: Cornell University Press, 2017).

40. Marc Abélès, "The Politics of Survival" (lecture, Life Configurations, April 2–4, 2012, Luján, Argentina), 2, 3, https://www.scribd.com/document/93813724/Marc-Abeles-The-Politics-of-Survival.

41. Franco "Bifo" Berardi, *Precarious Rhapsody: Semiocapitalism and the Pathologies of the Post-Alpha Generation*, trans. Arianna Bove et al. (London: Minor Compositions, 2009), 55 (sec. "Hope").

42. Wolfgang Streeck, *How Will Capitalism End? Essays on a Failing System* (London: Verso, 2016), 93.

43. Temporary Autonomous Zones. See Hakim Bey, *T.A.Z.: The Temporary Autonomous Zone, Ontological Anarchy, Poetic Terrorism* (New York: Autonomedia, 1991).

Epilogue: The Displaced Imagination

1. Agamben, *The Use of Bodies: Homo Sacer IV, 2*, trans. Adam Kotsko (Stanford: Stanford University Press, 2016), xxi.

2. Plato, *The Laws*, ed. Malcolm Schofield, trans. Tom Griffith (Cambridge: Cambridge University Press, 2016), 186 (739c–e).

3. In body-utopian dreaming and prefiguration, desires that can be instantly gratified only by perpetrating suffering in oneself or in others, and hence be socially unacceptable, are sublimated, refined, or converted. The highest expression of civilization (i.e., universal utopia) is thus reached in out-and-out dystopia, as if human happiness and history were about to part ways. Dystopia, however, is a social-critical, not a scientific, term; what turns the world now into a dystopia is the stringency of critique.

4. Bookchin, *Toward an Ecological Society* (Montreal: Black Rose, 1980), 285–86.

5. Diogenes Laertius, *Lives of the Eminent Philosophers*, trans. Pamela Mensch and James Miller (Oxford: Oxford University Press, 2018), 2.25.

6. Compare Judith Butler's distinction between precariousness and precarity in Butler, *Precarious Life: The Powers of Mourning and Violence* (New York: Verso, 2004) and *Frames of War: When Is Life Grievable?* (New York: Verso, 2009). Lives are precarious by definition (*Frames of War*, 25). Butler links precarity with bodily persistence and resistance, and the political power of physical popular assemblies, in her *Notes toward a Performative Theory of Assembly* (Cambridge, MA: Harvard University Press, 2015).

7. Butler, *Frames of War*, 46.

8. Guy Standing, *The Precariat: The New Dangerous Class* (London: Bloomsbury, 2011), 8, 155. For details of the proposed program, see chap. 7, "A Politics of Paradise," 155–83.

9. Raoul Vaneigem, "Nous n'avons d'autre alternative que d'oser l'impossible," interview by Nicolas Truong, *Le Monde*, August 31, 2019.

10. Charles Baudelaire, "Invitation to the Voyage," in Baudelaire, *The Flowers of Evil* (1857), trans. James McGowan (Oxford: Oxford University Press, 2008), 108–9, trans. mod.

11. See Florence Bernault and Joseph Tonda, "Le Gabon: Une dystopie tropicale," *Politique africaine* 115 (2009): 7–26; and Joseph Tonda,

L'Impérialisme postcolonial: Critique de la société des éblouissements (Paris: Karthala, 2015).

12. Barbara Ehrenreich, "The Humanoid Stain: Art Lessons from Our Cave-Dwelling Ancestors," *The Baffler* 48 (2019).

13. Margaret Mead, "Towards More Vivid Utopias," *Science* 126, no. 3280 (1957): 958. Mead says we need our utopias to be more vivid to unite and guide our enormous powers of destruction and construction, though nowhere does she question the role of utopias in modern societies, noting only their plurality and that people still "live by" them. The vividness of good visions will not spur us to put them into effect any more than the vividness of bad ones has deterred us from putting these last into practice or motivated us to militate against their recurrence in such forms as war.

14. Frye, "Varieties of Literary Utopias," *Daedalus* 94, no. 2 (1965): 347.

15. Adorno, *Minima Moralia: Reflections on a Damaged Life*, trans. E. F. N. Jephcott (New York: Verso, 2005), 61.

16. Theodor W. Adorno, *Negative Dialectics*, trans. E. B. Ashton (New York: Continuum, 1995), 203, trans. mod.

17. The expression "corporeality of *thought*" is Romantic in origin; its author was Samuel Taylor Coleridge, quoted in Roy Porter, *Flesh in the Age of Reason* (London: Penguin, 2003), 405.

18. I refer the reader to the work of and literature about Otto Gross, the anarchist psychoanalyst, whose revolutionary ideas—especially, liberated sexuality as the precondition for political and social emancipation—were inspired by Johann Bachofen and anticipated those, better known, of Wilhelm Reich. For translated excerpts of his reply to Gustav Landauer, "Zur Überwindung der kulturellen Krise" (1913), see Robert Graham, ed., *Anarchism: A Documentary History of Libertarian Ideas*, vol. 1: *From Anarchy to Anarchism (300 CE to 1939)* (Montreal: Black Rose, 2005), 281–84.

19. See my "Serious, Not All That Serious: Utopia beyond Realism and Normativity in Contemporary Critical Theory," *Constellations* 26, no. 2 (2019): 330–43. As I wrote there, "the value of utopia for critique is not exhausted by its complementing normativity and realism; it is also necessary to recognize utopia's structural importance to Critical Theory's realist-normative project." Yet to assimilate utopia to Critical Theory in

these ways is to contain the utopian spirit's more practical, experimental, and political potencies. "Utopia understood as a complement, dimension, or moment of Critical Theory . . . is enclosed and domesticated, rhyming happiness with home rather than new horizons." When not thus reduced, however, utopia becomes "an impulse within the activity of thought (worthy of the name) to point beyond itself, to trace the horizon of hope against which reality appears dark as in *contre-jour*. It is upon this horizon that Theory's practical telos of universal freedom and happiness comes into view" (338–339). I defend, in other words, a conception of utopia as *conceptual play* that strengthens the political purchase of utopia without translating it into a particular version of emancipatory politics. My account represents less a "solution" than a different and underexposed way of conceptualizing utopia, addressing the internal limitations on contemporary Critical Theory's emancipatory goals. While drawing on a thread in Adorno, it accentuates dialectics over negativity to advance a more robust, ludic utopianism, latent in his work, as an active modality of anticipatory thinking.

It should be clear from this that I disagree with Jameson's way of framing the utopia-ideology dialectic, wherein utopia becomes ideology's positive hermeneutical counterpart in a "properly Marxian" hermeneutics of meaning, that is, one that resists the temptation of an instrumental conception of culture. Fredric Jameson, *The Political Unconscious: Narrative as a Socially Symbolic Act* (1981) (London: Routledge, 2002), 276. For Jameson, dialectical thought is "the anticipation of the logic of a collectivity that has not yet come into being"; its "vocation" is the transcendence of the opposition between the positive and the negative. This "collective dialectic" is the only conceivable answer to the question formulated by "project[ing] an imperative to thought in which the ideological would be grasped as somehow at one with the Utopian, and the Utopian at one with the ideological." What is elided in his initially typecasting utopia as ideology's antagonist—and as (in a Blochian vein) coexistent with ideology in even the most degraded mass culture texts, which use the gratification of utopian impulses (now managed and defused) as bait or "incentives . . . for ideological adherence"—is, first, the capacity of the texts' creators themselves for dialectical thought or a cynical consciousness of using the utopian aspiration to happiness for ideological ends, and, second, the dialectical capacity of the apparently passive spectators (no "blank slate[s]," they, incapable of grasping their own solidarity, as he acknowledges), not to mention the negative-dialectical structure of utopianism itself (the determinate negation of what is and of what can be imagined as better than what is, seeing the limits of both) as the most powerful motor of negative dialectics. Jameson, then, insists on the "profound identity" of utopian and ideological dimensions/functions (at least in some cultural artifacts), since their separation "is not possible for any worldview—whether conservative or radical and revolutionary—that takes politics seriously" (277, 278–79). The problem, however, is that this identity of ideology and utopia again presupposes an undialectical creator/spectator, the revolutionary politics of whose worldview is therefore highly questionable, to say the least. Jameson proposes that "all class consciousness—or in other words, all ideology in the strongest sense, including the most exclusive forms of ruling-class consciousness just as much as that of oppositional or oppressed classes—is in its very nature Utopian" (for example, the text of the state presenting a "vision of the state or the public sector as a collectivity in its own right") (279, 288). Once state institutions are read as embodiments of utopian values, the transgressive, negative dialectic of utopian hope is arrested and sacrificed on the altar of identity thinking—and not, as Jameson thinks, of Marxist "political praxis" (290). Such structural Althusserian ambivalence is what ultimately sinks Jameson's cultural-Marxist rescue mission, his theorization of utopia. This last he would later nondialectically define as "the absolute opposite of our history as a whole . . .[,] the absolute negation of that fully realized absolute which our own system has attained" that "cannot now be imagined as lying ahead of us in historical time as an evolutionary or even as revolutionary possibility. Indeed, it cannot be imagined at all . . . It would be best, perhaps, to think of an alternate world—better to say the alternate world, our alternate world—as one contiguous with ours but without any connection or access to it. Then, from time to time, like a diseased eyeball in which disturbing flashes of light are perceived or like those baroque sunbursts in which rays from another world suddenly break into this one, we are reminded that Utopia exists and that other systems, other spaces, are still possible." Fredric Jameson, *Valences of the Dialectic* (New York: Verso, 2009), 612. The absolute, incurable negativity of such a vision, its quasi-mystical lens, should not be confused with anything like embodied utopian hope. Missing from it are that "double negation" of the negative dialectic previously admitted by Jameson and its incarnation in daily life. For Jameson, utopia emerges at the moment of the suspension and separation of the political from "the social field" or totality, "from daily life and even from the world of the lived and the existential," and its "modification or abolition" of political institutions and structures is confined to mental play, given that "reality paralysis" without any prospect of real-world reform or revolution. Jameson, "The Politics of Utopia," *New Left Review* 25 (2004): 50–51, 45, 43–44. For me, contrariwise, utopia qua conceptual play emerges as "a liminal, transitional activity in the practical process of emancipation, on an agonistic or anarchistic conception of democracy." Chrostowska, "Serious, Not All That Serious," 336. See also note 24, below.

20. See, for instance, the muted (to put it mildly) appreciation of "real utopias" in Dylan Riley, "An Anticapitalism That Can Win," *Jacobin Magazine*, July 1, 2016.

21. Corey Robin, "Socialism: Converting Hysterical Misery into Ordinary Unhappiness," *Jacobin Magazine*, October 12, 2013.

22. Russell Jacoby fortunately employs the expression "anti-utopian utopianism" to mean *iconoclastic utopianism* and to unpack his valuable concept only once, in Jacoby, *Picture Imperfect: Utopian Thought for an Anti-Utopian Age* (New York: Columbia University Press, 2005), 85. "Anti-utopian utopianism" is perhaps best suited to describe, not a Marxian utopianism that dare not speak its name, but one in denial about itself; a self-contradictory closeted utopianism that denounces utopianism left, right, and center.

23. Fredric Jameson, "Of Islands and Trenches: Neutralization and the Production of Utopian Discourse" (1977), in Jameson, *The Ideologies of Theory*, rev. ed. (London: Verso, 2008), 388.

24. In his magnum opus devoted to "the desire called utopia," Jameson celebrates utopia's "recovered . . . vitality as a political slogan and a politically energizing perspective," and to its "fellow-travelers" suggests "the slogan of anti-anti-Utopianism"—navigating between the Scylla of utopianism (flawed) and the Charybdis of anti-utopianism (unacceptable)—as the best working discursive strategy. Fredric Jameson, *Archaeologies of the Future: The Desire Called Utopia and Other Science Fictions* (London: Verso, 2005), xvi, xii, xvi, 232. This curious formulation is indebted to Robert C. Elliott's *The Shape of Utopia* (1970), credited in a

recent reedition with reinventing utopia as practice and with responding to the fear of utopia (a fear nearly behind us now that the likelihood of realizing utopia seems to have plummeted). Elliott, *The Shape of Utopia*, ed. Phillip E. Wegner (Oxford: Peter Lang, 2013). As Jameson develops it in response to the contemporary widespread sense that it is easier to imagine the end of the world than to imagine the end of capitalism, utopia understood formally, as a "break" or "disruption" (as *Novum*, not terroristic violence), fulfills, in his words, "a vital political function"; forcing us "to think the break itself" (instead of "offering a more traditional picture of what things would be like after the break"), it is a "meditation on the impossible, on the unrealizable in its own right," and becomes "a rattling of the bars [of capitalism] and an intense spiritual concentration and preparation for another stage which has not yet arrived." Jameson, *Archaeologies of the Future*, 232–33. The compensatory turn of attention to form, which cannot be accomplished without returning to old utopian visions and ideologies (e.g., the abolition of money), comes out most clearly in the following, densely layered passages: "This is indeed how Utopia recovers its vocation at the very moment where the undesirability of change is everywhere dogmatically affirmed . . . And this is now the temporal situation in which the Utopian form proper—the radical closure of a system of difference in time, the experience of the total formal break and discontinuity—has its political role to play, and in fact becomes a new kind of content in its own right . . . Paradoxically, therefore, this increasing inability to imagine a different future enhances rather than diminishes the appeal and also the function of Utopia. The very political weakness of Utopia in previous generations—namely that it furnished nothing like an account of agency, nor did it have a coherent historical and practical-political picture of transition—now becomes a strength in a situation in which neither of these problems seems currently to offer candidates for a solution. The radical break or secession of Utopia from political possibilities as well as from reality itself now more accurately reflects our current ideological state of mind . . . Utopia thus now better expresses our relationship to a genuinely political future than any current program of action, where we are for the moment only at the stage of massive protests and demonstrations, without any conception of how a globalized transformation might then proceed. But at this same time, Utopia also serves a vital political function today which goes well beyond mere ideological expression or replication. The formal flaw—how to articulate the Utopian break in such a way that it is transformed into a practical-political transition—now becomes a rhetorical and political strength—in that it forces us precisely to concentrate on the break itself." "Mark[ing] the rupture and open[ing] up a space into which Utopia may enter" is the decisionism "in which we are forced to invent new Utopian ideologies," with the familiar "ideological impasses of Utopian content" that this implies (231–32, 212). Just as a global "pluralism of utopias" (a proposal Jameson takes from Robert Nozick [218]) fits unsettlingly well with the neoliberal mantra of free, *à la carte* choice, so Jameson's defense of utopia against its reputation as a shell game turns it into a salutary and energizing exercise in which old ideals become, by revealing collective solidarity, socializing thought-experiments—and nothing more. That this is a stratagem uncoupling utopia from performativity and political forms or even just ideological shadowboxing, leaving us idle rather than "compel[ling] us to action," needs no belaboring (xiv). The argument boils down to the disappointing claim that utopias compel us to act by leaving much to be desired. It will have few disciples among those who, fearing not utopia but inaction, put things in absolutist terms: utopia or nothing.

25. Laurent Jeanpierre, *In girum: Les Leçons politiques des ronds-points* (Paris: La Découverte, 2019).

26. The French translations of Wright's *Envisioning Real Utopias* and the posthumous *How to Be an Anti-Capitalist in the 21st Century* appeared in 2017 and 2020, respectively, in the "L'Horizon des possibles" series coedited (and, for the 2020 title, postfaced), by Jeanpierre at Éditions La Découverte.

27. "Symbiotic," "interstitial," and "ruptural" refer to Wright's three emancipatory strategic logics (the first two of which he endorses) for transforming capitalism, as laid out in his *Envisioning Real Utopias* (New York: Verso, 2010). Wright prefers the "symbiotic" as a means of metamorphosis through compromise between the capitalist and the working classes. The other two strategies advocate discontinuity. In his primer, *How to Be an Anti-Capitalist in the 21st Century* (London: Verso, 2019), capitalism is not to be "smashed," but "eroded" by a combination of "dismantling," "taming," "resisting," and "escaping."

28. To be fair, Wright's conclusion is not exactly Panglossian: "*What we are left with, then, is a menu of strategic logics and an indeterminate*

prognosis for the future. The pessimistic view is that this condition is our fate, living in a world in which capitalism remains hegemonic . . . The optimistic view is that we don't know what system challenges and transformative possibilities there will be in the future." Wright, *Envisioning Real Utopias*, 364–65.

29. Joël Gayraud, *L'Homme sans horizon: Matériaux sur l'utopie* (Montreuil: Libertalia, 2019), 61–93.

30. Yona Friedman, *Utopies réalisables: Vers une cité conçue par ses habitants eux-mêmes (1958–2000)* (Paris: L'Éclat, 2000).

31. Pierre Rosanvallon, *Le Capitalisme utopique: Histoire de l'idée de marché* (Paris: Seuil, 1999). (Expanded edition of 1979 original.)

32. *Collapsology* (French *collapsologie*, synonymous with *effondrisme*) names a younger current of thought and a transdisciplinary approach to the global collapse of industrial civilization: its risk, its possible anthropic causes, and how it ought to be navigated. It counts among its precursors Jared Diamond's 2005 book *Collapse*, whose two subtitles, *How Societies Choose to Fail or Succeed* (in the US edition [New York: Viking]) and *How Societies Choose to Fail or Survive* (in the UK edition), suggest that surviving would already be a success, if not exactly a utopia. Collapsology does overlap with survivalism, for which the highest good is survival (of all or just the select few, capable of building a postapocalyptic utopia). Christopher Lasch, *The Minimal Self: Psychic Survival in Troubled Times* (New York: W. W. Norton, 1984), 82, 83. (Lasch was quick to add, however, that given the threat of nuclear Armageddon and a discredited ethic of sacrifice, *criticism* of the survival ethic, or the preservation of life as an end in itself, has a moral claim on us only when such criticism appeals to and identifies itself with the peace and environmental movements [79–81].) To overcome the dread and fascination of the coming catastrophe(s), collapsologues propose acting as if the catastrophe were already upon us (there is a symmetry here with prefigurative utopianism's acting as if the alternative society were already here). They advise mourning in advance and acceptance over than defeatism, but also (at their best) cultivating desirable forms of life critical of capitalism, along with the collective "arts of uprising and montage." Yves Citton and Jacopo Rasmi, *Générations collapsonautes: Naviguer par temps d'effondrement* (Paris: Seuil, 2020). For a more political angle, see Renaud Duterme, *De quoi l'effondrement est-il le nom? La Fragmentation du monde* (Paris:

Utopia, 2016), published by the antigrowth, anticonsumerism, and antilabor Mouvement Utopia, whose primary objective is "the collective elaboration of a great project of society" (http://www.editions-utopia.org/le-mouvement-utopia/). The titles of two influential primers in collapsology—Pablo Servigne and Raphaël Stevens's *Comment tout peut s'effondrer: Petit manuel de collapsologie à l'usage des générations présentes* (Paris: Seuil, 2015), and Servigne, Stevens, and Gauthier Chapelle's *Une autre fin du monde est possible: Vivre l'effondrement (et pas seulement y survivre)* (Paris: Seuil, 2018)—are allusions to, respectively, Vaneigem's 1967 classic and the slogan of the World Social Forum (whose *détournement* as "another end of the world is possible" is a perfect expression of the apocalyptic anti-apocalypticism espoused by collapsology). See also José Ardillo, "Pour une écologie sans compte à rebours," *Réfractions, recherches et expressions anarchistes* 44 (2020): 25–40, for an appreciation of 1970s radical, left-libertarian ecology and the comparative political poverty of collapsology, which, despite its ecological core, in counting down to the end of the world, counts on civilizational collapse rather than social transformation or political emancipation (e.g., individual or collective secession from capitalism or from the state). In a similar vein, Renaud Garcia's *La Collapsologie ou l'écologie mutilée* (Paris: L'Échappée, 2020) chastises the abdication of social critique by the majority of collapsologues. Responding to his critics, Servigne underlines collapsology's "anarchism" and plurality (its fight against the myth of *a* collapse). He challenges anarchists to take advantage of the breakdown of social order afforded by the expected multiple collapses—as so many opportunities for social revolution. He is open to "catastrophist political movements (Degrowth, Transition Initiatives, Collapso[logy])" reviving the ideas of Peter Kropotkin and Elisée Reclus, or, more recently, Bookchin and Janet Biehl. "In short, anarchists of all lands, instead of bashing collapsology, enrich it, and participate in the elaboration of a true politics of the twenty-first century!" Servigne, "Faire de la fin du monde une brèche," *Réfractions, recherches et expressions anarchistes* 44 (2020): 92, 94.

Postscript

1. Maurice Blanchot, *Political Writings, 1953–1993*, trans. Zakir Paul (New York: Fordham University Press, 2010), 95.

2. Gilles Deleuze, "Postscript on the Societies of Control" (1990), *October* 59 (1992): 3–7.

3. See Hartmut Rosa and Christoph Henning, eds., *The Good Life beyond Growth: New Perspectives* (London: Routledge, 2018). Ashish Kothari, whose essay concludes the volume, stresses that "the lure of 'growth' as an engine of well-being still holds sway, even within the new paradigms of 'green economy' and 'sustainable development'" (251).

4. Perry Anderson, "Editorial: Renewals," *New Left Review* n.s. 1 (2000): 15.

5. Adorno, *Minima Moralia: Reflections on a Damaged Life*, trans. E. F. N. Jephcott (New York: Verso, 2005), 230.

6. CrimethInc., "Surviving the Virus: An Anarchist Guide," CrimethInc., March 18, 2020.

7. Jean-Baptiste François Xavier Cousin de Grainville, *The Last Man*, trans. I. F. Clarke and M. Clarke (Middletown, CT: Wesleyan University Press, 2002), 44, trans. mod.

8. Oscar Wilde, *The Soul of Man under Socialism* (Boston: J. W. Luce, 1910), 27.

9. Bruno Latour, "What Protective Measures Can You Think of So We Don't Go Back to the Pre-crisis Production Model?" trans. Stephen Muecke, http://www.bruno-latour.fr/sites/default/files/downloads/P-202-AOC-ENGLISH_1.pdf.

BIBLIOGRAPHY

Abélès, Marc. *The Politics of Survival*. Translated by Julie Kleinman. Durham, NC: Duke University Press, 2010.
Abélès, Marc. "The Politics of Survival." Lecture. Life Configurations, April 2–4, 2012, Luján, Argentina. https://www.scribd.com/document/93813724/Marc-Abeles-The-Politics-of-Survival.
Abélès, Marc. *Thinking beyond the State*. Translated by Phillip Rousseau and Marie-Claude Haince. Ithaca, NY: Cornell University Press, 2017.
Abensour, Miguel. "Les Formes de l'utopie socialiste-communiste." 2 vols. PhD diss./thèse pour le Doctorat d'État en science politique, Panthéon-Sorbonne, 1973. Unpublished.
Abensour, Miguel. *L'Histoire de l'utopie et le destin de sa critique: Utopiques 4*. Paris: Sens & Tonka, 2016.
Abensour, Miguel. "William Morris: The Politics of Romance." Translated by Max Blechman. In Blechman, ed., *Revolutionary Romanticism: A Drunken Boat Anthology*, 125–61. San Francisco: City Lights, 1999.
Abensour, Miguel. "William Morris, utopie libertaire et novation technique." In [collective], *L'Imaginaire subversif: Interrogations sur l'utopie*, 113–50. Geneva: Éditions Noir, 1982.
Adorno, Theodor W. *Aesthetic Theory*. Edited by Gretel Adorno and

Rolf Tiedemann. Translated by R. Hullot-Kentor. London: Continuum, 2004.

Adorno, Theodor W. *Critical Models: Interventions and Catchwords*. Translated by H. W. Pickford. New York: Columbia University Press, 2005.

Adorno, Theodor W. *Minima Moralia: Reflections on a Damaged Life*. Translated by E. F. N. Jephcott. New York: Verso, 2005.

Adorno, Theodor W. *Negative Dialectics*. Translated by E. B. Ashton. New York: Continuum, 1995.

Adorno, Theodor W. *Prisms*. Translated by Samuel Weber and Shierry Weber. Cambridge, MA: MIT Press, 1981.

Adorno, Theodor W. "Theses on Need." Translated by Martin Shuster and Iain Macdonald. *Adorno Studies* 1, no. 1 (2017): 102–4.

Adorno, Theodor W., and Elisabeth Lenk. *The Challenge of Surrealism: The Correspondence of Theodor W. Adorno and Elisabeth Lenk*. Edited and translated by Susan H. Gillespie. Minneapolis: University of Minnesota Press, 2015.

Agamben, Giorgio. *The Coming Community*. Translated by Michael Hardt. Minneapolis: University of Minnesota Press, 1993.

Agamben, Giorgio. *Homo Sacer: Sovereign Power and Bare Life*. Translated by Daniel Heller-Roazen. Stanford: Stanford University Press, 1998.

Agamben, Giorgio. *The Use of Bodies: Homo Sacer IV, 2*. Translated by Adam Kotsko. Stanford: Stanford University Press, 2016.

Alperovitz, Gar. "America beyond Capitalism: Reclaiming Our Wealth, Our Liberty, and Our Democracy." *Philosophy and Public Policy Quarterly* 25, nos. 1–2 (2005): 25–35.

Alperovitz, Gar. *What Then Must We Do? Straight Talk about the Next American Revolution*. White River Junction, VT: Chelsea Green, 2013.

Anderson, Perry. *Arguments within English Marxism*. London: Verso, 1980.

Anderson, Perry. "Editorial: Renewals." *New Left Review* n.s. 1 (2000): 1–20.

Aragon, Louis. *Le Paysan de Paris*. Paris: Gallimard, 1926.

Ardillo, José. "Pour une écologie sans compte à rebours: Aventures et

mésaventures de l'effondrement." *Réfractions, recherches et expressions anarchistes* 44 (2020): 25–40.
Arendt, Hannah. "The Freedom to Be Free." *New England Review* 38, no. 2 (2017): 56–69.
Bachelard, Gaston. *Air and Dreams: An Essay on the Imagination of Movement.* Translated by Edith R. Farrell and C. Frederick Farrell. Dallas: Dallas Institute Publications, 2002.
Bachelard, Gaston. *The Dialectic of Duration.* Translated by Mary McAllester Jones. Manchester, UK: Clinamen, 2000.
Bachelard, Gaston. *Le Droit de rêver.* Paris: PUF, 1970.
Bachelard, Gaston. *Intuition of the Instant.* Translated by Eileen Rizo-Patron. Evanston, IL: Northwestern University Press, 2013.
Baczko, Bronislaw. *Utopian Lights: The Evolution of the Idea of Social Progress.* Translated by Judith L. Greenberg. New York: Paragon House, 1989.
Bailly, Jean-Christophe. "68, année philosophique?" Episodes 3–4, "Un printemps à Nanterre." *Les Nouveaux chemins de la philosophie*, April 25, 2018, Radio France Culture.
Balibar, Étienne. *Equaliberty: Political Essays.* Translated by James D. Ingram. Durham, NC: Duke University Press, 2014.
Bargu, Banu. *Starve and Immolate: The Politics of Human Weapons.* New York: Columbia University Press, 2014.
Bargu, Banu. "Why Did Bouazizi Burn Himself? The Politics of Fate and Fatal Politics." *Constellations: An International Journal of Critical and Democratic Theory* 23, no. 1 (2016): 27–36.
Barthes, Roland. *Mythologies.* Paris: Seuil, 1996.
Barthes, Roland. *Mythologies.* Translated by Annette Lavers. New York: Noonday Press of Farrar, Straus & Giroux, 1972.
Baudelaire, Charles. *The Flowers of Evil.* Translated by James McGowan. Oxford: Oxford University Press, 2008.
Bellamy, Edward. *Looking Backward, 2000–1887.* Edited by Matthew Beaumont. Oxford: Oxford University Press, 2009.
Benjamin, Walter. *The Origin of German Tragic Drama.* Translated by John Osborne. London: Verso, 1998.
Benjamin, Walter. *Selected Writings.* 4 vols. Edited by Michael W.

Jennings et al. Cambridge, MA: Belknap Press of Harvard University Press, 1996–2003.

Berardi, Franco "Bifo." *Precarious Rhapsody: Semiocapitalism and the Pathologies of the Post-Alpha Generation*. Translated by Arianna Bove et al. London: Minor Compositions, 2009.

Berlin, Isaiah. *The Sense of Reality: Studies in Ideas and Their History*. Edited by Henry Hardy. New York: Farrar, Straus & Giroux, 1996.

Bernault, Florence, and Joseph Tonda. "Le Gabon: Une dystopie tropicale." *Politique africaine* 3, no. 115 (2009): 7–26.

Berréby, Gérard, ed. *Documents relatifs à la fondation de l'Internationale situationniste 1948–1957*. Paris: Allia, 1985.

Bey, Hakim. *T.A.Z.: The Temporary Autonomous Zone, Ontological Anarchy, Poetic Terrorism*. New York: Autonomedia, 1991.

Blanchot, Maurice. *Political Writings, 1953–1993*. Translated by Zakir Paul. New York: Fordham University Press, 2010.

Blanqui, Auguste. *Oeuvres complètes*. Vol. 1: *Écrits sur la révolution: Textes politiques et lettres de prison*. Edited by Arno Münster. Paris: Galilée, 1977.

Blanqui, Louis-Auguste. *Eternity by the Stars: An Astronomical Hypothesis*. Translated by Frank Chouraqui. New York: Contra Mundum, 2013.

Bloch, Ernst. *The Principle of Hope*. Translated by Neville Plaice, Stephen Plaice, and Paul Knight. 3 vols. Cambridge, MA: MIT Press, 1995.

Blumenberg, Hans. *Präfiguration: Arbeit am politischen Mythos*. Edited by Angus Nicholls and Felix Heidenreich. Berlin: Suhrkamp, 2014.

Blumenberg, Hans. *Work on Myth*. Translated by Robert M. Wallace. Cambridge, MA: MIT Press, 1988.

Boggs, Carl. "Marxism, Prefigurative Communism, and the Problem of Workers' Control." *Radical America* 11, no. 6 and 12, no. 1 (1977–78): 99–122.

Bookchin, Murray. *Toward an Ecological Society*. Montreal: Black Rose, 1980.

Bottici, Chiara. *A Philosophy of Political Myth*. Cambridge: Cambridge University Press, 2007.

Bouquin, Stephen, Mireille Court, and Chris Den Hond, eds. and trans. *La Commune du Rojava: L'Alternative kurde à l'état-nation*. Paris: Syllepse, 2017.

Boyd, Andrew. "Tactic: Prefigurative Intervention." In Andrew Boyd and Dave Oswald Mitchell, eds., *Beautiful Trouble: A Toolbox for Revolution*, 82–85. New York: OR, 2012.
Braidotti, Rosi. "Biopower and Necro-Politics: Reflections on an Ethics of Sustainability." *Springerin: Hefte fur Gegenwartskunst* 13, no. 2 (2007): 18–23. Special issue on Leben/Überleben. https://www.springerin.at/en/2007/2/biomacht-und-nekro-politik/.
Bregman, Rutger. *Utopia for Realists: And How We Can Get There*. Translated by Elizabeth Manton. London: Bloomsbury, 2018.
Breines, Wini. *Community and Organization in the New Left, 1962–1968: The Great Refusal*. New Brunswick, NJ: Rutgers University Press, 1989.
Breton, André. *Free Rein (La Clé des champs)*. Translated by Michel Parmentier and Jacqueline D'Amboise. Lincoln: University of Nebraska Press, 1995.
Breton, André. *Manifestoes of Surrealism*. Translated by Richard Seaver and Helen R. Lane. Ann Arbor: University of Michigan Press, 1969.
Breton, André. *Ode to Charles Fourier*. Translated by Kenneth White. London: Cape Golliard, 1969.
Breton, André. *Oeuvres complètes*. 4 vols. Paris: Gallimard, 1988–2008.
Breton, André. *What Is Surrealism? Selected Writings*. Edited by Franklin Rosemont. New York: Pathfinder, 1978.
Breton, André, and Benjamin Péret. *Correspondance 1920–59*. Paris: Gallimard, 2017.
Brown, Wendy. "Resisting Left Melancholy." *boundary 2* 26, no. 3 (1999): 19–27.
Buck-Morss, Susan. *Dreamworld and Catastrophe: The Passing of Mass Utopia in East and West*. Cambridge, MA: MIT Press, 2000.
Butler, Judith. *Frames of War: When Is Life Grievable?* New York: Verso, 2009.
Butler, Judith. *Notes toward a Performative Theory of Assembly*. Cambridge, MA: Harvard University Press, 2015.
Butler, Judith. *Precarious Life: The Powers of Mourning and Violence*. New York: Verso, 2004.
Canetti, Elias. *Crowds and Power*. Translated by Carol Stewart. New York: Continuum, 1981.

Carrier, Aurélie. *Le Grand Soir: Voyage dans l'imaginaire révolutionnaire et libertaire de la Belle Époque.* Montreuil: Libertalia, 2017.
Cerutti, Furio. "Humankind's First Fundamental Right: Survival." *Constellations* 22, no. 1 (2015): 59–67.
Cesarano, Giorgio. *Critica dell'utopia capitale.* Milan: Colibri, 1993.
Cesarano, Giorgio. *Manuale di sopravvivenza.* Bari: Dedalo libri, 1974.
Cesarano, Giorgio. *Manuel de survie.* Translated by Benjamin Villari. Rev. ed. Bordeaux: La Tempête, 2019.
Chrostowska, S. D. "Coda: Utopia, Alibi." In Chrostowska and James D. Ingram, eds., *Political Uses of Utopia: New Marxist, Anarchist, and Radical Democratic Perspectives*, 269–310. New York: Columbia University Press, 2017.
Chrostowska, S. D. "The Flesh Is *Not* Sad: Returns of the Body in the Utopian Tradition." *diacritics* 46, no. 3 (2018): 4–30.
Chrostowska, S. D. "Serious, Not All That Serious: Utopia beyond Realism and Normativity in Contemporary Critical Theory." *Constellations* 26, no. 2 (2019): 330–43.
Chrostowska, S. D. "Utopia and Political Theology in the 'Oldest Systematic Program of German Idealism.'" In Kirill Chepurin and Alex Dubilet, eds., *Nothing Absolute: German Idealism and the Question of Political Theology*, 54–72. New York: Fordham University Press, 2021.
Citton, Yves, and Jacopo Rasmi. *Générations collapsonautes: Naviguer par temps d'effondrement.* Paris: Seuil, 2020.
Clark, T. J. "For a Left with No Future." *New Left Review* 74 (2012): 53–75.
Clark, T. J. Foreword to *Guy Debord* by Anselm Jappe, translated by Donald Nicholson-Smith. Berkeley: University of California Press, 1999.
Clark, T. J. *Heaven on Earth: Painting and the Life to Come.* London: Thames & Hudson, 2018.
Clastres, Pierre. *Archeology of Violence.* Translated by Jeanine Herman. New York: Semiotext(e), 1994.
Clastres, Pierre. *Society against the State: Essays in Political Anthropology.* Translated by Robert Hurley and Abe Stein. New York: Zone, 1989.
Cobra. *Cobra 1948–1951.* Paris: Jean-Michel Place, 1980.
Cohn, Norman. *The Pursuit of the Millennium: Revolutionary Messianism in Medieval and Reformation Europe and Its Bearing on*

Modern Totalitarian Movements. 2d ed. New York: Harper & Brothers, 1961.

Cohn-Bendit, Daniel, and Jean-Pierre Duteuil. *La Révolte étudiante: Les Animateurs parlent*. Paris: Seuil, 1968.

CrimethInc. "Surviving the Virus: An Anarchist Guide." CrimethInc. March 18, 2020. https://crimethinc.com/2020/03/18/surviving-the-virus-an-anarchist-guide-capitalism-in-crisis-rising-totalitarianism-strategies-of-resistance.

Danaher, John. *Automation and Utopia: Human Flourishing in a World without Work*. Cambridge, MA: Harvard University Press, 2019.

Dardot, Pierre, and Christian Laval. *Commun: Essai sur la révolution au XXIe siècle*. Paris: La Découverte, 2014.

Debord, Guy. *Correspondance*. Vols. 6 (1979–87) and 7 (1988–94). Paris: Fayard, 2006–8.

Debord, Guy. "Report on the Construction of Situations and on the Terms of Organization and Action of the International Situationist Tendency." Translated by Tom McDonough. In McDonough, ed., *Guy Debord and the Situationist International: Texts and Documents*, 29–50. Cambridge, MA: MIT Press, 2002.

Debord, Guy. *The Society of the Spectacle*. Translated by Ken Knabb. Berkeley, CA: Bureau of Public Secrets, 2014.

Debout, Simone, and André Breton. *Simone Debout et André Breton, correspondance 1958–1966*. Edited by Florent Perrier. Paris: Claire Paulhan, 2019.

Deleuze, Gilles. "Postscript on the Societies of Control." *October* 59 (1992): 3–7.

Deleuze, Gilles, and Félix Guattari. *Kafka: Toward a Minor Literature*. Translated by Dana Polan. Minneapolis: University of Minnesota Press, 1986.

Diamond, Jared. *Collapse: How Societies Choose to Fail or Succeed*. New York: Viking, 2005.

Diem, Rebecca. "Hopepunk and the New Science of Stress." *Tor.com*, March 2, 2020. https://www.tor.com/2020/03/02/hopepunk-and-the-new-science-of-stress.

Diogenes Laertius. *Lives of the Eminent Philosophers*. Translated by Pamela Mensch and James Miller. Oxford: Oxford University Press, 2018.

Dumont, René. *L'Utopie ou la mort!* Paris: Seuil, 1973.
Duterme, Renaud. *De quoi l'effondrement est-il le nom? La Fragmentation du monde.* Paris: Utopia, 2016.
Eagleton, Terry. *Hope without Optimism.* Charlottesville: University of Virginia Press, 2015.
Eaton, George. "'I Want the State to Think Like an Anarchist': Dutch Historian Rutger Bregman on Why the Left Must Reclaim Utopianism." *New Statesman*, February 19, 2018. https://www.newstatesman.com/culture/observations/2018/02/i-want-state-think-anarchist-dutch-historian-rutger-bregman-why-left.
Ehrenreich, Barbara. "The Humanoid Stain: Art Lessons from Our Cave-Dwelling Ancestors." *The Baffler* 48 (2019). https://thebaffler.com/salvos/the-humanoid-stain-ehrenreich.
Elliott, Robert C. *The Shape of Utopia.* Edited by Phillip E. Wegner. Oxford: Peter Lang, 2013.
Engels, Frederick. "Anti-Dühring." In Karl Marx and Engels, *Collected Works*, vol. 25: *Frederick Engels: Anti-Dühring, Dialectics of Nature*, 5–309. New York: International, 1975.
Esposito, Roberto. *Categories of the Impolitical.* Translated by Connal Parsley. New York: Fordham University Press, 2015.
Esposito, Roberto. *Persons and Things: From the Body's Point of View.* Translated by Zakiya Hanafi. Cambridge: Polity, 2015.
Fassin, Didier. "Another Politics of Life Is Possible." *Theory, Culture and Society* 26, no. 5 (2009): 44–60.
Fassin, Didier. "Ethics of Survival: A Democratic Approach to the Politics of Life." *Humanity* 1, no. 1 (2010): 81–95.
Fierke, K. M. *Political Self-Sacrifice: Agency, Body and Emotion in International Relations.* Cambridge: Cambridge University Press, 2013.
Foucault, Michel. *Politics, Philosophy, Culture: Interviews and Other Writings, 1977–1984.* Edited by Lawrence D. Kritzman. New York: Routledge, 1988.
Foucault, Michel. *"Society Must Be Defended": Lectures at the Collège de France, 1975–1976.* Edited by Mauro Bertani and Alessandro Fontana. Translated by David Macey. New York: Picador, 2003.
Fourier, Charles. *Oeuvres complètes.* Vol. 7: *Le Nouveau monde amoureux.* Edited by Simone Debout-Oleszkiewicz. Paris: Anthropos, 1972.

Fourier, Charles. *The Theory of the Four Movements*. Edited by Gareth Stedman Jones and Ian Patterson. Translated by Ian Patterson. Cambridge: Cambridge University Press, 1996.

Frase, Peter. *Four Futures: Visions of the World After Capitalism*. London: Verso, 2016.

Friedman, Yona. *Utopies réalisables: Vers une cité conçue par ses habitants eux-mêmes (1958–2000)*. Paris: L'Éclat, 2000.

Frye, Northrop. "Varieties of Literary Utopias." *Daedalus* 94, no. 2 (1965): 323–47.

Fuller, R. Buckminster. *Utopia or Oblivion: The Prospects for Humanity*. 2d ed. Zürich: Lars Müller, 2019.

Garcia, Renaud. *La Collapsologie ou l'écologie mutilée*. Paris: L'Échappée, 2020.

Gayraud, Joël. *L'Homme sans horizon: Matériaux sur l'utopie*. Montreuil: Libertalia, 2019.

Geuss, Raymond. "Realism, Wishful Thinking, Utopia." In S. D. Chrostowska and James D. Ingram, eds., *Political Uses of Utopia: New Marxist, Anarchist, and Radical Democratic Perspectives*, 233–47. New York: Columbia University Press, 2017.

Goldmann, Lucien. *The Hidden God: A Study of Tragic Vision in the Pensées of Pascal and the Tragedies of Racine*. Translated by Philip Thody. London: Verso, 2016.

Goldsmith, Edward, Robert Allen, Michael Allaby, John Davoll, and Sam Lawrence. *Blueprint for Survival*. Harmondsworth, UK: Penguin, 1972.

Gordon, Uri. "Prefigurative Politics between Ethical Practice and Absent Promise." *Political Studies* 66, no. 2 (2018): 521–37.

Graeber, David. *Revolutions in Reverse: Essays on Politics, Violence, Art, and Imagination*. London: Minor Compositions, 2011.

Grainville, Jean-Baptiste François Xavier Cousin de. *The Last Man*. Translated by I. F. Clarke and M. Clarke. Middletown, CT: Wesleyan University Press, 2002.

Graus, František. "Social Utopias in the Middle Ages." Translated by Bernard Standring. *Past and Present* 38 (1967): 3–19.

Gross, Otto. "Overcoming Cultural Crisis." Translated by John Turner. In Robert Graham, ed., *Anarchism: A Documentary History of*

Libertarian Ideas, vol. 1: *From Anarchy to Anarchism (300 CE to 1939)*, 281–84. Montreal: Black Rose, 2005.

Guattari, Félix. *The Guattari Reader*. Edited by Gary Genosko. Oxford: Blackwell, 1996.

Habermas. Jürgen. "Modernity: An Unfinished Project." Translated by Nicholas Walker. In Maurizio Passerin d'Entrèves and Seyla Benhabib, eds., *Habermas and the Unfinished Project of Modernity: Critical Essays on* The Philosophical Discourse of Modernity, 38–55. Cambridge, MA: MIT Press, 1997.

Habermas. Jürgen. "Questions and Counterquestions." In Richard J. Bernstein, ed., *Habermas and Modernity*, 192–216. Cambridge, MA: MIT Press, 1985.

Hardt, Michael, and Antonio Negri. *Assembly*. Oxford: Oxford University Press, 2017.

Hardt, Michael, and Antonio Negri. *Commonwealth*. Cambridge, MA: Harvard University Press, 2009.

Hardt, Michael, and Antonio Negri. *Empire*. Cambridge, MA: Harvard University Press, 2000.

Hardt, Michael, and Antonio Negri. *Multitude: War and Democracy in the Age of Empire*. New York: Penguin, 2004.

Harvey, David. *Spaces of Hope*. Edinburgh: Edinburgh University Press, 2000.

Herbert, R. L., Anne-Marie Rougerie, and Jacques Rougerie. "Les Artistes et l'Anarchisme d'après les lettres inédites de Pissaro, Signac et autres." *Le Mouvement social* 36 (1961): 2–19.

Heron, Kai, and Jodi Dean. "Revolution or Ruin." *e-flux* 110 (2020). https://www.c-flux.com/journal/110/335242/revolution-or-ruin.

Hobbes, Thomas. *Leviathan: Revised Student Edition*. Edited by Richard Tuck. Cambridge: Cambridge University Press, 1996.

Hobbes, Thomas. *Leviathan: With Selected Variants from the Latin Edition of 1668*. Edited by Edwin Curley. Indianapolis: Hackett, 1994.

Horkheimer, Max, and Theodor W. Adorno. *Dialectic of Enlightenment: Philosophical Fragments*. Edited by Gunzelin Schmid Noerr. Translated by Edmund Jephcott. Stanford: Stanford University Press, 2002.

Huxley, Aldous. *Island*. New York: Harper Perennial, 2009.

Internationale lettriste. *Potlatch, 1954–1957*. Paris: Gérard Lebovici, 1985.

Internationale situationniste. *Internationale situationniste, 1958–1969.* Amsterdam: Van Gennep, 1972.

The Invisible Committee. *The Coming Insurrection.* Anonymous translation. New York: Semiotext(e), 2009.

Jacoby, Russell. *The End of Utopia: Politics and Culture in an Age of Apathy.* New York: Basic, 1999.

Jacoby, Russell. *Picture Imperfect: Utopian Thought for an Anti-Utopian Age.* New York: Columbia University Press, 2005.

Jameson, Fredric. *Archaeologies of the Future: The Desire Called Utopia and Other Science Fictions.* London: Verso, 2005.

Jameson, Fredric. *The Ideologies of Theory.* Rev. ed. London: Verso, 2008.

Jameson, Fredric. *Marxism and Form: Twentieth-Century Dialectical Theories of Literature.* Princeton, NJ: Princeton University Press, 1971.

Jameson, Fredric. *The Political Unconscious: Narrative as a Socially Symbolic Act.* London: Routledge, 2002.

Jameson, Fredric. "The Politics of Utopia." *New Left Review* 25 (2004): 35–54.

Jameson, Fredric. *Valences of the Dialectic.* New York: Verso, 2009.

Jeanpierre, Laurent. *In girum: Les Leçons politiques des ronds-points.* Paris: La Découverte, 2019.

Kinna, Ruth. "Utopianism and Prefiguration." In S. D. Chrostowska and James D. Ingram, eds., *Political Uses of Utopia: New Marxist, Anarchist, and Radical Democratic Perspectives,* 198–215. New York: Columbia University Press, 2017.

Knabb, Ken, ed. and trans. *Situationist International Anthology: Revised and Expanded Edition.* Berkeley, CA: Bureau of Public Secrets, 2006.

Kompridis, Nikolas. *Critique and Disclosure: Critical Theory between Past and Future.* Cambridge, MA: MIT Press, 2006.

Kunkel, Benjamin. *Utopia or Bust: A Guide to the Present Crisis.* New York: Verso, 2014.

Landauer, Gustav. *Revolution and Other Writings: A Political Reader.* Translated and edited by Gabriel Kuhn. Oakland, CA: PM, 2010.

Lasch, Christopher. *The Minimal Self: Psychic Survival in Troubled Times.* New York: Norton, 1984.

Lash, Scott. "Life (Vitalism)." *Theory, Culture and Society* 23, nos. 2–3 (2006): 323–49.

Latour, Bruno. "What Protective Measures Can You Think of So We Don't Go Back to the Pre-Crisis Production Model?" Translated by Stephen Muecke. http://www.bruno-latour.fr/sites/default/files/downloads/P-202-AOC-ENGLISH_1.pdf. [Originally published in *Analyse Opinion Critique*, March 29, 2020.]

Laudani, Raffaele. *Disobedience in Western Political Thought: A Genealogy*. Translated by Jason Francis McGimsey. Cambridge: Cambridge University Press, 2013.

Lear, Jonathan. *Radical Hope: Ethics in the Face of Cultural Devastation*. Cambridge, MA: Harvard University Press, 2006.

Lears, Jackson. *Fables of Abundance: A Cultural History of Advertising in America*. New York: Basic, 1994.

Le Guin, Ursula K. *The Dispossessed*. New York: Harper & Row, 1974.

Levinas, Emmanuel. Preface to *Utopie et socialisme*, by Martin Buber translated by Paul Corset and François Girard, 7–11. Paris: Aubier Montaigne, 1977.

Levitas, Ruth. *The Concept of Utopia*. Witney, UK: Peter Lang, 2011.

Levitas, Ruth. "Educated Hope: Ernst Bloch on Abstract and Concrete Utopia." *Utopian Studies* 1, no. 2 (1990): 13–26.

Levitas, Ruth. *Utopia as Method: The Imaginary Reconstitution of Society*. London: Palgrave Macmillan, 2013.

Löwy, Michael. *Morning Star: Surrealism, Marxism, Anarchism, Situationism, Utopia*. Austin: University of Texas Press, 2009.

Löwy, Michael. "Oiseau hermétique: La Réponse des surréalistes à Jürgen Habermas." In Guy Girard, ed., *Insoumission poétique: Tracts, affiches et déclarations du groupe de Paris du mouvement surréaliste 1970–2010*, 42–43. Paris: Le Temps des Cerises, 2011.

Magritte, René, ed. *La Carte d'après nature*. Special issue. Brussels, June 1954.

Mannheim, Karl. *Ideology and Utopia: An Introduction to the Sociology of Knowledge*. Translated by Louis Wirth and Edward Shils. New York: Harcourt, Brace, 1954.

Marcuse, Herbert. *Eros and Civilization: A Philosophical Inquiry into Freud*. London: Routledge, 1998.

Marcuse, Herbert. *Five Lectures: Psychoanalysis, Politics and Utopia*.

Translated by Jeremy Shapiro and Shierry M. Weber. Boston: Beacon Press, 1970.
Marcuse, Herbert. *One-Dimensional Man: Studies in the Ideology of Advanced Industrial Society.* Boston: Beacon Press, 1964.
Marcuse, Herbert. *Transvaluation of Values and Radical Social Change: Five New Lectures, 1966–1976.* Edited by Peter-Erwin Jansen, Sarah Surak, and Charles Reitz. Toronto: International Herbert Marcuse Society, 2017.
Marx, Karl. *Capital: A Critique of Political Economy.* Vol. 3. Translated by David Fernbach. London: Penguin, 1991.
Marx, Karl. "First Outline of *The Civil War in France*." In Marx and Frederick Engels, *On the Paris Commune*, 102–81. Moscow: Progress, 1971.
Marx, Karl, and Frederick Engels. *Collected Works.* Vol. 3: *1843–1844.* New York: International, 1975.
Marx, Karl, and Friedrich Engels. *The Communist Manifesto.* Translated by Samuel Moore. London: Pluto, 2008.
Mason, Paul. *Postcapitalism: A Guide to Our Future.* London: Allen Lane, 2015.
Mavelli, Luca. "Governing Populations through the Humanitarian Government of Refugees: Biopolitical Care and Racism in the European Refugee Crisis." *Review of International Studies* 43, no. 5 (2017): 809–32.
Mbembe, Achille. "Necropolitics." Translated by Libby Meintjes. *Public Culture* 15, no. 1 (2003): 11–40.
Mbembe, Achille. *Necropolitics.* Translated by Steven Corcoran. Durham, NC: Duke University Press, 2019.
Mbembe, Achille. *Politiques de l'inimitié.* Paris: La Découverte, 2016.
McKean, Benjamin L. "What Makes a Utopia Inconvenient? On the Advantages and Disadvantages of a Realist Orientation to Politics." *American Political Science Review* 110, no. 4 (2016): 876–88.
McQueen, Allison. *Political Realism in Apocalyptic Times.* Cambridge: Cambridge University Press, 2017.
Mead, Margaret. "Towards More Vivid Utopias." *Science* 126, no. 3280 (1957): 957–61.
Michelsen, Nicholas. *Politics and Suicide: The Philosophy of Political Self-Destruction.* New York: Routledge, 2016.

Miesseroff, Lola. *Voyage en outre-gauche*. Montreuil: Libertalia, 2018.

Minkowski, Eugène. *Lived Time: Phenomenological and Psychopathological Studies*. Translated by Nancy Metzel. Evanston, IL: Northwestern University Press, 1970.

More, Thomas. *Utopia*. Edited by George M. Logan and Robert M. Adams. Translated by Robert M. Adams. Rev. ed. Cambridge: Cambridge University Press, 2002.

More, Thomas. *Utopia: Latin Text and English Translation*. Edited by George M. Logan, Robert M. Adams, and Clarence H. Miller. Cambridge: Cambridge University Press, 2006.

Morris, William. *News from Nowhere: Or, an Epoch of Rest. Being Some Chapters from a Utopian Romance*. Oxford: Oxford University Press, 2009.

Morton, A. L. *The English Utopia*. London: Lawrence & Wishart, 1952.

Moyn, Samuel. *The Last Utopia: Human Rights in History*. Cambridge, MA: Harvard University Press, 2010.

Mumford, Lewis. *The Story of Utopias*. New York: Viking, 1962.

Murray, Stuart J. "Thanatopolitics: On the Use of Death for Mobilizing Political Life." *Polygraph* 18 (2006): 191–215.

Negt, Oskar. *L'Espace public oppositionnel*. Translated by Alexander Neumann. Paris: Payot, 2007.

Negt, Oskar. *Nur noch Utopien sind realistisch: Politische Interventionen*. Göttingen: Steidl, 2012.

Noys, Benjamin. "The Poverty of Vitalism (and the Vitalism of Poverty)." Paper presented at To Have Done with Life: Vitalism and Anti-vitalism in Contemporary Philosophy Conference, June 17–19, 2011, MaMa, Zagreb, Croatia. https://www.academia.edu/689255/The_Poverty_of_Vitalism_and_the_Vitalism_of_Poverty_.

Obama, Barack. Transcript of Keynote Address, 2004 Democratic National Convention, Fleet Center, Boston, MA, Tuesday, July 27, 2004. http://p2004.org/demconv04/obama072704spt.html.

Passerini, Luisa. *Memory and Utopia: The Primacy of Intersubjectivity*. London: Routledge, 2014.

Passerini, Luisa. "'Utopia' and Desire." *Thesis 11* 68, no. 1 (2002): 11–30.

Pensky, Max. "Contributions toward a Theory of Storms: Historical

Knowing and Historical Progress in Kant and Benjamin." *Philosophical Forum* 41, nos. 1–2 (2010): 149–74.
Pessis, Céline, ed. *Survivre et vivre: Critique de la science, naissance de l'écologie*. Paris: L'Échappée, 2014.
Pierre, José, ed. *Tracts surréalistes et déclarations collectives, 1922–1969*. Vol. 2: *1940–1969*. Paris: Terrain vague, 1982.
Pierret, Marc. *Utopies et perversions: Un dossier ouvert par Marc Pierret*. Paris: Nouvelles Éditions Debresse, 1969.
Piketty, Thomas. *Capital in the Twenty-First Century*. Translated by Arthur Goldhammer. Cambridge, MA: Belknap Press of Harvard University Press, 2014.
Plato. *The Laws*. Edited by Malcolm Schofield. Translated by Tom Griffith. Cambridge: Cambridge University Press, 2016.
Plonowska-Ziarek, Ewa. "Bare Life." In Henry Sussman, ed., *Impasses of the Post-Global: Theory in the Era of Climate Change*, vol. 2, 194–211. Ann Arbor: Open Humanities Press, 2012.
Polanyi, Karl. *The Great Transformation*. Boston: Beacon Press, 2001.
Porter, Roy. *Flesh in the Age of Reason*. London: Penguin, 2003.
Proudhon, Pierre-Joseph. *General Idea of the Revolution in the Nineteenth Century*. Translated by John Beverly Robinson. London: Dover, 2003.
Reeve, Charles. *Le Socialisme sauvage: Essai sur l'auto-organisation et la démocratie directe dans les luttes de 1789 à nos jours*. Paris: L'Échappée, 2018.
Richardson, Michael, and Krzysztof Fijałkowski, eds. *Surrealism against the Current: Tracts and Declarations*. London: Pluto, 2001.
Riley, Dylan. "An Anticapitalism That Can Win." *Jacobin Magazine*, July 1, 2016. https://www.jacobinmag.com/2016/01/olin-wright-real-utopias-socialism-capitalism-gramsci-lenin-luxemburg/.
Robin, Corey. "Socialism: Converting Hysterical Misery into Ordinary Unhappiness." *Jacobin Magazine*, October 12, 2013. https://www.jacobinmag.com/2013/12/socialism-converting-hysterical-misery-into-ordinary-unhappiness/.
Robinson, Marilynne. "Is Poverty Necessary? An Idea That Won't Go Away." *Harper's Magazine*, June 2019. https://harpers.org/archive/2019/06/is-poverty-necessary-marilynne-robinson/.
Romano, Aja. "Hopepunk, the Latest Storytelling Trend, Is All about

Weaponized Optimism." *Vox*, December 27, 2018. https://www.vox.com/2018/12/27/18137571/what-is-hopepunk-noblebright-grimdark.

Rosa, Hartmut, and Christoph Henning, eds. *The Good Life beyond Growth: New Perspectives*. London: Routledge, 2017.

Rosanvallon, Pierre. *Le Capitalisme utopique: Histoire de l'idée de marché*. Paris: Seuil, 1999.

Rousseau, Jean-Jacques. *The Collected Writings of Rousseau*, vol. 9: Letter to Beaumont, Letters Written from the Mountain and Related Writings. Edited by Christopher Kelly and Eve Grace. Translated by Christopher Kelly and Judith R. Bush. Hanover, NH: University Press of New England, 2001.

Rousseau, Jean-Jacques. *The Social Contract*. Translated by Christopher Betts. Oxford: Oxford University Press, 1994.

Sahlins, Marshall. "La Première société d'abondance." *Les Temps modernes* 268 (1968): 641–80.

Sahlins, Marshall. *Stone Age Economics*. London: Routledge, 2017.

Salomon, Albert. "The Religion of Progress." *Social Research* 13, no. 4 (1946): 441–62.

Sargent, Lyman Tower. "The Three Faces of Utopianism." *Minnesota Review* 7, no. 3 (1967): 222–30.

Sargent, Lyman Tower. "The Three Faces of Utopianism Revisited." *Utopian Studies* 5, no. 1 (1994): 1–37.

Sargisson, Lucy. *Fool's Gold? Utopianism in the Twenty-First Century*. Basingstoke, UK: Palgrave Macmillan, 2012.

Sargisson, Lucy. *Utopian Bodies and the Politics of Transgression*. New York: Routledge, 2000.

Schweickart, David. *After Capitalism*. Lanham, MD: Rowman & Littlefield, 2002.

Servigne, Pablo. "Faire de la fin du monde une brèche." *Réfractions, recherches et expressions anarchistes* 44 (2020): 81–94.

Servigne, Pablo, and Raphaël Stevens. *Comment tout peut s'effondrer: Petit manuel de collapsologie à l'usage des générations présentes*. Paris: Seuil, 2015.

Servigne, Pablo, Raphaël Stevens, and Gauthier Chapelle. *Une autre fin du monde est possible: Vivre l'effondrement (et pas seulement y survivre)*. Paris: Seuil, 2018.

Shemon. "The Rise of Black Counter-Insurgency." Ill Will Editions. July 30, 2020. https://illwilleditions.com/the-rise-of-black-counter-insurgency/.

Sorel, Georges. *Reflections on Violence*. Edited and translated by Jeremy Jennings. Cambridge: Cambridge University Press, 1999.

Spinoza, Benedict de. *The Collected Works of Spinoza*. Vol. 2. Edited and translated by Edwin Curley. Princeton, NJ: Princeton University Press, 2016.

Spinoza, Benedict de. *A Spinoza Reader: The* Ethics *and Other Works*. Edited and translated by Edwin Curley. Princeton, NJ: Princeton University Press, 1994.

Standing, Guy. *The Precariat: The New Dangerous Class*. London: Bloomsbury, 2011.

Streeck, Wolfgang. *How Will Capitalism End? Essays on a Failing System*. London: Verso, 2016.

Survivre et vivre. "Fin de l'économie." *Survivre . . . et vivre* 19 (1975): 4–7.

Suvin, Darko. "Erkenntnis: Keystones for an Epistemology (11 Theses and 1 Indication)." Version 8 (2012). https://darkosuvin.com/2015/05/23/erkenntnis-keystones-for-an-epistemology-11-theses-and-1-indication/.

Suvin, Darko. "Locus, Horizon, and Orientation: The Concept of Possible Worlds as a Key to Utopian Studies." In Jamie Owen Daniel and Tom Moylan, eds., *Not Yet: Reconsidering Ernst Bloch*, 122–37. London: Verso, 1997.

Swain, Dan. "Not Not But Not Yet: Present and Future in Prefigurative Politics." *Political Studies* 67, no. 1 (2019): 47–62.

Thaler, Mathias. "Hope Abjuring Hope: On the Place of Utopia in Realist Political Theory." *Political Theory* 46, no. 5 (2018): 671–97.

Thompson, E. P. *William Morris: Romantic to Revolutionary*. Rev. ed. New York: Pantheon, 1977.

Thompson, Peter. "What Is Concrete about Ernst Bloch's 'Concrete Utopia'?" In Michael Hviid Jacobsen and Keith Tester, eds., *Utopia: Social Theory and the Future*, 33–46. Burlington, VT: Ashgate, 2012.

Tischler, Sergio. "Detotalization and Subject: On Zapatismo and Critical Theory." *South Atlantic Quarterly* 113, no. 2 (2014): 327–38.

Tomba, Massimiliano. *Insurgent Universality: An Alternative Legacy of Modernity*. New York: Oxford University Press, 2019.

Tonda, Joseph. *L'Impérialisme postcolonial: Critique de la société des éblouissements*. Paris: Karthala, 2015.

Tournier, Maurice. "'Le Grand Soir,' un mythe de fin de siècle." *Mots* 19 (1989): 79–94.

Traverso, Enzo. *Left-Wing Melancholia: Marxism, History, and Memory*. New York: Columbia University Press, 2016.

Turchin, Peter. *Historical Dynamics: Why States Rise and Fall*. Princeton, NJ: Princeton University Press, 2003.

Tuveson, Ernest Lee. *Millennium and Utopia: A Study in the Background of the Idea of Progress*. Berkeley: University of California Press, 1949.

Vaneigem, Raoul. "Basic Banalities" [parts I and II]. In Ken Knabb, ed. and trans., *Situationist International Anthology: Revised and Expanded Edition*, 117–30, 154–73. Berkeley, CA: Bureau of Public Secrets, 2006.

Vaneigem, Raoul. "Nous n'avons d'autre alternative que d'oser l'impossible." Interview by Nicolas Truong. *Le Monde*, August 31, 2019. https://www.lemonde.fr/idees/article/2019/08/30/raoul-vaneigem-nous-n-avons-d-autre-alternative-que-d-oser-l-impossible_5504332_3232.html.

Vaneigem, Raoul. *The Revolution of Everyday Life*. Translated by Donald Nicholson-Smith. London: Rebel, 2001.

Vaneigem, Raoul. *Voyage à Oarystis*. Blandain-Tournai: Estuaire, 2005.

Vatter, Miguel. *The Republic of the Living: Biopolitics and the Critique of Civil Society*. New York: Fordham University Press, 2014.

Vatter, Miguel, and Vanessa Lemm, eds. *The Government of Life: Foucault, Biopolitics, and Neoliberalism*. New York: Fordham University Press, 2014.

Vázquez-Arroyo, Antonio Y. *Political Responsibility: Responding to Predicaments of Power*. New York: Columbia University Press, 2016.

Viénet, René, ed. *Enragés et situationnistes dans le mouvement des occupations*. Paris: Gallimard, 1968.

Vrignon, Alexis. *La Naissance de l'écologie politique en France: Une nébuleuse au coeur des années 68*. Rennes: Presses Universitaires de Rennes, 2017.

Watkins, Susan. "Presentism? Reply to T. J. Clark." *New Left Review* 74 (2012): 77–102.

Weil, Simone. *Oeuvres complètes*. Vol. II, pt. 3: *Écrits historiques et politiques: Vers la guerre (1937–1940)*. Edited by André A. Devaux and Florence de Lussy. Paris: Gallimard, 1989.

Weil, Simone. *Oppression and Liberty*. Translated by Arthur Wills and John Petrie. London: Routledge, 2001.

Weil, Simone. *Simone Weil: An Anthology*. Edited by Siân Miles. London: Penguin, 2009.

Wigley, Mark, and Constant. *Constant's New Babylon: The Hyper-Architecture of Desire*. Rotterdam: Witte de With Center for Contemporary Art and 010 Publishers, 1998.

Wilde, Oscar. *The Soul of Man under Socialism*. Boston: J. W. Luce, 1910.

Williams, Raymond. *Politics and Letters: Interviews with New Left Review*. London: Verso, 2015.

Winter, Jay. *Dreams of Peace and Freedom: Utopian Moments in the Twentieth Century*. New Haven: Yale University Press, 2006.

Wright, Erik Olin. *Envisioning Real Utopias*. New York: Verso, 2010.

Wright, Erik Olin. *How to Be an Anti-Capitalist in the 21st Century*. London: Verso, 2019.

Yassour, Avraham. "Communism and Utopia: Marx, Engels and Fourier." *Studies in Soviet Thought* 26, no. 3 (1983): 217–27.

Youl, Edward. "The Golden Age." *Howitt's Journal of Literature and Social Progress* 2 (1847): 118.

Žižek, Slavoj. *Slavoj Žižek: The Reality of the Virtual*. Directed by Ben Wright. 74 minutes. Ben Wright Film Production, UK, 2004.

Žižek, Slavoj. *The Year of Dreaming Dangerously*. London: Verso, 2012.

Žižek, Slavoj. *Žižek!* Directed by Astra Taylor. 71 minutes. Hidden Driver Productions, Documentary Campaign, US, 2005.

INDEX

Abélès, Marc, 95–96. *See also* survivance, politics of
Abensour, Miguel, 8, 17, 55, 66–68, 76, 83, 98. *See also* education of desire
Adorno, Theodor W., 21, 27, 58–60, 69, 107, 117, 136n29, 150n15, 156n66, 167n19
aesthetics, 58–60
Agamben, Giorgio, 83, 91–92, 100. *See also* coming community, the
Amazon (multinational corporation), 122, 134n14; (website), 134n14
American Dream mall, 6
Amsterdam, 63
anarchism, 44, 79, 118, 128n26, 129n32, 134n14, 173n32. *See also* prefiguration
anarchoprimitivism, 26
Anderson, Perry, 68
anticonsumerism, 103, 172n32. *See also* consumerism
antisemitism, 51, 103
anti-utopianism/anti-utopian, 108; anti-, 108, 169n24; of Cohn, 139n55; politics that is, 30; utopianism that is, 108, 169n22. *See also* utopianism
Arab Spring, 30
Ardillo, José, 173n32
Arendt, Hannah, 83, 87–88, 161n13
assembléisme, 87. *See also* democracy; Yellow Vests
atheist, 10, 60
autogestion, 157n87; as *autogestion généralisée*, 157n87. *See also* Vaneigem, Raoul
automation, 143n79

Bachelard, Gaston, 52–53
Baczko, Bronislaw, 42
Bailly, Jean-Christophe, 66
Balibar, Étienne, 84
bare life: as abject "death-in-life," 92; of the *homo sacer*, 162n22;

bare life (*continued*)
as the horizon of all subjection to power, 84; as incompatible with radical utopian politics, 20; as the original nucleus of sovereign power, 91; survival as, 69, 90, 100. See also *bios* vs. *zoē*
Bargu, Banu: *Starve and Immolate*, 91–95, 164n37. See also necroresistance
baroque: Benjamin's melancholy of history as, 134n17; vision of utopia as, 168n19
Barthes, Roland: *Mythologies*, 37–43, 46
Bataille, Georges, 60, 64
Baudelaire, Charles, 103, 135n17
Bellamy, Edward, 56, 135n23
Benjamin, Walter, 30, 32–33, 35, 59, 90, 96, 134n17. See also messianism/messianic
Bensaïd, Daniel, 32, 49
Berardi, Franco "Bifo," 98
Bergson, Henri, 52
Berlin, Isaiah, 4–5
Biden, Joe, 12
Biehl, Janet, 173n32
biopoliticization: and the necropoliticization of resistance, 94; of sovereignty, 21, 91–94. See also biopolitics
biopolitics: apparatus of, 86; and body politics, 86–89; Foucault's concept of, 162n20; necropolitics and, 91. See also biopoliticization; politics
biosovereignty, 91–92; assemblage of, 95; new power regime of, 94 *bios* vs. *zoē*, 90–91, 100, 162n22. See also bare life
Birthstrike (movement), 25
Björk: *Utopia* (album), 5
Black Lives Matter, 11
Blanchot, Maurice, 45, 113, 140n62. See also great refusal, the
Blanqui, Auguste: *Eternity by the Stars*, 3
Blumenberg, Hans, 36, 43, 136n29, 137n39, 144n81
Bloch, Ernst: *The Principle of Hope*, 3, 7–8, 19, 22, 49, 67, 126n6, 136n29, 142n74, 146n1. See also *docta spes*
Boccaccio: *Decameron*, 117–18
body: creative power of the, 68; desiring, 64; suffering of the, 19; and revolution, 64–65; survival of the, 19; and utopia, 21, 100, 107, 131n38; weaponization of the, 28, 164n37. See also body utopia; embodiment; sexuality
body utopia: and city utopia, 19, 146n3; and the corporal constitution of community, 21; definition of, 131n36; desire-driven, 56–60; and dystopia, 165n3; and material luxury, 80–82; in the revolutionary artistic and intellectual movements of the twentieth century, 68–71. See also body; city utopia; Cockaigne/Cokaygne; utopia

INDEX 197

Bookchin, Murray, 83, 102, 109, 147n4, 173n32
Bouazizi, Mohamed, 164n37
Boulez, Pierre, 5
Braidotti, Rosi, 94
Brazil, 122
Bregman, Rutger: *Utopia for Realists*, 134n14
Breton, André, 59–61, 63–66, 144n84; *Ode à Charles Fourier* of, 59–61
Brown, Wendy, 33, 84
Butler, Judith, 90, 103, 161n13, 165n6

Cahun, Claude, 60
Canada, 114
Canetti, Elias, 96
capitalism, 38, 41, 58, 70, 75, 106; abundance generated by, 81; crises of, 11, 19; deformation of desire in, 16, 74; ecofascism of, 80; end of, 170n24; as the enemy of utopia, 44; erosion of, 109; liberal principle of laissez-faire, 155n55; mediation of needs in, 69; opposition of the left to, 31–32, 97, 161n11; passage from industrial to finance, 158n91; predictions about the end of, 31; private dreamworlds of, 50; revolutionary capacity of, 47; self-critical, 75; social relations of, 71; survival and, 71, 97; techno-, 6; utopian, 111; visions of a new social order after, 11; wilderness of, 16. *See also* consumerism; free market; state

Carrouges, Michel, 66
Castro, Fidel, 29
Cesarano, Giorgio: *Manuale di sopravvivenza*, 75–77
Chiapas, 108, 110. *See also* neo-Zapatism; Zapatism
Chile, 117
China, 122; Maoist, 8
Chtcheglov, Ivan: "Formulary for a New Urbanism," 62
city utopia: as ascetic, 86, 102; vs. body utopia, 19, 146n3; as a fundamental tradition of utopian literature, 146n3. *See also* body utopia; utopia
civic-mindedness, 113
civil rights movement, 11
civil society: and the individual, 94; state and, 160n9; or state order, 90; and utopia, 37
Clark, T. J., 30–35, 48–49, 133n10, 134n14, 145n93
Clastres, Pierre, 80, 82–83, 89
climate: catastrophe of, 25, 102; change of, 82, 116; crisis of, 11, 57, 87; and neutrality as goal, 102
CoBrA (avant-garde group), 63
Cockaigne/Cokaygne, 18, 111, 145n93, 147n6; counterintuitive nature of, 57; dreams of, 130n35; land of, 56–57; main motifs of, 146n3; "pastoralism" of, 56; plebeian, 18. *See also* body utopia; English Peasants' Revolt; Kildare Poems; *pays de Cocagne*; utopia
Cohn, Norman: *The Pursuit of the Millennium*, 139n55

Cold War, 6
collapsology/collapsologues: abdication of social critique in, 173n32; anarchists and, 173n32; apocalyptic antiapocalypticism espoused by, 173n32; comparative political poverty of, 173n32; and survivalism, 172n32; survivalists and, 111; as a transdisciplinary approach to the global collapse of industrial civilization, 172n32
coming community, the, 49, 162n22. See also Agamben, Giorgio; revolution
common, the, 49, 141n71. See also revolution
communism, 3, 44, 107; disaster, 11; of Marx, 80; party, 11; principles of, 17; regimes of, 68; true, 77. See also Communist Party; socialism
Communist Manifesto, The, 59. See also communism
Communist Party, manifesto of the, 3. See also communism; *Communist Manifesto, The*; French Communist Party
constellation: new social, 149n9; of utopia, 22
construction of situations, 62–74, 152n33. See also Situationists, the
consumerism, 44, 57, 70, 74. See also anticonsumerism; capitalism
Contre-Attaque (left-wing antifascist group), 59–60

counterculture, 74; critiques by the, 74
counter-myth, 38, 40, 51. See also myth
counterrevolution, 75. See also revolution
Covid-19. See pandemic/Covid-19
Crevel, René, 66
crisis: "balance of terror" of the nuclear threat and the ecosocial, 22; political stakes in the ecosocial, 22
critical theory, 21, 23, 32, 47, 107, 141n66, 166n19; of capitalist society as spectacle, 64; myth-hunting, 51; realist, 133n3; against the state, 83–99. See also Frankfurt School/Critical Theory; social theory
Cynics, 7
Cyrenaics, 7

Dadaism, 149n10
Danaher, John, 143n79
death, 19, 104, 119
Debord, Guy, 30, 63–64, 66, 71, 83, 139n55, 152n33. See also Situationist International; spectacle
Debout-Oleszkiewicz, Simone: *Le Nouveau monde amoureux*, 60
Declaration of the Rights of Man and of the Citizen: of 1789, 87; in Constitution of 1793, 42
Degrowth/degrowth, 116, 173n32; as antigrowth, 172n32
Deleuze, Gilles: *Anti-Oedipus* of, 66; influence of Surrealism on, 66; and the society of

control, 115; and theorist of politics of survival, 94
democracy: direct, 87, 109; individual participation in representative, 86; insurgent, 98; radical, 17–18, 21; suspension of, 98. *See also* social movements
desire: capture by economic forces of, 70; corporal, 19, 57, 67, 71, 77; critique of, 69; disembodiment of, 70; education of, 55, 69, 76; the emancipation of, 55–82; fetishism of, 57; as founded on expenditure and abundance, 17; hope and, 11–12, 15; ideology of, 79; individualistic cult of, 79; and lack, 20, 67, 75, 164n37; liberation of, 79; micropolitics of, 66; modalities of utopian, 21; moralization of, 102; need and, 63, 67, 69, 72, 107, 146n3; and pleasure, 70; politics of, 67; and revolution, 62–66; romantic, 63; as structured by lack, 16; supreme value of, 61; Surrealists' notion of freedom and, 149n11; and survival, 71–82; unlimited experience of, 74; for utopia, 13, 15–16, 36, 44, 53; utopia as the education of, 67; utopian expressions of, 86; utopian promise of, 70; whims and velleities as, 16. *See also* education of desire; fetishism; love; sexuality
destituent power, 49. *See also* revolution

desublimation: art and, 59; of desire, 58; libidinal energy of, 74; Surrealist view of, 149n10. *See also* sublimation
determinate negation, 167n19–68n19
dialectical materialism, 63. *See also* materialism
disembodiment: of desire, 70 for utopia; or spiritualization, 17; of utopian theory, 57. *See also* embodiment; spiritualization
displacement: desire-driven, 104; in governmentality and resistance, 96; of the imagination, 100–112; physical or imaginary, 21; and postponement of determinate "blueprint" utopias, 52
dissensus, 28, 119
distimacy, 115
docta spes (educated hope), 142n74. *See also* Bloch, Ernst
Duchamp, Marcel, 66
Dumont, René: *L'Utopie ou la mort!*, 156n76
dystopia, 1–2, 31, 104, 165n3; present, 7; super, 14; utopia as the opposite of, 5. *See also* utopia

Eagleton, Terry, 36
Earth/earth: destruction of the, 26, 46; extreme constraints on survival for the inhabitants of the, 111; fictional dying of the, 120; the globalized twenty-first century's heaven on, 105; humankind as a species bound to, 112; and outer space, 102; planetary

Earth/earth (*continued*)
apocalypse of, 22; saving, 122; uninhabitable, 119; wretched of the, 41. *See also* geoengineering, solar; terraforming
éblouissements (amazement): of modern society, 104; of postcolonial capitalism, 104. *See also* spectacle; Tonda, Joseph
écart absolu (absolute deviation, absolute separation), 46, 60; (absolute departure), 68
ecological Leninism, 107. *See also* ecology; environmentalism
ecology, 78–79, 87; left-libertarian, 173n32; political, 156n76. *See also* ecological Leninism; environment; environmentalism; zadism
economy: capitalist, 16; of desires, 72; end of the, 80; green, 174n3; and liberal society, 5; libidinal, 70; predatory growth of the, 6; of profit, 72; of survival, 82. *See also* free market; global economic system; political economy; socialism
education of desire, 55, 69, 76; image of utopia as, 67; utopian, 69. *See also* Abensour, Miguel; desire; utopia
e-economy, 118
Elliott, Robert C., 137n30, 169n24
embodiment, 17; New Left forms of radicalism as prefigurative, 129n32; partial active, 87; state institutions as utopian, 168n19. *See also* body; disembodiment; politics

Engels, Friedrich, 17, 29, 85, 141n64
English Peasants' Revolt, 18. *See also* Cockaigne/Cokaygne
Enlightenment, the: hopes and promises of the, 60; political philosophers of the, 3; as project, 32; reconstructed, 111; revolutionary goals of the, 59
environment: harm to the, 7; pollution of the, 45, 116, 143; radical ecology and the, 20. *See also* ecology; environmentalism
environmentalism, 20, 78, 172n32. *See also* ecological Leninism; ecology; environment
Esposito, Roberto, 87–88, 94
étatisation (state formation), 98
eudaemonia, 111. *See also* happiness
eugenics, 71
Europe: barbarism and feudalism in, 68; Old, 4; "spectre of communism" haunting, 3; utopian dream of, 105
everyday life: construction of situations of, 72; the critical mythology proposed by Barthes and, 40; passional revolution of, 20; of Surrealism, 63; transformation of, 29
excess: Bataillean, 78; and lack, 16; relative, 16; and waste, 107
Extinction Rebellion (movement), 25, 88. *See also* social movements

Fassin, Didier, 90, 94
Femen (movement), 88. *See also* social movements

fetishism: commodity, 6; of desire, 57. *See also* desire
fiction: hopepunk, 14, 129n28; solarpunk, 14
Floyd, George, 48
form of life, 87, 91; collective, 149n9; communitarian experimentation with new, 79; conforming to society's "programmed lack," 20; critical of capitalism, 172n32; delineating the contours of a, 100
Foucault, Michel, 84, 86, 90, 93–94; economy of power relations of, 154n45
Fourier, Charles, 18, 46, 51, 58–62, 67–68, 85–86, 141n64, 150n13; corporal utopia of, 57; *Théorie des quatre mouvements et des destinées générales* of, 60. *See also* Fourierism/Fourierist
Fourierism/Fourierist: ideas on social organization of, 61; the post-Marxist phase of Surrealism as inspired by, 19–20, 61. *See also* Fourier, Charles
France, 44, 55–82, 103, 114, 135n23
Frankfurt School/Critical Theory, 23, 59, 141n66; emancipatory goals of, 167n19; Geuss's conception of utopia's place in realist, 133n3; interest in utopia of, 107, 166n19; realist-normative project of, 166n19. *See also* critical theory
freedom: desire for, 63; and equality, 86; individual, 93–94; in love and ecstasy, 76; personal, 58; public spaces of, 99; of sexual expression, 74; social, 58; techno-scientific dreams of, 71
free market: and religion, 70; "utopia" of the, 6. *See also* capitalism; economy
French Communist Party, 60. *See also* Communist Party
French Revolution, 39–40, 42, 67, 83, 87. *See also* revolution
French Revolution of 1848, 3–4, 43. *See also* June Days Uprising; revolution
Freud, Sigmund, 66, 107–8, 142n74
Friedman, Yona, 110. *See also* realizable utopia
Frye, Northrop, 37, 106, 147n6
Fuller, R. Buckminster, 26
Garcia, Renaud: *La Collapsologie ou l'écologie mutilée*, 173n32
Gayraud, Joël, 110
general strike (*grève générale*): as a final myth, 137n39; as a social myth, 39; of Sorel, 44, 51–52
genocide, 32
geoengineering, solar, 102. *See also* Earth/earth; terraforming
Germany, 60
global economic system, 36. *See also* economy
Golden Age, 60; myth of, 35; of poets, 125n2, 135n23
Good Old Cause, 44. *See also* myth
Gordon, Uri, 128n26
Graeber, David, 83

Grainville, Jean-Baptiste Cousin
    de: *The Last Man*, 120
Gramsci, Antonio, 30
Great Night, the (*le Grand Soir*),
    44. *See also* myth
great refusal, the, 45, 130n32,
    140n62. *See also* Blanchot,
    Maurice; Marcuse, Herbert;
    New Left
Greco-Roman civilization, 89
Grenelle agreements, 74. *See also*
    France
Grothendieck, Alexandre, 78–79
Guattari, Félix: *Anti-Oedipus* of,
    66; influence of Surrealism
    on, 66
Geuss, Raymond, 132n3

Habermas, Jürgen, 58–59, 68,
    148n9
happiness: countless kinds of,
    104; definition of, 68–69; and
    history, 165n3; as the path to
    utopia, 68; personal safety
    and, 114; pleonectic social, 6;
    pursuit of, 2; social, 58; somatic, 68. *See also* eudaemonia
Hardt, Michael, 49, 94
Harmony: Fourier's mythology
    of, 51; Fourier's utopia of
    passional freedom and, 86;
    Fourier's vision of, 86
health fascism, critique of, 79
hedonism, 70, 74–75
Hegel, G. W. F., 51, 83, 159n3
history: Fourier's absolute
    separation from, 60; creative
    contempt for, 29; cyclical
    pattern of, 43, 60; departure from, 68; destruction
of, 43; economic, 40; end
    of, 45; happiness and, 165n3;
    of hope, 68; human, 9; of
    human rights, 158n91; of
    literature, 136n29; materialist,
    33; melancholy, 111, 134n17; of
    millenarianism, 139n55; myth
    of, 37; myth's naturalizing of,
    37; panorama of, 49; sociological, 78; utopian, 110; of
    utopianism, 106; of utopian
    literature, 18
Hobbes, Thomas, 89–90;
    Leviathan of, 125n2
Hoffman, Abbie: *Steal This Book*,
    74
Hölderlin, Friedrich, 83
Hong Kong, 117
hope, 8–12, 136n28; and anxiety,
    11, 128n26; collective, 35;
    defense of, 36; denigration of,
    10; despair and, 10, 47; educated, 55, 146n1; extensions
    into politics of, 110; history
    of, 68; for humanity, 13; "kairotic talent" and, 49; without
    optimism, 35; optimistic, 35;
    in the pandemic, 116; as a
    potent stimulant, 11; present,
    36; refusal of utopian, 30; and
    social vision, 115; of survival,
    121; suspicion by the Left of,
    36; and utopia, 10–13, 49, 65.
    See also optimism
horizon: active imagination oriented by hope toward a new,
    103; of actualizable human
    possibility, 44; and capitalism, 70; of corporal desire,
    57; critique that forgets the

mobile, 27; economic, 80; of educated hope, 146n1; of every reality, 142n74; the historical moment that affords a collective, 15; of hope, 167n19; locus and, 9; "lost," 110; making "bare life" the, 84; and new collective hopes, 33; and orientation, 9; of possibility, 136n29, 143n79; regulating, 49; removal from sight of, 32, 44, 110; as a spatial category, 8–9; of utopianism, 3, 19, 23, 27, 32, 110, 167n19. *See also* utopia
Horkheimer, Max, 21
Huizinga, Johan, 64
humanitarianism, 81
humanity: hope for, 13; menace to, 116; universal destiny of, 60; visual representation of, 106
human rights, 26; and governmentality, 94; history of, 158n91; international movement of, 158n91; liberal utopia of, 81
Huxley, Aldous, 29; *Island* of, 80–81

Idealism: aesthetic, 136n29; German, 51, 85; "Oldest Systematic Program of German Idealism" (1796–97), 85
illuminisme, Fourier's mystical, 60
imagination: austerity in the realm of the, 109; displaced, 100–112; eclipse of the utopian, 49; free, 23; future of utopian social, 70; modern, 104; mythic utopian, 106; poverty of the, 136n29; social, 6, 70; universal creative power of, 60; unproductive, 41; utopian, 49, 85, 105, 147n6
impolitical, the, 160n8. *See also* politics
Indigenous communities, 122; Zapatista, 161n9
inequality, 50
instant: in Bachelard, 52–53, 145n86; in Benjamin's concept of now-time (*Jetztzeit*) as the messianic moment, 145n86; decision of the, 113; experience of time's verticality in the present, 52; fertility of the, 53; vs. horizontality, 52; messianic moment or, 145n86. *See also* temporality/time
insurrection, 49, 75; erotic, 76; as the last remaining mode of political expression for those devoid of market power, 98; popular, 85. *See also* revolution
Iran, 117
Ireland, 98

Jacobin (magazine), 108
Jacoby, Russell, 44–45, 169n22
Jameson, Fredric, 27, 108, 137n30, 141n67, 149n11, 167n19–69n19, 169n24
Jeanpierre, Laurent, 108–9
Jonas, Hans, 36, 136n29
June Days Uprising, 3. *See also* French Revolution of 1848

Khayati, Mustapha: *On the Poverty of Student Life* (pamphlet), 66, 153n35
kibbutzim, 108
Kildare Poems, 18. *See also* Cockaigne/Cokaygne
King Jr., Martin Luther, 11
Klossowski, Pierre, 60
Kompridis, Nick, 47, 141n66
Korea, 122
Kropotkin, Peter, 173n32
Kurds, 98. *See also* Öcalan, Abdullah

Lacan, Jacques, 66; sense of "Real" of, 131n39
Landauer, Gustav, 47–48
language: of emancipation, 41; freedom of, 40; mythical, 38; myth-prone leftist, 40; of religion, 139n55; revolutionary, 38, 41; of utopianism, 22
Latour, Bruno, 121
Lears, Jackson, 70
Lenin, Vladimir, 29
left, the: boundless optimism of the, 134n14; critique and utopia on the, 25; future of the, 24–25; historians and theorists on the, 8; international, 24; libertarians of the, 17, 61–62, 78, 173n32; old ideological contests of the right and, 158n91; parties of the, 161n11; politics of the, 21, 29–30, 47; public, 11; recovery from the Soviet experiment of the, 20; revolution by the, 29, 141n71; socialist, 61, 108; and social movements, 28–29; utopias of the, 29, 46, 49–50, 53, 68, 134n14, 142n73, 169n22; visionary, 61. *See also* left-wing intellectuals; New Left
Left Front, 59; as a movement in Czechoslovakia, 59
left-wing intellectuals: historians and theorists of the, 8; left-wing melancholy of, 30, 32–33, 49, 84; left-wing politics of, 30, 36; myths of, 40–41, 46; speculation about the possible disappearance of politics by, 84; suspicion of hope by, 36. *See also* left, the; libertarians; Marxism/Marxist; neo-Marxism; political theory; post-Marxism/post-Marxist; Romanticism; socialism; Surrealism/Surrealist; utopian thinking
Lenk, Elisabeth, 60, 153n33
liberticidal, 114
Lettrist International, 62, 152n33
Levinas, Emmanuel, 35
Levitas, Ruth, 8; *The Concept of Utopia* of, 12
liberalism/liberal, 5, 93; façade of, 22; individualistic, 69
libertaire, 154n41
libertarians: of the left, 11, 17, 61–62, 78; public left, 11; socialist, 61; and telling utopia by its level of freedom, 56
logos: mythos and, 105; pure opposite of, 51
love: as the passion of unreason, 61; and pleasure, 65; religion of, 68; and revolution, 77; and

subversion, 65, 76. *See also* desire

Mannheim, Karl, 78
Mao Zedong, 29
Marc, Alexandre, 52
Marcuse, Herbert, 23, 45, 64–65, 140n62, 153n34; *Eros and Civilization* of, 65. *See also* great refusal, the
Marin, Louis, 137n30
Marquis de Sade, 18
martyrdom, as a counter-logic, 92
Marx, Karl, 17, 36, 44, 46, 50, 58, 80, 86, 141n64, 148n8; *The Civil War in France* of, 85. *See also* Marxian
Marxian: ambivalence that is, 108; hermeneutics of meaning that is, 167n19; utopianism that is, 169n22. *See also* Marx, Karl
Marxism/Marxist, 11, 79, 107–8; historiography of, 18; and the Pascalian wager, 142n73; political theory of, 17; Romantic, 151. *See also* left-wing intellectuals; Pascalian wager; post-Marxism/post-Marxist; socialism
materialism, 60. *See also* dialectical materialism
Mbembe, Achille, 91–92, 94. *See also* necropolitics
Mead, Margaret, 106, 166n13
melancholy, 30–34; heroic, 135n17; of history, 134n17; as "indolence of the heart" (*acedia*), 134n17; protean and polyvalent nature of, 134n17; as

"the quintessence of historical experience" (*spleen*), 135n17
messianism/messianic: moment, 145n86; revolutionary, 139n55; "weak," 27. *See also* Benjamin, Walter; millenarianism; millennialism; religion
metabolic rift, 36. *See also* Marx, Karl
metalanguage, 38–41; of myth, 38, 41
Mexico. *See* Chiapas; Neo-Zapatism; Zapatism
microsociety, 110
Miesseroff, Lola, 66
migration: crisis of, 160n7; economic, 105; human, 104; mass, 87; prehistoric, 106
millenarianism: Christian-, 44; critical history of, 139n55; heretical, 10, 44; movements of, 10; promise of, 44; religious passion of, 139n55. *See also* messianism/messianic; millennialism; religion
millennialism: progress myth as secular, 139n56; promise of, 44. *See also* messianism/messianic; millenarianism; religion
minimalism: as pursuit of minimalism-by-gadgets, 102; utopia and, 19, 158n91
Minkowski, Eugène, 10
misery: comedy distracting the masses from their, 145n93; a conception of felicity arising inside a condition of, 90; hysterical, 107–8; migration ending in, 105; sexual, 74; of the working condition, 160n8

modernity, 3, 102; ambivalent character of, 51; grand promises of, 31
More, Thomas: *Utopia*, 7–8, 18, 56, 125n2, 127n14, 146n3, 147n4
Morris, William, 56, 60, 67; *News from Nowhere* of, 147n5
Morrisian, 67
Morton, A. L., 18, 130n35
Mouvement Utopia (association), 172n32
Movement for Survival (MS), 127n10
Moyn, Samuel: *The Last Utopia: Human Rights in History*, 158n91
Murray, Stuart J., 94
myth, 36–46, 105, 136n29; and ancient social ideals, 35; artificial, 38; comedy of, 37; and criticism, 51; dialectical, 43; distinction between truth and, 39; of escape, 138n39; final, 137n39; fundamental, 36–37; general strike as a final, 137n39; left-wing, 40–41, 44, 46; meaning-making as, 43; modern collective, 51; modern popular, 42; political, 144n81; popular medieval, 56; progress, 139n56; proletarian, 138n39; of reconstruction, 138n39; of revolution, 39, 42–43, 109; secular, 37; social, 39, 49, 51, 137n39; speculative, 56; subversive, 40; of telos, 53, 106, 109, 111–12; tragic overtones of, 37; of utopia, 13, 21, 37, 40, 44, 49, 108, 110. *See also* counter-myth; Good Old Cause; Great Night, the; mythology; mythos
mythology: bourgeois, 41; and counter-mythification, 40; and counter-mythology, 38; critical, 40; as ideology, 38; new, 51; rational, 159n3; revolutionary-era, 42; as semiology, 38; of utopianism, 148n7. *See also* myth
mythos: and logos, 105; political myth as, 144n81. *See also* myth

naïve: assumption about utopia as, 108; the *hamartia* of trust that is, 36; hope as, 11; vs. the sentimental spirit of critical theory, 32; trust in an accelerating, greening global economic system that is, 36. *See also* sentimental
nationalism, 121
Nazi Germany, 8
necropolitics: biopoliticization of sovereignty and, 94; form of resistance of, 92, 94–95. *See also* Mbembe, Achille; necroresistance; politics; thanatopolitics
necroresistance, 91–94, 98–99. *See also* Bargu, Banu; politics; protest; thanatopolitics
need: and the animal order, 77; bodily, 86, 118; and desire, 63, 67, 69, 72, 107, 146n3; distorted, 50; lack-based notion of the satisfaction of, 69; legitimate and illegitimate, 69; lived experience of, 96;

material, 68, 70, 88; for a new telos, 31; the passion for life as a biological, 73; for politics, 28; of proletarian experience, 50; for realignment of the utopian wheel, 23; satisfaction of, 47, 71–72; situation and, 136n29; for social criticism, 28; transformation of, 47; unmet, 47, 88; value and, 69
Negri, Antonio, 30, 49, 94
Negt, Oskar, 45
neo-Marxism, 83. *See also* post-Marxism/post-Marxist
neo-Zapatism, 87. *See also* Chiapas; Zapatism
New Anticapitalist Party (NPA), 161n11
New Babylon, 63. *See also* Nieuwenhuys, Constant; unitary urbanism
New Left: forms of radicalism of the, 129n32; politics of the, 29, 34, 129n32. *See also* great refusal, the; left, the; prefiguration
New Left Review (journal), 30
New Man, secular, 68
New York, 59
New Zealand, 118
Nietzsche, Friedrich, 19
Nieuwenhuys, Constant, 62–63. *See also* New Babylon; unitary urbanism
nonplace, 125n1. *See also* utopia
nostalgia/nostalgic, 34–35, 48, 104, 111; childhood as nostalgic figure, 65; for a Golden Age, 60; spell of, 75; utopian, 35. *See also* sentiment

Nozick, Robert, 171n24
nuclear threat, 22

Oaristys, 133n5
Obama, Barack, 11–12
Öcalan, Abdullah, 98. *See also* Kurds; Rojava
Occupy (movement), 30
optimism: blind, 11; of Fourier's utopianism, 60; hope without, 35, 136n28; of the left, 134n14; Marxist, 79; pessimism or, 10, 120; as a political tonality, 133n10; radical, 75; of the will, 30. *See also* hope; pessimism/pessimist
other, the: altruism and care of, 116; fear of, 115

pandemic/Covid-19, 12, 114–22; and liberticidal restrictions, 114
Paradise: myths of, 35; "politics of paradise," 103; secular version of, 118; the superrich in their artificial, 118
Paris: May 1968 in, 56–82, 136n29; psychogeographic guide to, 63; revolutionaries of, 68; Surrealists of, 66
Paris Commune, 3, 44, 48, 85
Paris Surrealists, 66, 153n33; existence of the Group of, 154n44. *See also* Surrealism/Surrealist
Pascalian wager, 49, 142n73. *See also* Marxism/Marxist
Passerini, Luisa: *Memory and Utopia: The Primacy of Intersubjectivity*, 148n7

pays de Cocagne, 18. *See also* Cockaigne/Cokaygne
pessimism/pessimist: and capitalism, 120, 171n28; and disappointed hopes, 30; and hope for the return of utopia, 32; or optimism, 10; without solace, 30; utopian, 160n8. *See also* optimism
Pierret, Marc: *Utopies et perversions*, 74
Piketty, Thomas, 11
Plain people, 103
Plato: *Laws* of, 13, 101; *Republic* of, 13, 125n2
play, 63–64; utopia as conceptual, 167n19, 169n19. *See also* pleasure
pleasure: collective, 63; desire and, 70; individual, 63; love and, 65; and pain, 107; principle of, 77; restrictions and, 66; of sex, 156n66; somatic, 107. *See also* play
Plonowska-Ziarek, Ewa, 90
pluralism, 97; bland "utopia" of value, 5; of globalized societies, 6; of utopias, 171n24
Polanyi, Karl, 70, 155n55
political economy, 71; in surviving Neolithic hunter-gatherer societies, 82. *See also* economy
political realism, 49; argument of Mathias Thaler for, 132n3; compatibility of utopia with, 132n3; limits of the tragic sensibility that goes with, 145n93
political theory: early modern, 3, 125n2; Enlightenment, 3, 126n2; Marxist, 17; post-Marxist, 17; revolution in, 49; Western, 49. *See also* left-wing intellectuals; utopian thinking
political writing: as instrumental, 30; as utopian, 30
politics: antistate, 83, 89, 96; anti-utopian, 30; of ascesis, 87, 160n8; body, 86–89, 161n13; of coexistence, 94–95, 167n19; comic, 54, 145n93; of death, 91, 94; defeat of proletarian, 84; of desire, 67; disappearance/extinction/end of, 84, 94; emancipatory, 131n38, 167n19; high, 84; human rights as new, 158n91; as an inquiry into the desirability of revolution, 84; left-wing, 21, 36, 47; of life, 88, 91, 93, 96; of living on, 92, 94; new left, 34, 129n32; polemics and, 3; "politics of paradise," 103; practical, 141n67; prefigurative, 130n32; as the public exercise of freedom, 28; radical, 17–18, 42, 109, 129n32, 141n67; radical utopian, 20, 31, 45; reinvention of, 84–85; renewal of, 30; revolutionary, 29, 31, 45, 52, 150n15; as separate sphere of human activity, 42, 83; space of, 97; specialized, 83; state-based, 84; state-sanctioned varieties of, 30; of survival, 21, 88–99; of survivance, 95–96; tragic, 30–35, 54, 145n93; utopia and, 17–20, 129n32, 132n3; utopian, 36, 52; utopianizing,

74, 88, 95–96; vitalist, 92, 94; vitalization of, 163n29; as we know it, 29, 84, 119; working definitions of, 28. *See also* biopolitics; embodiment; impolitical, the; necropolitics; necroresistance; radical politics; state; thanatopolitics
postapocalyptic: alarmist or, 11; utopia that is, 172n32
postcritique, 26
post-Marxism/post-Marxist, 17, 21, 83; phase of Surrealism of, 19–20. *See also* Marxism/Marxist; neo-Marxism
postrevolutionary apocalypticism, 84
post-Situationism, 79
posttheory, 26
posttruth, 26
poverty, 40, 66, 73, 82, 102; existential, 74; extreme, 142n78; ignorance and, 117; of the imagination, 136n29; legalistic (human rights), 158n91; material, 158n91; new, 71–72; of student life, 153n35; ultimate, 72; wealth and, 50
precariat, the: of existence, 103; in France, 103; as a political wildcard, 103
precariousness: of condition of existence, 164n37; heightening of, 103; and precarity, 165n6
precarity: as assimilable to survival, 103; and bodily persistence, 165n6; collapse of, 104; economic, 95, 103; environmental degradation and, 87; and fragmentation of the working class, 50; nomadism of economic migrants as, 105; and performativity, 161n13; politics and, 97; and precariousness, 165n6
prefiguration, 87, 100, 106, 128n26, 129n32–30n32, 160n8, 165n3. *See also* anarchism; New Left
protest: hunger strike as, 88, 98, 161n14; lip-sewing as, 88; martyrdom as, 161n14; of migrants to the European Union, 88; self-destruction as an act of, 88–89; self-immolation as, 88, 161n14, 164n37; site of, 28. *See also* necroresistance
Proudhon, Pierre-Joseph, 43
psychoanalysis/psychoanalysts: Adorno on, 156n66; anarchist, 166n18; Freudian, 107
public assembly, 49, 84–85, 165n6. See also *assembléisme*; revolution
Pythagoreans, 101

reality principle, 107; limitations imposed upon freedom and happiness by the, 153n34
realizable utopia, 110. *See also* Friedman, Yona; utopia
realm of freedom, 50, 63, 86, 147n4
realm of necessity, 50, 86, 147n4, 161n13
real utopia, 70–71, 107, 109–10, 143n79; in the Lacanian sense of "Real," 131n39; muted appreciation of, 169n20. *See also* utopia; Wright, Erik Olin

Reclus, Elisée, 173n32
reform/reformism: 14, 31; manifesto of, 127n10; prospect of real-world, 169n19; revolutionary, 49, 85, 110; subversive, 49; utopian, 42, 45, 80; vanguard of ideology of, 74. *See also* revolution
religion: free market and, 70; of love, 68; revolutionary class struggle speaking the language of, 139n55. *See also* messianism/messianic; millenarianism; millennialism; theology
repression: of desire, 71; of the pleasure instincts, 58; sexual, 65; socially necessary vs. surplus, 79; Surrealist critique of, 20; the transformation of desires and, 15
revolt: against biopolitical state power, 88; English peasant, 18; ethos of, 74; of modernity, 51; open, 119; prison, 119; Reformation-era peasant, 139n55; and revolution, 88; social, 61, 117; taboo-breaking perversions in a purely instinctual, 74, 81; talking of, 39. *See also* revolution
revolution: by Americans, 138n39; body and, 64–65; and class struggle, 65; desire and, 62–66; of everyday life, 20, 57, 62; international, 11; language of, 38; love and, 77; myth of, 39, 42–43, 109; in the Reformation peasant revolts, 139n55; sexual, 74, 156n66; social, 130n32, 173n32; socialist, 52; in social relations, 29; survival and, 74; unfinished, 42, 142n74; utopia and, 47–48, 64. *See also* coming community, the; common, the; counterrevolution; destituent power; French Revolution; French Revolution of 1848; insurrection; public assembly; reform/reformism; revolt
Revolution, the. *See* French Revolution
Robin, Corey, 108
Robinson, Marilynne, 50
Rojava, 87, 109–10; communalist, 87, 109; confederalist, 109. *See also* Kurds; Öcalan, Abdullah
Romanticism, 51, 152n33, 166n17; revolutionary, 51, 153n33
Rousseau, Jean-Jacques, 37; *The Social Contract* of, 126n2, 133n3

Sahlins, Marshall: *Stone Age Economics*, 81–82, 89, 158n92, 159n93
Saint-Simon, Henri de, 56
Samuel, Pierre, 79
Schelling, Friedrich Wilhelm Joseph von, 83
Schmitt, Carl, 90
science, 19, 53; complexity, 43; instruction in, 78; Marxist, 67
Scudéry, Madeleine de: *Carte du pays de Tendre*, 63
Sears, Roebuck & Co. catalog, 29
sentiment: evolution of, 36; of nostalgia, 34; as path out of the past and the present, 34.

See also nostalgia/nostalgic;
sentimental
sentimental: vs. naïve, 32; nostalgia rather than melancholy as, 34; as resting on a reconstruction of the Enlightenment project, 32; Surrealists as, 58. See also naïve; sentiment
Servigne, Pablo, 173n32
sexuality: fetishism of desire in, 57; liberation of, 20, 76, 131n2, 166n18; neutralization of, 75, 156n66. See also body; desire
Signac, Paul, 135n23
Situationist International (SI), 20, 30, 62–67, 71–72, 75, 79; foundation of the, 152n33; microsociety of the, 64. See also Debord, Guy; Situationists, the
Situationists, the: on consumerism, 74; the emphasis on "radical subjectivity" among, 65; the impact on the "Enragés" of, 65; and social theorists, 75; utopianism of, 62, 67, 71, 74. See also construction of situations; Situationist International; utopia
sixty-eighters, the, 20
social codes, upper-class, 145n93
social contract, 3, 37, 111
social criticism, 28, 51
socialism: American, 108; aspirations of, 137n39; combination of internationalism and redistributive, 81; Corey Robin on the point of, 108; critique of utopian, 17; democratic, 155n55; enemies of, 108;
legacies of, 25, 32, 36; "*nostalgie du juste*" of, 35; opposition to capitalism of, 161n11; postwar disillusionment with, 44; quest for emancipation of, 46; revolutionary, 3; utopias of, 6, 46, 51, 68, 109, 153n34; visionary left-libertarian, 61. *See also* communism; economy; Marxism/Marxist
social movements, 28–29, 83–84, 97, 128n26; as [driven] into regression, 68; horizontality of, 97; on the left, 28. *See also* democracy; society
social theory, 17, 37; utopian, 129n29. *See also* critical theory; society; utopian thinking
society: bourgeois, 38; capitalist, 81; of control, 115; corporal prefiguration of harmony in, 100; critique of capitalist, 70; free and democratic, 130n32; images of a stateless, 56; and the individual, 147n4; injustice in, 88; model, 8; Neolithic, 80; reconstitution of, 99; telos of, 37; utopian, 61; vision of the good, 56; visions of new post-capitalist, 11. *See also* social movements; social theory
sociology, 60
Sorel, Georges, 38–40, 42, 44, 51–52, 137n39, 144n83
Soviet Russia, 8
spectacle: critical theory of capitalist society as, 20, 64; erotic, 74; mainstream media, 46; of mass mobilizations in

spectacle (*continued*)
social movements, 25; virtual, 48. See also Debord, Guy; *éblouissements*
Spinoza, Benedict de, 10, 125n2, 126n2
spiritualization: of desire and pleasure, 70, 76; of the utopian project, 17, 20. See also disembodiment
Stalin, Josef, 29
state: critical theory against the, 83–99; critique of the, 85; institutions of the, 168n19; power of the biopolitical, 88; surviving capitalism in opposition to the, 97. See also capitalism; politics
Streeck, Wolfgang, 98
sublimation: abstraction and, 16; artistic, 58; dependence of freedom on non-repressive, 153n34; of desire, 58, 165n3; of mimetic powers in the work of art, 149n9; of sensuousness, 65. See also desublimation
suicide, 98
Surrealism/Surrealist, 20, 51, 57–66, 148n9, 149n10, 152n33; everyday life of, 63; great rendezvous with history of, 144n84; Group in Chicago, 154n44; Group in Prague, 154n44; manifestoes of, 59, 61–62; origins and fate of, 150n15; reading of Freud by, 153n34; rediscovery of the corporal utopia of Fourier by, 57; simplest act of, 62. See also Paris Surrealists

survival: augmented, 71–72; as "bare life," 69, 90; biological, 88; blueprint for, 7, 127n10; capitalist hegemony of, 95; collapse and, 172n32; collective, 100; connections to utopia of, 16–17; desire and, 71–82; dialectical view of, 78; dialectic of life and, 72; dramas of, 36; economy of, 82; experience of, 15, 100; as foundation of politics, 88; as ground or condition of possibility for politics, 94–95; hope of, 121; human concern with survival as necessary for politics, 90; of the left, 30; logic of, 129n30; notion of, 20; as a political-anthropological constant, 93; political recognition of biological, 86; politics of, 21, 88–99; psychology of, 86; and revolution, 74; struggle for, 2, 16, 21, 81; theories of politicized, 92; training of desire in, 17; utopia and, 16, 83–99, 156n76; Vaneigem's moral aversion to, 75
survivance, politics of, 95–96. See also Abélès, Marc
Survivre et vivre (movement), 79–80
Survivre/Survivre et vivre (journal), 78–80
Suvin, Darko, 8

technology: high, 65; military uses of nuclear, 78; science and, 19; technolatry as worship of, 79; utopian hope in, 71 telos, 8, 31; emancipation and, 67; generic concept of utopia as a, 55; myth of, 37, 47, 52–53, 106, 109–12, 147n6; practical, 167n19; of social progress, 85; of society, 37; ultimate utopian, 19. *See also* utopia

temporality/time, 42, 52–53, 164, 170; cyclical, 80; dead, 64; duration as, 52; of dystopia, 9; experience of, 52; framing of a future in some indeterminate, 39; the gold of, 50; horizontal vs. vertical, 52; of instrumentality, 30; now-, 145n86; perceived, 52–53; and place, 28; revolution and, 47, 52; of the self, 52; space and, 72; suffering the pain of, 53; of utopia, 112, 120; of utopia's reinvention, 23; vertical, 52. *See also* instant

Temporary Autonomous Zone (TAZ), 99, 164n43

terraforming: Faustianism of, 102; as solar geoengineering to combat the greenhouse effect, 102. *See also* Earth/earth; geoengineering, solar

thanatopolitics, 94. *See also* necropolitics; necroresistance; politics

theology: economic, 70; monotheistic, 10; political, 44, 70. *See also* messianism/messianic; millenarianism; millennialism; religion

Thompson, E. P., 67–68

Thunberg, Greta, 46

Tonda, Joseph, 104. *See also éblouissements*

totalitarianism, 6, 32

transhumanism, 71; scientific fantasy of, 26

Transition Initiatives, 173n32

Traverso, Enzo: *Left-Wing Melancholia*, 32–33, 49

Trump, Donald, 12

truth: inconvenient, 2; and myth, 39; social, 39

Turkey, 98

unitary urbanism, 63. *See also* New Babylon; Nieuwenhuys, Constant

United Nations Conference on the Human Environment, 127n10

United States: hope in the, 11; mass student movement in the, 129n32; writing in the, 126n6. *See also* US

urbanism, critique of, 63

US: federal administration, 117; foreign policy, 118. *See also* United States

utopia: abstract, 142n74; as alibi, 17; applied, 68; art and, 148n9; ascetic, 102; blueprint tradition of, 63, 139n58; as a buzzword, 5; city, 19, 86, 146n3; collective, 50, 100, 138n39; concrete, 49, 75, 142n74; definition of, 125n1; desire for, 13, 15–16, 36, 44; disembodiment of, 17; dreaming of, 3, 12, 18, 26; dreamworld as, 50, 145n93; dynamic, 9; emancipation and, 67;

utopia (*continued*)
end of, 45–46; of escape, 71; evocation of the aspirations of, 2; and experiments in society-making, 8; fate of, 9–10; fear of, 169n24; of the free market, 6; historical, 107; historical divergence of politics and, 17; hope and, 10–13, 49; as hypothesis, 14, 54; iconoclasm of, 21; iconoclastic tradition of, 45, 82, 105, 139n58, 169n22; identity of ideology and, 168n19; and intellectual elitism, 5; as a jocoserious creation, 8; left, 36, 46; and the level of freedom, 56; mass, 50, 158n91; melancholy, 32–33; as method, 8; minimalist, 19, 158n91; as a myth, 13, 21, 37, 40, 44, 49, 108, 110; negativist theorization of, 107; nexus of desire and, 56; or oblivion, 27; as the opposite of dystopia, 5; persistence of, 85–86; Platonic ideal state as, 7; pluralism of, 171n24; and political realism, 132n3; and politics, 17–20, 129n32, 132n3; private, 50; of rational communication, 77; real, 108, 169n20; rebooting of, 112; rejection of, 39; and revolution, 47–48, 64; of sexual liberation, 20; Situationist, 64; social, 40, 53; socialist, 6, 46, 51, 68, 109; of social labor, 110; sociological history of, 78; as a sociological method, 8; as speculation, 14–15; spiritualization of, 17; and survival, 16, 83–99, 156n76; as a term of abuse, 5; as topos, 18, 135n23; ubiquity of, 55; useful, 11; and utopianism, 126n3; Virtual, 143n79; visions of, 20, 27, 87; writers of, 3. *See also* body utopia; city utopia; dystopia; education of desire; horizon; nonplace; realizable utopia; real utopia; Situationists, the; telos; utopian hypothesis; utopianism; utopian studies; utopian thinking; utopist/utopian; Wikipedia; world-making, utopian

utopian fiction, 132n3, 133n3, 147n5

utopian hypothesis, 54. *See also* utopia

utopianism: anti-anti-, 108, 169n24; anti-utopian, 108, 169n22; atheist, 10; body, 58; charge of, 3, 49; defeated, 108; without dogmatism, 134n14; historians of, 106; historical, 64; hypothetical facet of, 14; language of, 22; ludic, 167n19; Marxian, 169n22; negative-dialectical structure of, 167n19; practice of, 64; and realist political theory, 132n3; resistance to the spiritualization of, 20; speculative facet of, 14–15, 106, 109; subversive strand of popular, 80; the three faces of, 129n29; total social transformation of, 46–47; transgressive, 131n38; utopia

and, 126n3. *See also* anti-utopianism/anti-utopian; utopia; utopian thinking
utopian studies, 9, 131n40, 137n36. *See also* utopia; utopian thinking
utopian thinking, 2–5, 7, 19, 22; contemporary, 47; critical, 17; desire-based conception of, 67; emancipatory, 68; rebooting of, 70. *See also* left-wing intellectuals; political theory; social theory; utopia; utopianism; utopian studies; utopist/utopian
utopist/utopian, 3–4, 15, 46, 112; defensible, 108; iconoclastic, 139n58; major/minor, 157n87; and the poet, 111; sensible, 108. *See also* utopia; utopian thinking

vampire, 19
Vaneigem, Raoul, 10, 71–77, 79, 103, 133n5, 157n86; *Traité de savoir-vivre à l'usage des jeunes générations* (*The Revolution of Everyday Life*) of, 64–65, 67, 76–77, 157n86. *See also autogestion généralisée*
Vatter, Miguel, 94
violence: popular, 3; of the state, 97, 117; Surrealist, 61–62; symbolic, 104
VR gaming, 26

war, 32
Weil, Simone, 160n8
West: capitalism of the, 38; civilization of the, 89; decentering of conceptions of life of the, 81; new economic policy of the, 44; political theory of the, 49, 90
Wikipedia, 109. *See also* utopia
Wilde, Oscar: "The Soul of Man under Socialism," 120
Williams, Raymond, 56, 147n5
world-making, utopian, 8. *See also* utopia
World Social Forum, slogan of, 173n32
World War II, 44, 59, 116
Wright, Erik Olin, 109, 171n27. *See also* real utopia

Yellow Vests (*Gilets Jaunes*), 83, 87, 97, 108, 114. *See also assembléisme*; social movements

zadism (ZADs), 87, 97, 99, 161n11. *See also* ecology
Zapatism, 87, 108, 160n9. *See also* Chiapas; neo-Zapatism
Zionism, 7
Žižek, Slavoj, 22–23, 31, 131n39, 134n14
zoē vs. *bios*, 90–91, 100, 162n22
zombie, 19
zone à défendre (ZAD). *See* zadism

Lightning Source UK Ltd.
Milton Keynes UK
UKHW010422260921
391056UK00012B/542